I GOT SCHOOLED

The Unlikely Story of How a Moonlighting Movie
Maker Learned the Five Keys to Closing
America's Education Gap

M. NIGHT SHYAMALAN

SIMON & SCHUSTER

NEW YORK   LONDON   TORONTO   SYDNEY   NEW DELHI

Simon & Schuster
1230 Avenue of the Americas
New York, NY 10020

First Simon & Schuster hardcover edition September 2013

SIMON & SCHUSTER and colophon are registered trademarks
of Simon & Schuster, Inc.

For information about special discounts for bulk purchases,
please contact Simon & Schuster Special Sales at
1-866-506-1949 or business@simonandschuster.com.

The Simon & Schuster Speakers Bureau can bring authors
to your live event. For more information or to book an event,
contact the Simon & Schuster Speakers Bureau at
1-866-248-3049 or visit our website at www.simonspeakers.com.

Designed by Ruth Lee-Mui

Manufactured in the United States of America

10 9 8 7 6 5 4 3 2 1

Library of Congress Cataloging-in-Publication Data is available.

ISBN 978-1-4767-1645-9
ISBN 978-1-4767-1647-3 (ebook)

To Bhavna and her keen sense of injustice.

CONTENTS

PART THREE: CONCLUSION

PROLOGUE

Everyone who decides to give money away makes missteps. A long time ago, I contributed to a passionate and well-meaning low-income housing initiative. I read their proposal, met with them, went to their church, walked the blocks that were going to be transformed, and wrote a check—a big one. Many years later, all I had bought with it was a raft of lost promises, intricate excuses, and bewilderment about where the funds went.

I licked my wounds. In due time, my interest in doing something to help my hometown of Philadelphia slowly migrated to education. Again, I chose to accomplish this by writing more checks. My wife, Bhavna, and I identified four exceptional public high school students from low-income schools and informed them we were going to help pay for their four years of college. To celebrate our candidates, I arranged to host a dinner with them at a popular and well-known restaurant to commemorate this auspicious beginning.

One thing you need to know about me is I'm seriously, clinically sentimental. I keep all the napkins I write ideas down on. Sunsets are a must on vacation. My house is filled with photos from every moment in my family's history. I keep a special bottle of Champagne for every script I complete. This list of sentimental rituals is long and getting longer; this dinner was going to become one of them. My wife and I were going to have an inspiring dinner with exceptional kids that were one day going to change the city of Philadelphia.

This is not what happened.

Bhavna and I waited at the restaurant as one by one the scholarship awardees arrived. One was escorted in by a very suspicious and protective aunt. The aunt clearly didn't want to leave, but eventually relented. So there we were, Bhavna, me, our awardees, and utter silence. I am considered a loquacious guy. I sallied forth with my best icebreakers and never-fail-me jokes. These had no effect.

I took stock of our guests. All four stared with hurt, pained eyes. Through the course of the barely eaten meal, a few morsels of information spilled from their otherwise sewn-shut lips. The most important was this: They were scared and unprepared for college. These children were not ready. They were deeply struggling. They were suspicious of Bhavna and me, and suspicious of the world.

That's when I began to recall things from their applications and letters, things that I had chosen to ignore. The uneven scores in their academics. The low percentiles of their standardized test scores as compared to public school kids not in the inner city. I remembered the darkness that stained their letters. The system had failed them and shoved them out the door with ribbons saying they had won.

It didn't take much to see that the immediate future for them would be very difficult and they would feel every day like they were barely breathing. As they shook our hands politely and left, Bhavna looked at me and saw I was shaken.

I was looking to be inspired. These children needed saving, but our money wasn't going to do the trick. The system had beaten them badly enough that no amount of money could undo the scars.

There are moments when you think you are somewhere on a road close to your destination until you see a road sign that tells you that you have drastically miscalculated the length of your journey. Bhavna and I left that restaurant feeling as so many others before us must have felt as they stared down the road and knew that their destination had somehow gotten further away. If we wanted to fix Philadelphia's broken educational system—to say nothing of America's—we needed a new map.

PART ONE

THE GAP

1

AS JOHN ADAMS SAID . . .

Some filmmakers love location scouting. I'm not one of them. You drive in a van or fly a plane for eternity just to get out, look around, and say, "This isn't it." You do this over and over till you find the place where you know the characters can live and breathe and walk around.

Which is what I was doing in the spring of 2007, with a team of location managers and scouts who were ferrying me around Philadelphia, looking at potential filming locations for *The Happening,* which was going to star Mark Wahlberg as a teacher in a Philadelphia high school. Our search had taken us to the Julia R. Masterman Middle and High School, a public school located at 17th and Spring Garden, right in the middle of the city. This is a flat-out beautiful building and beautiful school. I knew right away when I stepped out that this was the place. It just felt right. There was light there.

I'm not superfamous, but people know my movies. Once it got around that we were scouting Masterman High School, the kids went crazy. They started coming out of the classrooms, circling, asking questions. "Are you making a movie here?" "Is someone going to die here?" "Can I die?" The usual inquiries. It was a pied piper–like scene as we moved through the building. We took our notes, talked to the principal, and left.

Then we drove fifteen minutes to Overbrook High School in West Philadelphia. It is a towering, imposing building. Inside, it's all fluorescent lights and metal detectors. The classrooms had bars on their doors and windows, and each one had to be unlocked before we could see them.

Something you should know about me is that I'm a pretty selfish guy. Not a great citizen of the world. I care about my family and films. That's it. Someone needs saving, countries need assistance, I'm sympathetic, but it doesn't penetrate me. But when they showed me the floor of the school that was closed because of too much drug use and sexual activity, something dark wrapped in outrage started growing in my stomach. It kept growing as they showed me the school theater that was being renovated because of a suspiciously set fire.

Something happened to me standing in the hallway in Overbrook High School. My arms became tight. My jaw set. It's exactly what happens when someone elbows me in a basketball game. It gets my attention.

Which is more than we got at Overbrook. When we walked down the halls, only one boy even looked at us. Something akin to recognition flickered in his eyes and then vanished. He looked back down and kept walking. That was the only moment of acknowledgment that a film-location crew was in the building.

I'm certain that the students of Overbrook watch just as many movies as the kids at Masterman. Just as many of them want to be actors or directors or producers. To Masterman's students, though, while a visit from a film crew wasn't an everyday event, it was exactly the sort of thing they expected to happen. Their entire lives had taught them that things like that were possible. That *anything* was possible. Overbrook's students *didn't even believe we were there*. If the kids at Masterman had spent their lives being taught that anything was possible, Overbrook's student body had learned the opposite.

That's one reason that the achievement gap that separates inner-city schools from suburban ones doesn't exist at Masterman. Which meant they had opened up a cavernous gap between themselves and Overbrook. In 2010, Masterman was one of only two high schools in the state of Pennsylvania to be awarded a National Blue Ribbon, which means just what it sounds like. Masterman students take enriched math and foreign language programs, participate in half a dozen different music ensembles, and can try out for nationally ranked chess and National Academic League teams. The school has a 100 percent graduation rate, and nine out of ten Masterman graduates are headed to a four-year college. Overbrook? Only 54 percent of Overbrook's students get a diploma. At Masterman, nearly one student in four takes the Advanced Placement test in English, and 90 percent receive a score of 3, 4, or 5: enough for college credit. At Overbrook, only one student in fifty takes it and, the last time anyone checked, none got as high as a 3.

It's not apples to apples. Masterman is a magnet school, and a very selective one. Even to *apply* to Masterman, a fourth-grader—almost every student starts in the fifth grade, and continues to graduation—needs to test in the top 12 percent of all students in the city of Philadelphia. But neither school has an especially affluent student body; the percentage of poor kids at Masterman is around 40 percent; at Overbrook a little more than 60 percent. The teachers at Overbrook work just as hard as their colleagues at Masterman, and care just as much. The schools use the same standards for language arts and mathematics. Only about four miles separates them. And a sense of possibility.

Here's another thing about me: My mind is hardwired to see possibilities everywhere. I look up in the night sky and *expect* to see a UFO. I was the kid who stared at the paper cup for hours convinced I'd move it with my mind. (Never happened.) I'm also the guy who saw my wife for the first time and knew she was the one. (Married twenty years.) I went to my first dance at a girls' school when I was twelve and knew my kids would go there one day. (All three do today.) I'm that guy. The eternal optimist on steroids.

The visit to the two schools made something crystal clear to me: I was now invested in the struggles of education, and I was going to figure out what Masterman's kids were getting that Overbrook's weren't. I wasn't sure how to do it. But I had a notion of where to start.

Six years before visiting the two schools, in October of 2001, my wife, Bhavna (who is a *great* citizen of the world), and I had signed the various documents—and written the check— that launched the M. Night Shyamalan Foundation (MNS Foundation). Its mission is "to support remarkable leaders working to remove the barriers created by poverty and inequality, which prevent individuals and communities from unleashing their full potential." Bhavna and I believe that every person on the planet is born with an unknowably great potential for knowledge, growth, and success, and that we are all responsible for helping turn that potential into actuality.

Over the years, the Foundation has mounted initiatives to fight hunger and improve access to livable housing in Philadelphia. We've supported single mothers in their efforts to get

GEDs. We've funded programs of self-empowerment around the world, investing in community leaders like Usha, a woman from the slum community of Nagpur, India, who stood up to the gang that had terrorized her community for years and came to MNS when she needed help training her neighbors in job skills. The Foundation invested in the Sudanese secondary school for boys and girls built by Valentino Achak Deng (the subject of Dave Eggers's *What Is the What*). The Foundation has given orphans in Africa access to a daily multivitamin that, all by itself, prevents a whole raft of potentially life-threatening deficiency diseases like scurvy and pellagra. We provided a grant to the Samburu Project, started by Kristen Kosinski, a former Paramount executive who left her job, flew to Kenya, and is now working to provide fresh water to an entire region.

So, when we decided that America's educational failures were the biggest obstacle "preventing individuals and communities from unleashing their full potential," we had an organization in place that could examine the scope of those failures. The first thing the foundation came back with was a reminder—the first of many—that what I knew just wasn't so. In this case, what *everyone* knew just wasn't so. Despite the impression left by thousands of research studies, tens of thousands of blog posts, and millions of words in every newspaper and magazine in the country, America's schools aren't failing.

I know how this sounds to you. But it's true. The country's high school graduation rate, college graduation rate, and average performance on those work-of-the-devil standardized tests are the highest they've ever been. Elementary and middle school students in the United States have been tested on their proficiency in math and science every four years since 1995, and have improved every single time. (A separate problem is that America's best students, our top 10 percent, are starting to fall behind the best European and Asian students. A good book could be written about this problem, but this isn't that book.)

OK. So maybe the problem is only that American schools are in *relative* decline. Maybe our schools shouldn't be compared to what they were twenty years ago, but with what other countries are doing today. If you read the *New York Times,* or the *Wall Street Journal,* or listen to National Public Radio, or just about anything else, you've already heard about how they do education better everywhere else—Finland and Singapore are favorite examples. But, again, there's a lot less to this than meets the eye.

The most important international comparison of educational performance is the Programme for International Student Assessment, or PISA, a test given every three years to fifteen-year-olds all over the world. Last time out, the U.S. average score was 500, just behind Poland and ahead of Liechtenstein.

However . . .

If America's scores were limited to those from schools in districts in which the poverty rate was less than 10 percent—Finland's poverty rate is less than 4 percent—the United States would lead the world, and it wouldn't be close: 551 on the latest PISA test, compared to Finland's 536, or South Korea's 539. In fact, if all you did was exclude the American schools that have student bodies that are more than three-quarters poor, U.S. schools would still score 513, just behind Australia, but ahead of the Netherlands, Belgium, Sweden, Germany, Iceland . . . well, you get the picture.

Unfortunately, nearly 20 percent of schools in the United States have student bodies that are more than 75 percent poor. That's a fifth—the bottom quintile—of all the 100,000 public schools in the country: 22 percent of America's elementary schools, and 11 percent of our secondary schools.

The top four-fifths of America's public schools are Norway. The bottom 18 percent—14,000 elementary schools, and more than 3,000 secondary schools—is Serbia. I knew there was a gap. But I didn't know that the gap was as big as the Grand Canyon. And, like the Grand Canyon, it was around for a long time before anyone actually "discovered" it. The first real evidence of what everyone already knew emerged only around fifty years ago, when the U.S. Department of Education issued the first comprehensive study of the subject, the 1966 *Equality of Educational Opportunity*. New studies have been coming out what seems like every few months ever since. A few highlights:

- A study by the Annie E. Casey Foundation found that third-graders who live in poverty—and remember, that's a fifth of the entire country—*and* read below grade level are three times as likely to drop out as students whose families have never fallen below the poverty line.

- In 2010, the average reading score on one test given to eighth-grade students in high-poverty schools was thirty-three points below the score in low-poverty schools. The gap in scores between poor and nonpoor students in math was thirty-six points. Every ten points is approximately equal to one grade level in performance.

- Twenty-two percent of children who have lived in poverty for more than a year or two don't graduate from high school (only 6 percent of those who have never lived in poverty fail to graduate). Spend more than half your childhood in poverty, and your chance of dropping out rises to an almost unbelievable 32 percent.

- It's mostly an urban problem: Only 29 percent of America's public school students attend schools in cities, but a whopping 58 percent of them are in high-poverty schools. Thirty-five percent of all public school students are in suburban schools, but only 23 percent of them are high-poverty schools. In towns, only 9 percent attend high-poverty schools, 11 percent in rural areas.

- The National Center for Education Statistics estimates that only 68 percent of twelfth-graders in what they defined as high-poverty schools—ones in which more than 75 percent of the students are eligible for a free or reduced-price lunch—ever graduate, as opposed to 91 percent everywhere else. Overbrook has a lot of company.
- Here's the really bad news. None of these numbers has improved in any real way for at least the last twenty years.

This was pretty depressing, even to an optimist like me. About the only good news I could extract from this research was that the problem was localized; that it seemed to happen everywhere you had a high percentage of low-income, urban families. That's what my Foundation researchers told me. And, since I don't live on Mars, and know that "low-income and urban" is code for "African-American and Latino," I then asked, "Is this a problem of poverty or racism?"

Well, it's both, obviously. In America, especially, they overlap. In California, black students are six times more likely than white students to attend the state's lowest-performing 30 percent of schools; Latino students four times more likely. But an honest look at the numbers shows that poverty is an even bigger part of the problem than race. The reading-score difference between low-poverty schools and high-poverty schools is nearly a third *higher* than the achievement gap separating African-Americans or Hispanics from white students.

That struck me as less of a daunting problem. We don't have to fix the problem of racial discrimination in America. Just the problem of poverty. (I'm being sarcastic.)

Or maybe not. I had another brainstorm. Paul Orfalea, the hyperactive (really hyperactive, as in diagnosed with ADHD) founder of Kinko's, used to say that his only secret was that he was so restless that he visited every Kinko's operation he could, found out what worked, and then told every other store manager about it. *We could do that,* I thought. If the problem is largely restricted to America's urban schools, let's look at a hundred or so urban school districts and find the ones that have the highest-achieving students. Then we'll figure out what they're doing that's different from the others and tell everyone about it, first in Philadelphia, then everywhere else.

A month later, I had my answer. The Foundation couldn't find a "best" urban school system. They had to move heaven and earth even to find a good one.

Again the eternal optimist on steroids took this as good news. To me, this said that these school systems have different rules than the rest of the education world, and that they are reacting uniformly—like a system. We just had to figure out the system's rules.

Actually, figuring out the rules wasn't all I had to do. I also had to figure out why I was looking for them in the first place. It wasn't enough to carry that dark ball of outrage in my stomach. I needed to get rid of it. After all, I wasn't in this just to satisfy my curiosity, as I believed in change. And when it comes to education, change means changing people's minds. If I had to change a bunch of minds, I needed to know my own.

So I started with one thing I knew for sure: America hadn't become a nation of educational apartheid entirely by chance. A big chunk of the problem was self-inflicted. We've done this to ourselves.

And when I say "we," I mean me, too. Remember that girls' school I visited when I was twelve, knowing that my daughters would go there someday? They're not going there just because I'm sentimental; it's probably one of the two or three best private schools in the state of Pennsylvania. I want my family to have the best, and I've been lucky enough to be able to afford it. And I don't think I'm very different from anyone else. We all want our schools to be great. None of us wants to send our kids to an average school, much less a below-average one.

The dark side of this equation is, if your school is above average, then someone else's has to be below average.

This isn't necessarily a bad thing. One hospital might be above average, another below, but we expect both of them to be able to remove an appendix or deliver a baby. The real problem with wanting your school to be above average is when that means "in comparison to another school." If what really matters to people isn't the *absolute* benefit of attending a particular school, or living in a particular school district, but the *relative* benefit—how your school compares with others— then they start to act as if they're playing a zero-sum game: If someone wins, someone else has to lose.

That's what was wrong with Masterman. It couldn't be the *solution*. It might have been part of the *problem:* If the most ambitious, motivated families in Overbrook's neighbor- hood apply to schools like Masterman, what happens to the kids whose families don't? It isn't just a Philadelphia problem: Thirty-seven of the top fifty schools in *Newsweek* magazine's most recent list of America's top thousand high schools had selective admission standards. They were there *because* they were selective, and selection is a zero-sum game. Which would be bad enough, but it becomes worse: You can't get the winners in a zero-sum game to help the losers when the stakes are good jobs or admissions to good colleges.

As I said, I'm just as vulnerable to this kind of thinking as anyone. I get it a lot: "Sure, it's easy for you to pontificate about public schools; your girls are never going to step inside one." The root of that objection, I guess, is the belief that improving underperforming schools has to come at the cost of everyone else. It just *has* to; that's what zero-sum games require: winners and losers.

Luckily, though, I have a wife, a family, and friends who were willing to give me three different solutions to that particular puzzle, one philosophical, one political, and the final one economic.

The philosophical answer—a liberal commitment to social justice—isn't going to surprise anyone who knows what I do professionally. One thing everyone believes about Hollywood that turns out to be mostly true is that its politics are pretty progressive. This gives a lot of people permission to call us hypocrites for talking about climate change while flying around the globe—or, in this case, having an opinion about public education and sending our kids to private schools.* I honestly don't know why so many people who tell stories for a living have liberal politics. I've heard it argued that it's because we reflexively take the side of the underdog, if only because it makes for superior drama.

But the philosophical case for social justice is even better. It has a lot of intellectual forebears,† but my favorite is a book that most people encounter in college and never pick up again. In simple terms, John Rawls's *A Theory of Justice* tells us that the most just society is one whose institutions are the ones its members would construct if they knew they were going to be born into the society but had no way of

---

* If I sent my daughters to private schools and then told you that public schools were superior, *that* would be hypocrisy.
† This is where my staff told me to put the "smarty-pants stuff." (Deep breath) Thomas Aquinas. John Stuart Mill. John Locke. Luigi Taparelli (who first used the phrase "social justice"). And especially Immanuel Kant.

predicting whether they'd be part of the most- or least-favored segments. If we had to build a society from behind Rawls's famous "veil of ignorance," where no one knows if he or she is going to be born smart, lucky, or wealthy—in a Mumbai slum or a Philadelphia suburb (or, more to the point, in a neighborhood where the public school is more than 90 percent poor or less than 10 percent)—what kind of education would everyone get?

For sure, we wouldn't be so quick to create a system like the one we have. We wouldn't have affluent suburban school districts surrounding poor urban ones if none of us knew which one our kids would be attending. Maybe most important, in Rawls's words, "greater resources would be spent for education of the less, rather than the more, favored . . ."

Fundamentally, this problem has arisen because we don't think of all of the members of our society as equal. This is a civil rights issue, and we have to be aware that we are complicit in its existence.

An adequate education is a civil right, just like the right to vote or to due process. You don't earn a civil right by doing anything except being born . . . and you definitely don't lose it because your parents were living in the wrong neighborhood *when* you were born. But there's another reason to support closing the achievement gap: a political one. Because if everyone has the right to vote, then we all have a powerful interest in making sure that every vote is an educated one.

I sometimes think that the most revolutionary thing about the American Revolution wasn't creating a constitutional republic or a democratic electoral system, but public education for everyone. Democracies have been around since ancient Athens, republics since Rome, but before the United States, the only people offering free public education were churchmen or wealthy families, and they were doing it out of charity.

America was the first place where government took on the responsibility of educating everyone, and we did it because our founders knew that, in a democracy, a basic education needs to be exactly as widespread as citizenship. John Adams, a hero of mine, sure thought so. In his 1779 *Constitution . . . for the Commonwealth of Massachusetts,* he wrote: ". . . the preservation of [the people's] rights and liberties . . . depend on spreading the opportunities and advantages of education in various parts of the country, and *among the different orders of the people . . .*" (emphasis added).

Revolutionary? Adam Smith, who published *The Wealth of Nations* the same year that Adams, Thomas Jefferson, and all the other founders were signing the Declaration of Independence, had some pretty revolutionary thoughts himself, but even he favored only schools with teachers "partly but not wholly paid by the public," but charging everyone fees meant that real public education in Britain would have to wait for another century. When the Frenchman Alexis de Tocqueville visited the United States half a dozen years after John Adams died, he recognized just how different America was from any other nation that had ever existed—and, remember, de Tocqueville knew a lot about revolution; his own country had experienced a pretty dramatic one only forty years earlier—he wrote, in *Democracy in America:*

> I do not think that the system of self-interest as it is professed in America is in all its parts self-evident, but it contains a great number of truths so evident that men, if they are only educated, cannot fail to see them. Educate, then, at any rate, for the age of implicit self-sacrifice and instinctive virtues is already flitting far away from us, and the time is fast approaching when freedom, public peace, and social order itself will not be able to exist without education.

Most people, including me, prior to immersing myself in this project, will tell themselves, *I'm all for education, it's fairly important, and I believe in democracy, too, but the inner-city problems are too daunting and I have my own problems. To be honest, they aren't really connected to me and my issues.*

Nope. That's actually what de Tocqueville was talking about when he came up with the American idea of "self-interest, rightly understood." We really are in this together. That's not my opinion: That's just what the evidence says. Remember PISA, the world's most widely taken test of cognitive skills? Well, the people who created it don't just collect test scores; they also calculate their impact. Here's how Andreas Schleicher, who directs those PISA tests, puts it: "The best way to find out whether what students have learned at school matters for their life is to actually watch what happens to them after they leave school."

Which is exactly what the Organisation for Economic Co-operation and Development does. They've been tracking the progress of tens of thousands of kids for years, following up every year to see what choices they've made and how successful they've been in college and at work.

In a not-surprising result, you find out that raising the scores of fifteen-year-old students is strongly correlated with success in later life. High scores: good; poor scores: bad. The higher their scores, the greater the impact. The PISA researchers have developed a baseline that allows them to estimate how much those scores matter to what they'd produce over the course of their working lives—how much they'd buy and sell; how much impact they'd have on the number known as the Gross Domestic Product.

This is why measures of parental satisfaction or student self-esteem aren't the focus of this book. Only measurable improvement in achievement scores is correlated with increased economic productivity and allows all of America's families to prosper.

So now I'm appealing to that side in all of us that is practical and economically conservative. (My goal is to systematically awaken every part of us that cares.) A twenty-five point overall improvement in the scores achieved by the world's fifteen-year-olds would add *$115 trillion* to the world economy over their working lifetimes. Twenty-five points. It's actually not a lot. Twenty-five points would raise only America's lowest-performing fifth, those schools that are more than 75 percent poor, to the level achieved by schools that are only a little less poor—those with poverty rates between 50 percent and 75 percent. Twenty-five points raises the score of the lowest quintile—446—to that of the second-lowest quintile: 471. (Remember, the U.S. average is 500, and students in schools where the poverty rate is under 10 percent score 551.) This is really aiming our sights low to make a point.

That movement would produce gigantic dividends for the United States. If all we did was raise the productivity of one-fifth of the U.S. economy to a level that *is still way below the national average,* it would add nearly *$7.8 trillion* to the American GDP over the next sixty years. In current dollars: *$130 billion* a year.

So again I am speaking only to that practical/economic side of ourselves. Wouldn't you want your kids to walk down any street in your city with that much more economic security? Wouldn't you want them in a job market with that much more prosperity to spread around? Wouldn't you want your loved ones to move about a city with that much less desperation?

Education is your issue unless you don't care about prosperity, safety, and stability in our economy.

Even in this little example, we gain $130 billion a year by letting our schools fail our inner-city kids, just fail them a little slower than they are now.

Can you even fathom what America would look like without the education gap? You wouldn't recognize this country.

2

I'M NOT A DOCTOR,
BUT I WATCH A LOT OF *HOUSE, M.D.*

I'm obsessive. My Ph.D. wife would say clinically so. My growing interest in education spilled out in conversations with friends at birthday parties and dinners. One of our friends is a Social Genius. She immediately seized one of these moments in conversation to plan a "think tank" on education. She set it at her beautiful home and invited very powerful and caring individuals from our Philadelphia circle of friends.

On the day of the think-tank dinner on education, we pulled up in the historic driveway of their estate and I felt like I was at the beginning of something big. This is how big things start, isn't it? Driving down a half-mile driveway to an estate? That's how the movie about this book would start anyway. It was so cinematic. Apple trees passed on either side as we parked on the gravel drive and were greeted by the Social Genius.

The food spread was tasteful and impeccable. The Social Genius was not just given her title; she earned it in countless social cage matches.

The assembled group was extremely impressive. One was the CEO of one of the biggest companies in the world. One was an almost legendary attorney who had worked a lot in social welfare. There was a very successful husband and wife who were among the most vocal advocates on behalf of charter schools in the country. And finally, there was the husband of the Social Genius, a brilliant businessman who has achieved enormous success despite a kind of undiagnosed Tourette's syndrome that manifests in ideas that are often off topic and sometimes shocking. Those that haven't been properly prepped can find themselves shaken by his quips. (He's one of my good friends, so I can rib him.) And, of course, Bhavna and me.

We all sat down with our plates of tasteful and impeccable food. The floor was opened up to me. I expressed the very unformed idea that there had to be something we could do about the huge gap in educational achievement in America or, really, some *things*. Perhaps we can make a list of what really works. There must be things that are obvious. There were murmurs of light approval. So I said, "What do you think the list is?" The very first answer came from the Legendary Lawyer, "Small classroom size." I wrote it down. That one seemed obvious to me as well. "Everybody already knows what works. The list is unnecessary," said the husband of the Charter School Couple. "The unions are corrupt. The mayor is a shill for them. You're being . . ." The wife of the Charter School Couple touched her husband's arm as if to silence him. The scars of their wars with the unions and the school boards and the politicians were suddenly clear on their faces as they looked at each other and found a way to ease their shared pain. The Businessman/Tourette's Husband of the Social Genius said, "We should have a World's Fair in Philadelphia. You know how many people would come to this city? Millions."

We all pondered the possibilities of hosting a world's fair with its World of Tomorrow exhibits and then returned to what we were talking about. The Charter School Couple volleyed into the conversation the idea that the ability to fire bad teachers has to be one of the items on the list. I wrote it down. The Social Genius said, "School spirit. Banners in schools. Good learning environments." I liked that one. I wrote it down. The CEO of One of the Biggest Companies said, "Higher pay for teachers." That one seemed obvious, too. I wrote it down. "Do you think I could get someone to sit on a chair in a room and do nothing for one year for one million dollars?" We all looked at the Businessman/Tourette's Husband of the Social Genius. We considered this fascinating subject and returned to education.

So we sat in the wood-paneled dining room and talked and talked. The conversation eventually landed on the topic of charter schools. The Charter School Couple and the Legendary Lawyer stressed that this was the only way. I said for the first time what I would repeat hundreds of times in the future when people got heated: "Please send me the research." I told the table truthfully, "If the facts are the way you say, you just got your poster boy for charter schools." The dinner finished in a flurry of promises of research and exclamations about the delicacy of the crème brûlée (I had half of Bhavna's as well), and promises to follow up and do this again.

As we drove away, I was dizzied by the number of opinions that had been proffered. I knew with even more clarity that I didn't want to produce another opinion. I wanted to find the list of what had been proven, and that was all.

I wondered whether the research I would receive tomorrow morning would end my journey before it began. I wondered whether research would just say charter schools were clearly the answer and the system is corrupt, which would mean there would be no need for a list at all. (I also wondered whether I knew anyone who would sit on a chair in a room for one year and do nothing for $1 million. I decided I knew many.)

The next morning no research arrived at my office. Just a brochure for a wonderful-looking charter school.

Looking back, it was probably just as well that no one tried to drown me with all the studies supposedly proving the value of charters. Not then. Because I wouldn't have been able to figure out what was important and what wasn't.

I wasn't a complete innocent. Long before I had attended the dinner hosted by the Social Genius, I had read plenty of stories in newspapers and magazines either debunking or advocating some silver bullet that was going to close America's educational achievement gap. All of the stories, like most of the ideas from the dinner (the ones that weren't World's Fair–related), sounded plausible enough. But I wanted proof.

I'm a dictionary fiend. It's the most used app on my phone. And when I first looked up the word "proof," I found out that it comes from a Latin root meaning "to test."

The gold standard for testing any kind of hypothesis that can't be experimentally controlled in a lab is a technique known as a "randomized field trial" (sometimes a "randomized clinical trial," or "randomized controlled trial"). They've been around since 1747, when a Royal Navy doctor named James Lind picked twelve sailors from the HMS *Salisbury*, gave six of them citrus juice, and waited to see whether they would get scurvy at the same rate as the six sailors who got nothing at all. (They didn't.) A century later, the American philosopher Charles Sanders Peirce added the idea of dividing the control group and the experimental group randomly, and science was off to the races. Randomized trials are how medical researchers find whether a new therapy is better than an alternative, and they're so popular (and so reliable) that hundreds of thousands of them have been published, and at least 10,000 more come out every year.

If what I wanted was evidence about closing the achievement gap, then randomized field trials were just the ticket. Unfortunately, field trials are about as common in the world of education research as successful urban schools: Though things have started to change over the past half dozen years, even now, no more than a few hundred have even been run. In 2000, the U.S. Department of Education funded 116 separate evaluations of national programs; only one of them was a randomized field trial. This shouldn't have surprised me, since if someone had found the solution already, the problem wouldn't be around anymore. We might want to cure the achievement gap, but we sure haven't been using the same methods that found the cure for polio.

This doesn't mean there haven't been a lot of other tests. The second-best option, where it's too hard (or unethical) to perform a clean randomized trial, is research from what's called an observational study, which is just what it sounds like: observation of subjects who've been sorted into two groups by circumstances—an example would be comparing some characteristic of everyone born in the year 1965 with everyone born in the year 1975—rather than by the decision of an experimenter. *Cross-sectional studies* take a snapshot of their subjects at a particular point in time; *longitudinal studies* do the same thing over a long period of time, sometimes a very long period of time: the Framingham Heart Study has been collecting statistics on cardiovascular disease in the town of Framingham since 1948 (and discovered, among other things, that cigarette smoking, high levels of cholesterol, and stress all increase the risk of heart disease).

Some scholars continue to argue for more data, better

studies, a higher standard for evidence. They're not wrong. But it *is* wrong to discount the consistent evidence from decades of observational data.

When you consider the history of tests and trials, there already is a lot of data. Even years before the federal government passed the No Child Left Behind Act in 2001, states and cities had been collecting carloads of data on student performance on standardized tests. There's so much statistical information on student performance that you can drown in it. It's because of all this data that we know the achievement gap exists at all. There's no problem finding a picture of the way things are. What I was after, though, was evidence of something that *changed* the picture, evidence that had been overlooked.

One thing I knew for sure was that if there was a list of what had been proven with data, no one could tell me what was on the list or where to find the elements of the list. That meant reviewing all the research out there. And that meant I needed a lot of help.

In the summer of 2008, Jennifer Walters-Michalec, our Foundation's director, set out to find that help. Her objective was to hire a researcher who could do what academics call a "literature review": a survey of all the scholarly research on closing the achievement gap in America's schools. Not just data, though; we wanted some guidance on the methods that policy-makers and academics used to define things like "achievement," which is not nearly as simple as it sounds. We had high standards for our candidates: a perfect mix of scary intellect, irrepressible enthusiasm, and outside-the-box curiosity. And one thing more: The right person had to believe that the project was even doable. Though Jennifer wanted someone who could balance my eternal optimism with a healthy dose of skepticism, our researcher needed to believe that the evidence was out there.

Two weeks later, Jenn introduced me to our newest researcher, James Richardson. Now I have to say, I trust Jenn's judgment completely. She has a real knack for spotting talent and with Bhavna has discovered some of our most celebrated grantees. But when she introduced me to James Richardson, I was dubious. I was dubious because Jenn used to spend a lot of time alone in her office room with our cat. And this new researcher was one of those *GQ* good-looking British dudes. Of all the résumés she picked a Hugh Grant look-alike? You can understand my suspicion. Everyone has weaknesses, even do-gooders.

After spending an afternoon with James, however, I knew why she had hired him. James had all the right academic credentials: experience in the classroom as a teacher; strong background in statistics and methodology; familiarity with the state-of-the-art in education research. James was working at the Graduate School of Education at the University of Pennsylvania and would be continuing his doctoral studies when he returned to England; in short, he was smart. But most of all, James believed a literature review was both possible and necessary and, most of all, useful. And he believed it would reveal the answers we were looking to find. The other candidates had tried to convince Jenn that our project was too immense or that our theory was too bold. Some were convinced that the evidence was going to be too ambiguous; others thought that unambiguous evidence might be found, but that the effort involved made it too large a challenge.

James was different. He was ready to do the work—a *lot* of work; hundreds if not thousands of papers, journals, reports, and books—and smart enough to make sense of it all.

He was confident we would find our answers, and wanted in on the project. Hugh Grant was our guy.

The first thing James required was that we develop a set of standards, which we would use to create our list of tenets that were valid while discarding others. What he recommended, and we adopted, was something called "effect size"—the statistical measure of the strength of a phenomenon. For patients with cardiovascular disease, a high-fat, high-calorie diet has a negative effect size on mortality. Quitting smoking, on the other hand, has an effect size of somewhere around +.75.*

The next thing James made us do was to assemble the potential candidates for inclusion on our list. So, we collected a dozen different books, and a year's worth of magazine and newspaper articles, along with papers from professional journals and conferences, all on various aspects of educational reform: scholarly and popular, practical and theoretical. We then created an index of the leading ideas—or, at least, those that were respectable enough to be written about.

For me, the big advantage of effect size is that it is a kind of standard measure that could be used to compare any different idea about closing the achievement gap with another, whether it was an "increase in school spirit" (I hadn't forgotten the Social Genius's dinner) or smaller class size: not just whether they had an effect, but how big the effect was.

For example, charter schools.

Charter schools—those publicly funded but privately managed schools that are, in theory, free of most of the regulatory red tape that is more common in typical public schools

---

* The number is a fraction of a single standard deviation. For more on the statistics behind effect size, see Appendix B: A Short Note on Statistical Significance, Standard Deviation, and Effect Size.

than lined notebook paper—are pretty much everywhere, in forty states plus the District of Columbia. By the end of 2009, the United States had around 4,700 charter schools, enrolling more than 1.4 million students. This meant that even though no one at that dinner party sent me the evidence that charter schools were the answer to America's achievement gap, there's a lot of information about them.

But there's a reason no one sent me the evidence that charters work: Even though there's a lot of evidence, it doesn't show that they work—not overall, anyway. The biggest study of charter school performance to date—covering some 70 percent of the country's charter school students—was done by the Center for Research on Education Outcomes at Stanford University in 2009. Here's what the study found:

- Using scores from the 2007 National Assessment of Educational Progress (NAEP) math tests, 17 percent of charter schools provided "superior educational opportunities"; 46 percent were no different from local public schools; and 37 percent were worse.
- Remember effect size? The overall effect size of charter schools was *negative:* Students in America's charter schools scored −.01 in reading, and −.03 in math. Though the first number is statistically and practically meaningless, and the second is barely meaningful, they sure don't suggest that charter schools, on average, are better than traditional ones.

Want more? The NAEP did the same sort of comparison in 2003, and found that the differences between traditional and charter schools were smaller than the error factor in the survey. The same year, the Department of Education published a report—the "Evaluation of the Public Charter Schools Program: Final Report"—that documented that traditional schools actually *outperform* charters. The National Center for Education Statistics found the same thing in 2006.

This doesn't mean there aren't success stories among charter schools. In fact, just about all of the real success stories we found in closing America's achievement gap were charters. Some cities, like New Orleans, have a lot of good news on the charter front. In New York, charter school students score higher in both math and reading than traditional public school students: In math, 50 percent do better than traditional public schools, a third do as well, and 16 percent do worse. In reading, 30 percent better, 60 percent the same, and 12 percent worse.*

So why all the passionate support? In the headache-inducing discipline of propositional logic, there's a term called either *affirming the consequent* or *denying the antecedent*. Put together, they comprise the formal fallacy known as the *undistributed middle:* a bad syllogism.

You know what a good syllogism looks like: I am a man. All men must die. Therefore, I must die. And I'll bet you can recognize a false one: I am going to die. All things that die are men. Therefore, I am a man.

This puts you one up on a lot of charter school advocates. Look at this (mostly) correct syllogism:

"All schools that succeed at closing the achievement gap are charters."

"This school closes the achievement gap."

"This is a charter school."

---

* The numbers are rounded off, which is why they total more than 100 percent.

Now, examine this incorrect one:

> "All schools that succeed at closing the achievement gap are
> charters."

> "This is a charter school."

> "This school closes the achievement gap."

The problem is that the middle term is in the wrong place. It
is "undistributed."

That's what happened with our meeting. Almost all of the
closing-the-gap stories *have* taken place in charter schools.
So many, in fact, that anyone would be forgiven for thinking
that these schools were successful *because* they were charter
schools. Belief in charter schooling, though, is a false syllogism. It's not the charter itself that's working the magic, but
something else. It's something you find in charters—in *some*
charters—that allows the magic to work.

When I learned this, I was both excited and confused: excited because it meant that there was still a need for that list
after all; and confused by my own reflexive skepticism about
the charter school support.

You see, I'm not a naturally skeptical person. The passion and confidence I saw at the Social Genius's dinner party
is usually exactly what inspires me. Ordinarily, I'm the one
steamrolling everyone's objections. Tell me I can't do something, and I'm going to prove you wrong: As I said, the eternal optimist. Normally, I am not the one demanding evidence.

But there was something about the kind of enthusiasm I
encountered at the dinner party that made me hold up a stop
sign. The guests definitely knew a lot. They were engaged,
sure. But they were also *pissed off.* They'd been butting heads
with the education bureaucracy for so long that they were

dizzy. But instead of being confused, they were more and more locked into their points of view. Their stories demanded villains: the mayor, the teachers' union, you name it.

And something in me just said no. I just couldn't accept that this was a story of good versus evil, no matter how impassioned the good guys seemed to be. So I did what I should actually do more often: I asked for the facts. Not long afterward, I asked Bhavna why I had acted so out of character. She looked at me sideways, and said (as if I already knew the answer), "You don't believe in enemies." After twenty years, she knows me pretty well. Because I really do want everyone to get along or, at least, not to be so angry they can't see straight.

It's not that I don't understand where a lot of the anger comes from. If you believe you really do know the way to get somewhere you need to be—to where America doesn't have an achievement gap, for example—and see anyone in your way, natural instincts take over: You get angry. Unfortunately, so does the guy in your way. Neither of you is a villain, definitely not in your own minds.

As a result, along with setting out the project's ground rules for evidence, I was determined to start our research with one other nonnegotiable principle: People who disagreed with our conclusions (whatever they might turn out to be) weren't evil. No one wants kids to leave school with inferior educations. The disagreement on how to prevent this (and, to be fair, how important it is to prevent this) doesn't come from bad intentions. It comes from somewhere else. It comes from bias.

Not racial bias; cognitive bias.

For lots of reasons, the human brain uses a lot of shortcuts and rules of thumb—the technical term is "heuristics"—in daily life. Most of the time, these shortcuts work OK. If I see a car decorated with a Confederate flag, I know I'm probably not going to get the driver to donate money to the ACLU. I'll be wrong some of the time, but not often. Sometimes, though, these rules confuse things more than they help. When they do, they become cognitive biases.

Researchers have been documenting different flavors of cognitive bias for more than thirty years now, and the list is now really long. There's *confirmation bias:* the tendency to cherry-pick information in favor of facts that confirm what we already believe. Or the *endowment effect,* where people value things more highly after they acquire them than they did before; whenever someone wants to sell something for more than he would pay to acquire it, that's an example. Or *hindsight bias,* which is what happens when people see past events in the light of present circumstances. Or the *frequency illusion,* the way a recent exposure to something—a song or a car or a breed of dog—makes us overestimate how often we're subsequently encountering it. For a rational species, we have a lot of irrational thinking tools.

The one that's most on display in any discussion of charter schools is known as the *affect heuristic,* which is what we depend on when we use a gut response to solve problems and arrive at conclusions. Like most heuristics, it might have offered an evolutionary advantage to our ancestors—when you're evaluating dangers in the Neolithic world, anything that speeds up your decision-making is probably a good idea— but it isn't so helpful today. For a lot of people, just hearing a presentation that includes the phrase "The teachers' union supports . . ." produces a bad-enough vibe that they don't even hear what comes next.

There's another problem with the affect heuristic, though: It's very bad at calculating. It has what psychologists call an "insensitivity to numbers." Which makes sense; a decision-making tool that evolved to remind our ancestors to avoid cave bears didn't have to be very good in counting up how many cave bears were needed to qualify as dangerous.

However, this also means that using the affect heuristic makes us a lot better at distinguishing between good and bad than at measuring "how good" or "how bad." Eating foods that are high in omega-3 fatty acids is good for you; so is not smoking. But their respective impacts aren't really comparable. In the same way, something that shows any effect at all on educational achievement—all those ideas at the Social Genius's dinner—usually has a lot of supporters, who find it a lot easier to see that something is doing good, without asking how much good.

This affect heuristic doesn't just infect civilians.* At least one scholar who's studied his colleagues in the social sciences pretty closely, John Hattie, points out that education research suffers because, well, "everything works." That is, 90 percent of all effect sizes in education are positive; and of the other 10 percent, half are the kind of things that you didn't expect to be positive in the first place, like poor behavior. By that standard, 95 percent of all educational interventions work, which means that it is as easy to find success stories as it is to find a block in Manhattan with a Starbucks; the real trick is finding a block without one. Just improving achievement isn't enough, since teachers who claim they are making a difference are usually right (they would have to be spectacularly bad to reduce learning). The key question is *how much* of a difference.

Another version of number insensitivity—one that appears in almost every popular account of educational reform—is

---

* Among studies that meet the most rigorous standard of evidence, very few have both positive effects and statistical significance.

the simplifying assumption formally known as the *linearity fallacy*, and that I call the if-some-is-good-more-is-better syndrome. We find it difficult to recognize threshold effects: phenomena that offer benefits only to a particular point. People who consume half as much vitamin A as they need can lose their vision to an ugly disease called xerophthalmia;* eating twice as much vitamin A as needed doesn't give them 20/10 vision. In the same way, a school that buys only half as many textbooks as it needs is in trouble, but one that buys twice as many as it needs is just wasting money.

These cognitive biases haven't been very helpful in changing educational policy, but learning about them definitely helped us. We didn't have to assume bad motives among people who were disagreeing with each other (or, as our ideas started to jell, with us). The conflicts didn't have to be about greed or self-interest or even ignorance—not usually, anyway. Most of them were the result of a cognitive bias: logical hiccups.

As we—and by "we," I mean James—began reviewing the literature on closing-the-gap efforts, and comparing results on the basis of effect size, a problem emerged. If our standard for evidence required that a particular practice have an obvious and direct effect on student achievement, we were going to be very disappointed. A lot of the effect sizes James was finding weren't direct; there wasn't a one-to-one correspondence between a particular practice and an effect, good or bad, on student achievement. A lot of the results were what statisticians call "mediated." Instead of experiments in which a change in an independent variable leads directly to a change

---

* A brief commercial for the M. Night Shyamalan Foundation: We've been funding vitamin therapy aimed directly at this problem for years.

in the dependent variable, the action, whatever it was, took a detour. The path didn't lead from a to b, but from a to c to b, and when c (the technical term is the *mediator variable*) is affected by other forces, finding the connection between a and b got more and more difficult.

Take charter schools. Even if the fact of attending a charter school really did have a large effect on student achievement—and, as we had discovered, it doesn't—it would be doing so by affecting some intermediate thing: how their teachers behave, or how much homework they assign, or how big the class sizes were. We not only didn't know the path between action and achievement; we didn't know how many different mediator variables were in between. The phenomenon was too complicated to understand, much less to implement.

So now I had the rudimentary tools to understand and evaluate research. Now I could understand what was working and what wasn't, but there had to be more to this problem. And I also knew this was a system—all the urban schools were working at the same level. What were the rules of this system? What were the invisible rules this system was functioning under?

Now this is where the story could have ended: me struggling over the search for these invisible rules and buried in contradictory data. And it did, until I ordered spinach gnocchi at Vetri.

Not long after the Social Genius's dinner, Bhavna and I were eating at this Italian restaurant with friends, another couple, both of them doctors. After eating a dinner portion of spinach gnocchi for my appetizer—I have no more self-discipline when it comes to buttery pasta than I do with crème brûlée—I asked Kevin Fosnocht, who is chief medical officer at Penn Presbyterian Medical Center, how his work was going. Kevin is a straight, no-nonsense guy, the guy you

turn to for advice in every situation. One of his most important jobs is teaching the hospital's sixteen residents, the best
and brightest from all over the country, during the last stage
of their clinical education. He casually said, while eating, that
the first thing he tells the residents, the first thing he tries to
inculcate in them, is the understanding that if your patients eat
a balanced diet, sleep eight hours a day, exercise three times
a week, don't smoke, and have a relatively stress-free work
environment, their chance of becoming seriously ill drops
dramatically. It beats every pill and drug ever concocted. He
mentioned that 50 percent of all mortality is directly related to
behavior. He also mentioned that there are related emotional
factors like structured critical self-reflection that can help as
well. And then Kevin offered, as he dipped his fresh-baked
bread into the extra virgin olive oil, the interesting fact that
*if you don't do all of those five behavioral things together, the
chance of your getting sick climbs right back up to the average.*

Occasionally, I watch the TV show *House, M.D.* And
there's always a moment, around minute thirty-eight, where
Dr. House is doing something seemingly irrelevant and gets
the answer to a seemingly unsolvable medical case. He might
be bowling and the dude who sprays the shoes before he
hands them out might make him think about a particular type
of bacteria in shoes that caused the patient's *Exorcist*-like
symptoms.

This was like that. I was like House, except Kevin gave me
the answer directly. I guess it was basically his idea. Fine.

You have to do them all. Doing four out of five doesn't
buy you 80 percent of the health improvement you get by
doing all five, but the effects of the remaining four tenets drop
exponentially. And you can't make up for a missing element
by doubling down on the remainder: If you try to make up
for an unhealthy diet with more exercise, that doesn't work.

Your body is a system. To operate properly, it needs to be treated systemically.

But if the problem was like health and could only be addressed systemically, how could we be sure what worked? The answer was hidden in the question: We could use the same kind of careful, longitudinal observational studies that have taught modern medicine just about everything known about heart disease, diabetes, and cancer.

That night, I thought again about Masterman and Overbrook. And I wondered if the difference between the healthy school and the unhealthy one might be just as system-sensitive as the difference between healthy and unhealthy people. What if classrooms "want" to be healthy? What if successful schools, like healthy people, shared a manageable number of characteristics that were so inextricably linked that missing one of them was nearly as bad as missing all of them? If this was the case, the results of each healthy tenet would be obfuscated and attenuated. Occasionally, when mixed with the right other tenets, the positive result would pop and then disappear again. If this was the case, the achievement gap between America's best-performing schools and its worst could be closed. And not just school by school, but everywhere.

Something went click inside of me, like when I know I have the right ending to a script.

So the research began. The papers and information were read and deciphered and presented to me week after week. There would be heated discussions between me, Bhavna, Jenn, and James about what each study meant and how it was or wasn't a part of a tenet. A picture started to emerge. Patterns. Categories. Some weeks, we would feel that we were on the doorstep of understanding what the tenets were and how many there were, and then there would be something that refused to fit. During this long process, I wanted to meet some of the prominent and respected leaders in the field of education. I wanted to sit with them for two reasons: one, to get advice and learn from them, and two, to see if they would laugh me out of the room when I told them my theory and the research we were doing. This was their life. I was just a tourist.

My coming-out party happened as a result of an invitation to attend the first annual Keystone Weekend in Hershey, Pennsylvania. This was described as a conference of Pennsylvanians who wanted to improve the state. They were having panels. They asked if I would be on one. I suggested that if they wanted to have a panel on education, I would be honored to attend. Unfortunately, they said yes. So Bhavna and I drove to Hershey to attend this conference where I was on a panel where I knew virtually nothing. I really had the sense I was a complete fraud. To compound my angst, my wife is a rabid zealot for Cadbury chocolate, and the thought of going to the city where they make "that sugary chocolate" was causing marital strife. Chocolate is a big deal to my wife and I'm sure to many wives. By the way, my wife has a British accent and was raised in Hong Kong, which explains the Cadbury fanaticism. We checked into the hotel, where there were Hershey confections of every variety in the room. Bhavna tried one, made a face. I said, "I know." She just shook her head.*

So there was a dinner. There was music. There were governors and senators. There were union heads. The panels started the next day. Ours was in the afternoon.

I remember being on the stage seated in the last of four chairs. I was on a panel with Marjorie Rendell, the wife of the governor of Pennsylvania, who was deeply involved in education reform, as well as Congressman Chaka Fattah and Roger

---

* I love Hershey chocolate. Don't tell my wife.

Dennis, dean at the Earle Mack School of Law of Drexel University. I remember the discussion became very inflamed very quickly. I felt the way I feel at the first audience preview for a film. You have no idea what the audience will think of your endeavor the first time it is screened, before you have a chance to fine-tune it and fix any of the problems. It may be a violent reaction or a quiet, warm acceptance. So my name was called and the floor was finally turned over to me. Everyone was very curious about what I was doing there. I told them all about my dinner with Kevin and my *House* moment. I told them I was going to search as much of the research as I could and see if there were these tenets, or keys, that have already been proven to close the achievement gap when done together and not separately. I told them I would tell them all what I found regardless of its implications to the life work of anyone in this room. I also told them I have no scars. I didn't think anyone in the room was the enemy. (And I still don't.) I just wanted to put things we really know on the table and see if the answer was already there. When the forum finished, there was an overwhelming number of union heads, politicians, and social do-gooders who came up and sincerely thought I was onto something. They felt instinctually from their experiences that there just might be this overlooked set of keys. It was a truly important moment for me. It gave me courage and it made me feel like everyone was on my side. I so badly wanted to help everyone in that room. I just wanted to be a list for them; a nonscarred, nonemotional list.

I felt like I got a good score on my first preview screening, but insecurity kept me going out and making sure my premise was sound. I called some superestablished people in the field of education to run my ideas by them and see if they felt there was merit in my endeavor.

I invited Wendy Kopp, the woman who created Teach

For America in her senior thesis at Princeton, to visit me at work. On one of her visits to Philly, she came. Wendy was so gracious to sit with Bhavna and me and listen to my nascent idea of whether there was an equivalent list of simple education practices that paralleled the medical ones that Kevin taught me about. Wendy thought carefully about it before she spoke. She said in her quiet way, "Maybe." I asked what, in her opinion, they might be. She told me about her strong belief that teacher training was the key. She was compiling a huge amount of data that would culminate in a report within a year. (This meeting was two years ago. The results of that report are referenced later in this book.) As we said goodbye to her that afternoon, my wife and I both felt her weariness. She was a mother and a trailblazer, and there were critics at every corner ready to undercut her achievements. She had asked us to support the Philadelphia branch of TFA, which we said we would. What really struck me as she drove away from the farm where I work was the fact that she thought it was possible that a list did exist. It made sense to her. I turned to Bhavna and said, "I guess we're not crazy."

In 2009 when this book began, Washington, D.C., was the epicenter for education reform. The person behind that explosion of controversy was Schools Chancellor Michelle Rhee. Michelle agreed to meet us for dinner in the middle of her busy schedule. Bhavna, Jenn, and I drove down to meet her. Michelle—surprise, surprise—was a TFA alum. Michelle at the time was pushing for radical changes in the teachers' union contracts. Forty percent of the students in the Washington, D.C., district were enrolled in charter schools, so with the great support of her mayor, she felt she could turn D.C. around from one of the lowest-performing districts in the country to one of the best. Her courage and lioness nature inspired me. She met us in an Asian-fusion restaurant. Bhavna and I love Asian food. I don't know what we expected, maybe some cold, machinelike individual who would chill us with her stare, but that's not who ate and spoke with us. Michelle came off as a funny and caring mother, and inspiring person. She listened as she ate, and when I finished with my "so it was like a *House* moment except Kevin just gave me the idea" joke, she smiled and said, "I'd be really interested to see your list when it's done." She said she suspected "human capital" would be on the list—teachers, principals, administrators, etc. She also said, "School choice should be one of them." She also stressed that data in some form would be on her list. We had a wonderful meal in the shadow of the Capitol building. We drank wine and joked and hoped to see each other again.

Jenn and Bhavna asked me early on to meet with Kate Walsh, the president of the National Council on Teacher Quality. Ever since it was founded in 2000, the organization has been a loud and sometimes controversial voice on behalf of everything from reforming teachers' education to standards-based teacher evaluations. Kate had come to NCTQ after running education programs in a boarding school in East Africa and one for at-risk students in her hometown of Baltimore. Kate turned out to be a very supportive person and I remember her smiling a lot. She also surprised me. She showed me copious amounts of literature not on teachers, but on tested curricula. She was convinced this had to be on the list and she had numbers to support it. I'll be honest. I heavily resisted this. This came early and I had certain prejudices. One of them was that all teachers needed freedom. But I promised I would consider it and thanked her for coming.

One of the best ways to slip me information is by feeding me articles, one at a time. Even better, by marking those articles with a highlighter. Or a Post-it note. That's what happened, about a year into our research project, when either James or Jennifer passed along a printout of an article entitled "Leadership as the Practice of Improvement." It was written by one of the most prominent educational researchers in the country, Richard Elmore at Harvard, who showed that there really aren't many direct effects in education that can be traced back to a single policy or program. What really happens is that a group of programs alters the distribution of effects around the mean. It shifts those curves of performance, usually in small and marginal ways.

What that means is that it isn't the direct effects that matter nearly as much as the *distribution of effects*. Moving the curve, a little bit at a time. But that doesn't mean that the effect isn't real. Here's his important quote:

> In the language of old-fashioned analysis of variance, interaction effects dominate main effects. *The effects most worth knowing about in policy analysis, and the least analyzed, are interaction effects* [emphasis added].

As a filmmaker, interaction effect is practically all we do. In the famous example, if you put a shot of a man staring and edit it to a steaming bowl of soup, we will feel the man is hungry. If we put a shot of a man staring and edit it to a voluptuous woman, who is undressing, we will think he is lusting after her. I've been making movies for more than twenty years, and I know that no one scene makes a movie work. In fact, I'd take it a step further: Improving any one scene won't necessarily make the movie better. It's just as likely to make it worse. Interactions are what matter.

If Professor Elmore was right, what we were looking for wasn't a list of policies that helped to close America's achievement gap independent of one another. We needed to find the practices that had their biggest impact from interacting with other practices. We needed a system. *"You have to do them all."*

Now, for the first time, I knew what the question had to be, and I took it back to James. "Is there a handful of tenets in education, like 'sleep eight hours a day' and 'exercise three times a week,' that interact in ways that multiply their impact?"

Answering that question took nearly another year.

3

WHY ISN'T *THAT* ON THE LIST?

There were a lot of ideas thrown into the mix at the Social Genius's dinner. To be fair, I didn't think all of them were equally promising. As it turned out, some were dead-on, some were improperly categorized, and some were just wrong. In the end, there are seven popular ideas about education reform that didn't make the final list. Some were surprises. There were ideas proposed at the dinner that were so clearly necessary for closing the achievement gap that I almost thought we didn't need to research them. Such as, for example, reducing the number of kids in every classroom. But you won't find it on the list.

CLASS SIZE?

All kinds of people believe in smaller class size. I did, and I had a lot of company. According to the Gallup Organization's survey "The Public's Attitudes Toward the Public Schools," the number-one choice for a change that would improve American education was reducing class size. I don't usually go with the crowd, but this one was common sense. Fewer kids per teacher? More time with each kid? Increased personal attention? You'd have to be irrational not to advocate for smaller classrooms.

I'm going to be irrational now. In the 1920s and '30s, researchers studied the importance of the number of kids in each classroom, which was a real issue at the time, as larger class sizes were starting to appear in America because of a fast-growing population. Out of all those dozens of studies (which were designed to ask the opposite question—was there a *disadvantage* to kids who take their lessons in larger classes), only two found that larger classes imposed any cost at all on student achievement, and those costs were so small that they were insignificant. Old information, but our first piece of evidence.

It didn't matter then. It doesn't matter now. Polls still show overwhelming support for reducing class size, and not just in America. James shared another study with me, one that compared the effect of class size on student performance in eighteen different countries. What the researchers who conducted the survey discovered was kind of underwhelming. Throughout the world, the only places students in smaller classes do significantly better than their peers are Greece and Iceland; and since the only other thing that those two countries had in common over the last ten years were gigantic financial bubbles, it's a good bet the class-size effect is pure coincidence. Eleven other countries *might* have some small effects from lowering class sizes, but they're so small that they disappear when compared to achievement gains in other ways. Data from outside the United States, but a second piece of evidence.

A 2000 study of 649 schools that compared classes of a

given size with others that were 10 percent smaller—classes of twenty kids versus other classes with eighteen, for example— found even less. Even when the bar is set very low—an effect size of +.02 to .04, or 2 to 4 percent of a standard deviation— there is no evidence that reducing class size has any noticeable impact.

You could even argue that the real problem with advocating for smaller class size is *we've already done it*. In 1960, the average class size in American schools was 25.8; in 1970, it had dropped to 22.3. In 1980, 18.7. In 1990, 17.2. And the trend shows no signs of stopping: Average class size fell from 17.2 students for every teacher in 1992 to 15.4 in 2005, and is expected to be at 14.6 in 2017. (Private schools have lowered class sizes even further, from 15.4 to 13.5 to 11.8.) If reductions in class size were going to improve student achievement, you might think they should have done so already. But there's hardly a single measure, from the National Assessment of Educational Progress to average scores on the SAT, that went up during those thirty years. Real-life information and our third piece of evidence.

You might not know this from reading newspaper accounts, since supporters of Class-Size Reduction (or CSR) still seem able to find at least *some* studies in support of their position. Here's the real report card: Out of 277 different estimates on the effect of teacher-pupil ratios, about 40 percent showed a small positive effect size, 40 percent a small negative, and 20 percent neutral.*

And there was the "Hawthorne Effect."

It's named for the Hawthorne Works, a telephone equip-

---

* Only about a third of the studies were even—and sorry for bringing it up again—statistically significant. That is, of the 40 percent that were positive, only 14 percent were probably more than just random noise.

ment factory near Cicero, Illinois, where, back in the 1920s, a bunch of industrial engineers and psychologists conducted a series of experiments on the workforce, like adjusting the amount of light on the factory floor in small ways, to see what impact, if any, more (or less) illumination had on productivity. The answers were confounding. Sure enough, when the light was increased, the workmen performed better. But they did the same thing when the light was turned down. Giving them more breaks raised productivity, but when the breaks were changed back, productivity increased then as well. The "Hawthorne Effect" has been part of the literature on motivational psychology ever since: Participants in studies alter their behavior when they feel they're being singled out. It wasn't the amount of light; it was the amount of attention.* Whether you put students into smaller or larger classes, and watch what happens, some of what you're going to see is just a result of the kids knowing they're being watched.

There's one big exception to this rule: In 1985, the state of Tennessee kicked off the STAR (for Student-Teacher Achievement Ratio) Project, which was, and remains, by far the largest class-size experiment ever: nearly 80 schools, more than 300 classrooms, and 6,500 students to start. Tennessee randomly assigned students and teachers to either large—22 to 25 students, with an average size of 23 students—or small classes, with between 13 and 17 students, averaging 15. The idea was to see whether the students who were assigned to smaller classes, from kindergarten through third grade, showed improvement in their subsequent educational achievement.

They did. The immediate impact, as measured by the tests

---

* Another worry, also well documented from a century's worth of social science research: the "demand effect," which occurs when participants change their behavior to give the researchers what they think the researchers want.

on math and literacy skills that the Tennessee students took, starting in 1989, was significant: an effect size of +.21 to .23 in reading, and +.13 to .27 in math, which translates into about twelve weeks' worth of additional schooling. And, though the kids were returned to "normal-sized" classrooms starting in the fourth grade, they were followed for at least the next thirteen years, and the STAR kids continued to see positive results. When the time came for college admissions tests like the SAT and ACT, Project STAR showed effect sizes of about +.12 to .13 as compared to kids who had never experienced smaller classes. This isn't actually all that big; but another feature of the follow-up studies was that black students who had been through the STAR small classes in their K–3 years were more likely to take college prep tests.

So, if the biggest and best study of class-size reduction showed such unambiguously solid results, would this be part of our list of gap-closing tenets? It looked like it would, but . . .

The closer you look at the Tennessee STAR Project, the more problems you find. First, the teachers involved received a lot of supplemental training, which makes it a little hard to untangle what was at the root of the students' performance improvement. Then there was the program's incremental cost, estimated at more than $7,000 per student. Since the average annual expenditure per student in the United States today, nearly thirty years after STAR, is only $11,000, this kind of reduction in class size looked unbelievably expensive.

However, since smaller classes are still one of the favorite tactics for parents and reformers alike, I needed to find out more about class-size reduction. The good news was that one scholar's name showed up more than anyone else's on the subject. The bad news—he didn't live near downtown Philly.

It was raining when I landed in San Francisco. This was my memory of the city when I lived there for a month when finishing the sound for *The Last Airbender* at Skywalker Ranch; rainy and slightly cold all the time. I drove the forty minutes to Stanford University, the only school in the country that I admired that I forbade my daughter to apply to because it was too far from me. (I know this is medieval. Leave me alone.) I flew here to meet with Professor Eric Hanushek, the Paul and Jean Hanna Senior Fellow at the Hoover Institution.

Professor Hanushek is an economist who has done copious amounts of research on the subject of education. He is quoted everywhere promiscuously. I pulled up in a continuing light rain, which I learned from the professor later is highly unusual for the area where Stanford University is located. The campus was immediately striking; similar sandstone architecture and red-tile roofing on every building. I later learned from the professor this was by design of the founders. I got a bit lost looking for his office. I asked a friendly university student. I judged the entire student body by her approachability and empathy, which lucky for the student body was commendable on both fronts. She guided me to the proximity of the Herbert Hoover building, where the professor does whatever professors do. I found his office right near the entrance. I didn't know what I expected, but the person that greeted me was a small, white-haired gentleman with a boyish, mischievous smile.

Professor Hanushek's office was modest and lined with books from floor to ceiling along all four walls, punctured by only a single window. I liked him immediately. I wanted to stay and peruse his collection, but my plane had landed thirty minutes late and we were in jeopardy of missing the one-thirty deadline for lunch at the faculty lounge. We began our walk through the Stanford campus. The professor seemed curious about me. "How did you come to be interested in this subject?" I told him about my personality. I told him I was a unifying theory kind of person. I told him about filmmaking and about how I needed to know the unifying theme of a film before beginning it so it permeated every scene and each piece of dialogue. He asked an example. I told him the unifying theory of *The Sixth Sense* was communication. He listened to me and simultaneously gave me a tour of the campus. He told me, "That's the tower where Herbert Hoover had an office after he was president." All around us as we walked, students crisscrossed us on bikes. I was wearing a baseball cap and a backpack. I felt like a student. I thought this would be a great place to go to school. I felt a pang of guilt about my daughter. It passed.

We were the last to be seated in the faculty cafeteria. I was starving. It was four-thirty East Coast time. I tortured myself with the menu as I often do. My wife finds this mildly annoying. I asked the waiter for his advice between the cheeseburger and the "Stanford Faculty Club." I did this hoping he would say, "Sir, you must have the burger. It is sublime." I do this to every waiter or waitress. I make them complicit in my bad choices. My wife finds this habit *completely* annoying. The professor was amused by my culinary vacillations. I settled on the club and said no to the fries reluctantly. I had told the professor about the health tenet model on the walk over, so he gave me the fist of solidarity for not choosing the fries. I dove right in with the questions. I asked him about classroom size. He immediately told me it has a minimal positive result but is dwarfed by so many other things, including quality teachers, that it isn't worth implementing. "Its value is too low for its cost." I realized again I was talking to an economist. I said off the cuff as I ordered the Stanford Faculty Club, "So that Tennessee STAR study really changed the country, didn't it?"

The professor said, "That is not true." And then he began

to tell me a very interesting story. Governor Pete Wilson of California, who took office in 1991, had a bit of an issue with the teachers' unions. They were demanding higher pay. Things got heated, and he decided to spend the money on something else in education to ensure the unions didn't get the money. In an attempt to spite them, he announced he would cut class sizes all across California. (Ironically, the unions would later love this move.) This was a move based on the intuitive feeling from the voting public that overpopulated classrooms were one of the major causes of the poor education system. The public believed that with fewer students, teachers can pinpoint their attention and efforts and produce strong results.

What followed was a huge natural experiment. California budgeted a billion dollars to pay local school districts that were able to keep class sizes in kindergarten through third grade below twenty kids per class.

The predictable consequence was a California Gold Rush in teacher hiring; the Los Angeles Unified School District, which had been hiring around 1,300 new elementary teachers a year, immediately hired more than 3,300 and, for the next five years, hired more than 2,500 annually. Teachers found themselves teaching in any space large enough to hold a dozen kids, sometimes windowless broom closets. The good news is that this huge influx of new teachers didn't lower the overall achievement for the state's five- through eight-year-olds. The bad news is that it didn't raise it, either. New teachers, old teachers, small classes, large ones: No change.

Even so, the governor's move worked—for him. His popularity rating went up twenty-five points virtually overnight. Governors in other states all across the country took note of this incredible swing in popularity and followed. Twenty governors passed their own small-class bills in their states very soon after, and twenty-four states now have some kind of CSR policy. We now had a movement and the voting public felt heard. To support all this governmental activism, officials looked to the research to find something to support what they all knew to be self-evident. They found it in the Tennessee study. Article after article after that made reference to the evidence for reduced classroom size, but in small print one can see they are referencing the same Tennessee study.

But the Tennessee STAR Project hasn't been replicated with anything like the same results, anywhere. The professor explained to me not only that the Tennessee study has never been duplicated but that, in his opinion, it was poorly done. "They didn't carefully document the students' achievements prior to the experiment, and they had very questionable grouping of the students." In his opinion, even if the findings were true, class-size reduction still didn't have enough of an impact to implement. "Their findings are dwarfed by the impact of good teachers. Why would you spend so much money to get such a small effect?" The cost, after all, is hundreds of billions of dollars—extrapolated to the entire country. Every one student decrease per teacher is about $12 billion annually—and the STAR Project reduced the count by eight kids, on average—for what amounts to a pretty modest effect size? There's nothing wrong with it. It's just not going to close the gap and it's unconscionably expensive for its gains.

I took a bite out of my Stanford Faculty Club sandwich, and bitterly regretted not choosing the burger and fries. The professor seemed pleased with his black bean burger.

When you think about it, you can see why CSR remains stubbornly popular. For lots of constituencies—teachers, for example, and probably even more important, teachers' unions—a belief in smaller class size has a perfectly rational basis: Smaller classes aren't necessarily less work, but they do allow more time with each student, which at least gives teachers the impression they're delivering a better teaching experience. And they demand, by definition, more teachers, which obviously is something teachers' unions would support.

But there's just as much support for CSR among scholars, who have no financial interest in the subject. For them, the reason might just be repetition—another of those cognitive biases, known as the "availability heuristic," which inclines us to make judgments based on how easy it is to find a confirming example, and, among educational researchers, hardly anything is easier to find than yet another mention of the STAR Project. The two best-known papers supporting the Tennessee STAR Project—one by Frederick Mosteller, a statistician at Harvard, the other by a team led by Alan Krueger, a Princeton economist—have been cited in the scholarly literature nearly nine hundred times between them.

But even the availability heuristic doesn't explain why parents and policy-makers remain so enthusiastic about smaller classes, so convinced by the simple math that fewer kids equals more education for each of them. Or, for that matter, why I did. Part of the enthusiasm is that it's intuitively obvious: We know, for example, that one-to-one tutoring has a huge effect on student achievement and assume that CSR gets us closer to a one-to-one relationship. Another, though, is that we're victims of a kind of thinking hiccup known as an *observational bias*—in this case, the "streetlight effect."

OK. You find a guy crawling around in the middle of the sidewalk looking for his keys under the nearest streetlight, even though he lost them in the park. You ask him why, and he says, "The light's better here."

That's a big part of the attraction of reducing class size.

It may not work, but it sure is easy to measure. The light's better there.

Finding out just how much it would cost to reduce class size in the United States by a third was a wake-up call, but not because of the expense. After all, we're spending more than $500 billion every year on primary and secondary education, so spending another $10 or $20 billion or so isn't as crazy as it sounds—as long, that is, as it actually closes the achievement gap. The real problem with class-size reduction isn't that it costs so much but that it buys so little: barely a fifth of the difference between the bottom quarter of America's schools and the top quarter.

In the health model, classroom size would be the equivalent of having a pet. Pet ownership is proven to increase life expectancy. But it is not one of the critical five things needed to be healthy. Not every person in America needs a pet to be healthy, but it wouldn't hurt you if you had one. This list is dedicated to the essential things needed to close the gap. Classroom size, once and for all, is not one of them.

INCREASED SCHOOL FUNDING?

Even if CSR didn't turn out to be worth the billions it would cost, that didn't mean that more money wasn't the answer for schools on the wrong side of the achievement gap. Maybe it just needed to be spent on different things, like higher salaries, or better technology. Maybe the people at the Social Genius's dinner who were saying that inner-city schools were underfunded had a point. Maybe the gap *could* be closed with money.

One of the things that happens when you're trying to assemble the best scholarship on a subject like reforming edu-

cation is that the same names start to appear over and over again. And we quickly found out that no one has thought more about the best (and worst) ways that schools spend money than Eric Hanushek. So I brought it up at our lunch.

"Tell me about funding for schools," I asked. The professor began telling me that he has found almost no correlation between school funding and student achievement. "Schools that are funded at $17,000 per student in the public schools do not do better than their peers who are being funded at $10,000 to $11,000 in the charter schools across the street." Hanushek attested to the fact that most additional funding is spent on administration costs and facilities, which do not have effects on student achievement. There are clear things that affect the children's capacity to learn, and the rest of the things are tangential. We discussed how for most people this will be surprising. Like the belief in classroom size, it is an instinctual belief that the problem with the schools is lack of funding. The professor noted that beyond a threshold that is really the minimum needed for basic education, it isn't the amount of money being spent but *where it is being spent* that will dictate its impact. This rang true to me. More money doesn't mean I make a better film. When the budget is tight, we often spend the monies on those areas that have the greatest impact on-screen. Actually, as an artist, I find some of the factors created by more money can actually distract me from the true storytelling. As a sign of knowing what is necessary and what is not, I flagged down our waiter and asked in a moment of contemptible weakness to bring a bowl of fries "for the table." The waiter told me the kitchen was closed.

We finished up our time together with a tour of the campus. Professor Hanushek told me about Stanford's collection of Rodin sculptures and wanted to show me *The Gates of Hell* on the other side of the campus. I told him that Rodin was a

particularly significant artist to me. I looked at the time and realized I might miss my flight if I did this. I reluctantly told him no. This was the second thing I wanted badly and couldn't have. The professor walked me to my car and waved to me like an uncle as I drove away. I felt the urge to go and spend the day with him eating fries and looking at Rodin sculptures.

What I took away from my lunch with Professor Hanushek was that the debate about whether America's schools have too much money, too little, or—like Goldilocks and the Three Bears—"just right" starts from one point that is definitely true, adds another one that is equally so, and then combines them in a way that isn't.

Point one is this: We know that for the typical American student, more years of schooling translates into a better life, at least in the only way that economics can measure it: higher incomes and more wealth. High school graduates earn more than high school dropouts. People with some college earn more than people with none, college graduates more than college dropouts, those with postgraduate education more than those without. Every additional year of education is worth tens of thousands of dollars over a person's working life and, therefore, it's worth a whole lot to the nation as a whole, since GDP is basically the sum of everyone's productive years.

Second point: We know, just as surely, that *better* schooling, as measured by test scores—or, in Eric Hanushek's words, "labor market returns to cognitive skills" (I mentioned that he was an economist, right?)—also equals higher earnings. Students who score higher on standardized tests will, on average, outearn students who score lower.

So far, so good. It's no great trick to calculate both the costs and benefits for an additional year of education. And it's nearly as easy to figure out the benefits of a *better* year: better grades and higher scores. But the cost of that better year is what the debate is about. And it's been going on since at least 1966, when the U.S. Department of Education commissioned a study of 150,000 American students and published it under the title *Equality of Educational Opportunity*. The report—usually known as the "Coleman Report" for its lead researcher, the sociologist James Coleman—is best remembered for concluding that school funding has next to no impact on educational achievement.

People have been taking potshots at this finding ever since, but it hasn't been knocked down. One reason is the sheer volume of evidence behind it. The most convincing piece, to a novice like me, isn't experimental results (like the Tennessee STAR Project), but just observation. For one thing, state-by-state spending is wildly different. Schools in Utah spend only about a third as much as schools in Vermont or New Jersey, but there is literally no relationship between their per-pupil spending and their scores on the standardized tests like the National Assessment of Educational Progress; and this is true even when we account for differences in income or the educational level of the students' parents. Anyway, in Utah, Vermont, and everywhere in between, real expenditures per pupil have been on a steady increase for a long time, from $278 (in current dollars) in 1890 to $1,308 in 1940 to $2,606 in 1960 to $4,622 in 1990 to $9,910 in 2005. That's more than 3 percent per year, every year, for more than a century.

The improvement in achievement? Not so much.

Now, I know there are a lot of reasons that we might want to spend more to educate our kids today than we did before World War II. A modern classroom isn't just home to a bunch of computers, but is probably air-conditioned, neither of which was true fifty years ago. And the kids they're educating have changed, too: Students today are more likely to come from low-income or single-parent households than they were fifty years ago and a lot more likely to speak a language at home that isn't English. Even more expensively, a whole lot more are in special education classrooms. When we spend money on a school today, we're really spending it on two parallel schools, since more than 13 percent of elementary and secondary students are now part of special education programs.

And this makes for a complication, because educating special education students costs more than twice as much as educating students in a traditional classroom. However, the special kids don't take the same standardized tests, and therefore the resources spent on special education don't show up in improved test scores. Any cost-benefit calculation that forgets this is going to be a little skewed.

Not so skewed as all that, though: Special education explains only 20 percent of the total increase in annual school budgets. Even less is explained by spending on extracurriculars like sports, art, or music, or English-as-a-second-language instruction.

Most of the remaining increase, almost all of it, is either personnel costs—teacher and administrator salaries, health insurance, pensions, and things like that—or building and maintaining the schools themselves. But as we reviewed the literature on increasing these parts of the educational budget, we found the same problem as we did with class-size reduction: When there was any effect at all—usually not—there were nearly as many negative results as positive ones:

- Out of 118 studies that tried to calculate the impact of increasing teacher salaries, 20 percent had a positive effect size, 7 percent negative, and 73 percent had no noticeable impact.

- There were 91 estimates for the effect of increased spending on facilities: 9 percent were positive, 5 percent negative, and 86 percent neutral.
- The 163 studies that estimated the value of increasing per pupil expenditures overall? Twenty-seven percent were positive, 7 percent negative, and 66 percent had no statistically significant impact at all.

DEGREES AND SALARY?

More money is definitely a common theme in education reform. It accounts for two more popular education reforms that aren't on the list. The first is rewards for advanced degrees. Each year, the Philadelphia School District spends nearly 40 percent of its entire professional development budget on bonuses for teachers who earn either masters or Ph.D. degrees; in 2007, American school districts spent more than $19 billion on them. Their impact on student achievement? Virtually undetectable. Eric Hanushek surveyed forty-one separate studies trying to find some correlation between educational attainment of teachers—primarily receiving a master's degree, primarily in education—and student achievement. Nothing. By the way, this is totally counterintuitive to me.

There were many things that shocked me in the research. This was one. Ten of the studies actually showed a *negative* effect. You read that correctly: There are studies showing that teacher performance declines with the acquisition of one of those expensive graduate degrees. *Very, very expensive*—more than 2 percent of *all* current expenditures on education are tied to compensation for master's degrees.

There are a lot of ideas that feel morally and intuitively right but aren't actually true. There were seven major reform platforms that didn't make the list. One of them is paying teachers more so they will be incentivized to improve student achievement.

Almost all performance bonus systems have the same nonexistent effect. It turns out that great teachers aren't motivated by money, at least not beyond a reasonably comfortable wage. Until we started researching this book, I didn't know the name for this particular bit of self-deception, but thanks to Google I do now. It's called the "extrinsic incentives bias," and it describes how people think others are motivated by things like pay and job security instead of intrinsic motivations like learning new things and pride in workmanship, while they describe themselves in exactly the opposite way.

Don't get me wrong. I know that teachers, just like clergymen, scientists, and military officers, like a nice salary as much as anyone else. They deserve one, too. But I also found that you won't get more eloquent sermons or better theories or more battlefield victories by paying more. Teachers are professionals, and the best of them—the ones we want—are motivated by intrinsic rewards more than money. Again, this is *after* a minimum level of pay is passed. Years ago, the Gallup Organization commissioned a survey of more than a million employees and 80,000 managers in every part of the American economy: manufacturers, retailers, and—yes—schools. They boiled down the core elements that successful organizations use to keep talented employees. It turns out that a good organization is one where people answer "yes" to twelve questions, and not one of them was about how much they were paid. The first three are always the same:

1. Do I know what's expected of me at work?
2. Do I have the materials and equipment I need to do my work right?
3. At work, do I have the opportunity to do what I do best every day?

Teachers want to know what's expected, to have the tools they need, and have the opportunity to do their best. Teachers want to teach kids how to learn better. Teachers have always been kind of holy to me. After learning the research about their selfless motivations, their apotheosis was complete.

More money might be needed to implement a system for closing the achievement gap. But we had to admit that until we knew where to spend it, there just wasn't any evidence that lack of money was the core problem, which meant that more money couldn't be the solution.

Now, for all those lifelong educators and activists for reform that are reading this and getting angry at me—please don't. I wanted classroom size to be on the list. I wanted teachers to get master's degrees. I wanted school funding to be there, too. I just didn't find the data to support it in the literature. I checked my answers with those schools closing the gap—their classrooms were big, their teachers didn't necessarily have master's degrees, and their funding per student was at or below state averages. I'm just trying to present my findings from the data with as little of my opinion as possible. OK, now that I've got you calmed down, let me piss you off some more.

SCHOOL CHOICE?

After all, everyone likes choices. If some choices are good, more must be better. Whether it makes us happier or not (and there are truckloads of research saying it doesn't), almost everyone, when asked, wants the maximum number of choices, and the maximum amount of freedom to pick among them.

Which is part of the reason that one of the ideas I jotted down at the Social Genius's dinner party was "Let parents choose where their kids go to school." Bhavna and I picked the school our daughters attend for the same reasons that any parent would: It provides a great education. And even though I know that we've been lucky enough to afford an academically rigorous private education for our girls, millions of parents make the same decision every time they move to a suburb or a different school district because of the quality of the local schools. So it's easy to see why so many reformers, particularly those who want to close America's achievement gap, believe in increasing parental choice. This isn't just an enthusiasm for charter schools; sometimes it takes the form of open enrollment, when residents can enroll kids in any public school where there's space rather than the one closest to home. Sometimes it's some kind of tax policy that reimburses parents for the costs of school. And, usually, school choice includes support for education vouchers.

School choice and particularly vouchers—those government-issued certificates that can be used by parents to pay for all or part of private school tuition (or, sometimes, home schooling)—have been around in parts of New England since the nineteenth century, where towns without schools issue them to parents who can use them to attend either private schools or public schools in neighboring towns. Hundreds of thousands of American families now use vouchers to pay for school.

Choice invokes unusually high levels of passion among supporters and opponents. It goes to the heart of what we consider to be fair—why should wealthy parents with the means to move to a better school district have a choice and the less well off be tied to the local school district? If choice already exists for the privileged, why can't choice be extended to all? Although the U.N. Universal Declaration of

Human Rights enshrines parents' right to choose the type of education their child receives, it is worth asking if diversity and choice are worthy goals in their own right or, as the political philosopher and president of the University of Pennsylvania Amy Gutmann suggests, if the pressure for choice derives more from a pressure for good public schools than a desire for choice.

There is evidence in support of vouchers and school choice. The City of Milwaukee has been making vouchers available since 1990, and the parents of more than 15,000 kids are now using them to pay for private schools. One 2002 study showed that not only do the students in voucher-chosen schools do well, but the vouchers have made the public schools more effective now that they have to compete for families. Which is another reason for people to support tax-funded vouchers. Americans, including myself, love competition. I'm an avid weekend warrior with two ACL surgeries to prove it.

The idea is that greater choice leads to competition and greater competition drives improvement. Two political scientists, John Chubb and Terry Moe, argued in an influential book, *Politics, Markets, and America's Schools,* that choice attacks the underlying cause of ineffective schooling because given the option, parents will remove their children from failing schools. If you replace the authority of school districts to assign children to schools with a diverse marketplace, only the good schools will survive.

But numerous studies suggest the opposite: Public, private, and charter schools remain open in spite of no discernible change in quality in these schools. A 2006 report from the U.S. Department of Education with the unimaginative title "Comparing Private Schools and Public Schools Using Hierarchical Linear Modeling" found that private elementary and secondary schools, like charter schools, didn't have any magic formula for effectiveness.* The method that the researchers used adjusted for family income, race, and gender, and found no real differences between private and public schools. After the adjustments, the average fourth-grade private school student scored the same in English and significantly *lower* than the average public school student in math: an effect size of −.12. For eighth-graders, there was no measurable difference in math, but an advantage for the private school students in English: an effect size of +.23. The researchers concluded that overall, there were no real differences between the average private and public school in student growth or achievement.

The other studies are just as inconclusive. Because so many of the voucher programs are oversubscribed—that is, demand exceeds supply—they are usually allocated by lottery, which makes for another natural experiment, like California's exercise in CSR in the 1990s, since the lottery randomly sorts the applicants into an experimental group—the winners; and a control group—the losers. Five large-scale lotteries—in New York City; Washington, D.C.; Dayton, Ohio; Milwaukee, Wisconsin; and Charlotte-Mecklenburg, North Carolina—have been analyzed a total of ten times to find the effect size for winning the lottery. Though a metastudy of the ten peer-reviewed analyses reported that "nine conclude that some or all of the participants benefited academically from using a voucher to attend a private school," the biggest "benefit" was in parental satisfaction: an effect size of +.3. And parental satisfaction, as we've learned, is a poor proxy for improved student achievement.

Most of the other effects were a lot more modest. Lottery winners did experience a modest increase in percentile rank-

* For more about hierarchical linear modeling, see Chapter 6.

ings of between 4 and 10—that is, students that were in the 40th percentile going in were able to see a jump to the 44th to 50th percentile after three to four years. An even bigger caution: The effects took place on a group that was already different from the overall population of students since they were from families that chose to apply for the lottery in the first place.

In fact, that Milwaukee study—of the Milwaukee Parental Choice Program—was starting to look a little like the Tennessee STAR study of class-size reduction: an outlier that hasn't been replicated with anything like the same effect sizes elsewhere. The Milwaukee numbers themselves have been diluted by further analysis. When the program was new enough that the Milwaukee system used a lottery to handle the excess demand, researchers benefited from having two separate groups—those who won the lottery and those who lost—to calculate the effect of voucher use. In a 2009 study by Cecilia Rouse and Lisa Barrow, researchers found effect sizes of +.14 in math, and +.01 in reading—essentially zero. Similar programs in Cleveland and the District of Columbia achieved even smaller effect sizes than Milwaukee, and were just as likely to be negative as positive. As the authors of the 2009 study put it, "The best research to date finds relatively small achievement gains for students offered education vouchers, most of which are not statistically different from zero." Vouchers don't have the data on their side.

And, even when presented with choices, parents don't always have the resources to choose wisely. Picking the best school for your children requires research, sometimes a lot; a 2011 study in Canada concluded that the poorer and less well educated the parents, the less likely they were to take advantage of the widest range of school choice. Which means that the benefits of choice flow to the families that need it the least, which is a recipe for expanding the achievement gap, not closing it.

It's not that parents don't want the best for their kids. They do. But *wanting* the best doesn't necessarily mean they *know* what's best. And even if they knew enough to choose the best, what they choose to do is to set up their own school districts.

On the route from San Francisco International Airport to meet with Eric Hanushek at the Hoover Institution in Palo Alto is the Woodside Elementary School District, in Redwood City, California. It's a very small district—one elementary school with 500 students—that has its own local education foundation. Between 1998 and 2009, the Woodside School Foundation raised $10 million in donations by its members. To no one's surprise, the elementary school received the top rating on California's Academic Performance Index every one of those years.

Less than ten miles from Woodside (and even closer to Palo Alto) is the Ravenswood City School District: 4,500 students, 94 percent of them from families poor enough to qualify for a free or reduced-price lunch, spread across six elementary schools and three middle schools.* Ravenswood, unsurprisingly, has no local education foundation. Also un-surprisingly: Half of Ravenswood schools earn the lowest API rating. Families can "choose" to move to Woodside and go to better schools. If they can afford it.

It's not that Woodside spends more on its students than Ravenswood. In fact, once you account for additional funding from the State of California and Title I money from the federal government, they don't, not really. And, as Eric Hanushek

---

* Ravenswood also feeds into a charter high school: the East Palo Alto Academy High School.

and dozens of other scholars have shown, money—or the lack of it—isn't behind the achievement gap. The important thing to take away from Woodside's local education foundation isn't what it does but that Woodside families can afford to put $10 million into it. Those families most likely will have multiple college graduates, they will have more books in their homes, they will have more trips to museums. The Woodside families have the resources to reinforce a high-achieving home learning environment. Choice in this situation wouldn't close the gap between Woodside and Ravenswood.

There is another big problem with looking to "choice" as a remedy for the achievement gap, whether in the form of giving money directly to parents (vouchers) or in the form of "capitation grants" (which is the technical term for how charter schools are funded: a fixed sum for every student that attends them). School choice does nothing about instruction, assuming that families—"education consumers"—will somehow inspire improvements in teaching. Choice programs leave the publicly governed systems to the "nonchoosers" and the unchosen. Richard Elmore of Harvard University compares this to the difference between public hospitals and private ones: Just as private hospitals get patients with the most money and best insurance, private schools get the cream, and the public schools get the rest . . . what Elmore calls the "overflow."

Another bizarre ramification of choice is the capriciousness of the way parents will pull their kids from one school to another if they don't feel immediate improvement. I spoke with teachers all over the country where vouchers and open enrollment are used and they were greatly hampered by students coming in and out of their schools; the parents were "trying schools on like clothes." In the end, from the evidence, choice was too broad a tool to be effective. It does not provide instructions on how to improve. It assumes schools will "figure it out." This has proven to produce inconsistent results. If choice were an essential part of closing the achievement gap and were powerful enough to cause the dominos of change to move, there would be evidence for this in multiple cities.

Giving more choice to parents wasn't exactly a complete dead end. But the evidence was clear: If "choice" was going to be part of any system for closing America's achievement gap, it needed to be the kind that included no bad choices. It's hard to oppose more choice. It's even harder to see how it's going to close the gap. When every school in America is able to properly educate its students, then, sure: Let parents choose which one has an environment that fits their child better. But until then, encouraging parents to find, on their own, the best education for their kids guarantees only one thing, which is to reward the families with the most resources. Since that's the system that created the gap in the first place, we can depend on choice to perpetuate it.

INTEGRATION?

Another practice that didn't make the list, despite a lot of support, was a push for more integration—not necessarily racial integration, but economic integration. If—as we learned, over and over again—the key driver of the achievement gap was that more affluent, better-educated families were concentrated in one group of schools while less affluent, less well-educated families concentrated in different ones, why not just cut through all the civil rights issues and put them in the same schools? Would it help to close the achievement gap? The evidence says it would.

There are dozens of studies over the last fifty years that

looked at whether eliminating segregation on economic grounds would close the achievement gap. One 2005 study of more than 14,000 students, selected from 913 American high schools, found that the schools' average socioeconomic level had as much impact on student achievement as the students' own families. If you wanted to predict the likely achievement of any group of students, the average social class—family income level, highest level of school completed—of their *schools* matters even more than that of their *families*. Another study, from 2010, reanalyzed the original data from the Coleman Report and found the same phenomenon had been true in 1966: Student achievement was more strongly correlated with the socioeconomic status of the 4,000 schools examined by Coleman than with the status of the study's 600,000 students. One of the most persuasive studies, performed in 2010 in Montgomery County, Maryland (one of the twenty wealthiest counties in America, but one that has a public housing policy that mixes low-income with high-income families), was even more powerful: Low-income students who attended high-income schools stayed even with those low-income students who didn't for the first two years. But after seven years in the district, the poorer kids' scores on standardized math tests showed an effect size of +.40 just from attending a school with more affluent classmates. Even better: The improvement in the standardized scores for kids on the wrong side of the achievement gap didn't do anything to harm the scores of kids on the right side. Middle-class students do just as well in schools that are a third low-income as they do in schools that are almost completely middle-class. More than eighty school districts in the United States with enrollment of more than 4 million students are now pursuing some sort of socioeconomic integration.

The reason that socioeconomic integration isn't on the list isn't analytical. It's political. It doesn't matter whether integration would help to close the gap if it isn't ever going to get the chance. Resistance to the concept is everywhere. Progressives, maybe understandably, find the idea that poor black kids can't learn without being surrounded by middle-class white ones to be borderline racist. Conservatives, also maybe understandably, see any policy of integration to be an example of governmental overreach.

Which means that support for socioeconomic integration as *the* answer to America's achievement gap isn't a viable policy. Another way of saying that until America has become economically equal, there's no way to make it educationally equal. I'm an incurable optimist. But even I'm not *that* optimistic. If that's what it was going to take to close the achievement gap, this battle was lost before it was even started.

GENERAL ACCOUNTABILITY?

One last thing I want to mention that isn't on the list is accountability on a school level. Ever since Congress passed the No Child Left Behind Act of 2001, just about the whole country has been holding schools to account for the performance of their students. For decades before that, individual states were doing so. Accountability was the magic wand that would cure what ailed all of America's schools, including the achievement gap. The logic was pretty persuasive: If you give everyone the same (or similar) tests, publish the results, and either reward schools (or school districts or states) that perform well, and punish those that don't, people responsible will stop practicing the things that fail and do more of the things that work. Incentives matter.

The stakes were serious: Schools that failed could be closed down. As a result, just about every public school in the United States now gives students, from the third grade on, some sort of high-stakes test every year. Almost all of them include multiple-choice standardized tests; a smaller number (though still most) add short-answer questions and essay questions. A couple even use panels of experts to assess complete portfolios of each student's work. In addition, a lot of accountability measures include attendance and dropout rates, or patterns of enrollment.

Like just about everyone, I support holding the people who teach America's kids—not just teachers, but administrators— accountable for the job they're doing. But holding schools responsible with an underlying premise that they will "figure it out" or "get their act together" is incorrect. This goes against everything I've found in the research and everything I feel as a human. This isn't about motivation of the adults to "do the right thing." They don't know what the right thing is and they are struggling to find it. No amount of sanctions from the outside will change that.

Richard Elmore is one of the people who showed us that accountability cannot, by itself, promote improvement in performance. I was lucky enough to speak with Mr. Elmore during a yearlong sabbatical he was taking. I actually spoke to him while he was snowed in during a blizzard in Boston. He was kind of my prisoner, so I took advantage. For decades, Mr. Elmore had been consulting with school districts around the country, and in his work and in conversation he describes schools that are held accountable for their students' math performance, but have no idea how to improve it.

To Elmore, this is because we fail to distinguish between instructional *accountability* and instructional *capacity:* the knowledge and skills needed to improve performance. In fact, the more resources we devote to accountability, the less we have to increase capacity. One thing that Elmore's research demonstrates is that, when capacity is present, students do well on just about any test.

Another thing is that when accountability scores aren't extremely precise, the "accountability" they demand acts in perverse ways. And precise, these scores are not. There's a lot of noise that gets collected in the data. First, the scores on all those high-stakes tests *within* a particular school are more variable than the differences *between* schools.* Not only that, but since the median elementary school in the United States has fewer than sixty students in each grade, a couple of really high scores, or low ones, can produce a huge amount of year-to-year variability. James showed me one study of schools in North Carolina where 74 percent of the difference from year to year in math, and 90 percent of the year-to-year difference in English, was completely transitory: a product of the natural fluctuations from one year to the next.

I wanted to believe that we could hold schools account-able, but even I could see that punishing a school for a one-year decline in math scores was a little too much like criticizing them for picking the wrong number on a roulette wheel.

That wasn't all. Since the biggest rewards and punish-ments for achieving or missing accountability measures go to the outliers—the schools with the biggest gains, or losses—the system tends to focus on the smallest schools, because they're almost always going to show the biggest fluctuations.

---

* This was a clue that the difference might be that some teachers are better than others; more on this in Chapter 4.

Even worse, most states also require schools to be account-able for the scores on those high-stakes tests not just for the entire school, but for subgroups within each school. If a school has 300 kids, but is accountable for the performance of any group that represents more than 15 percent of the total student body, then forty-five scores might be the difference between success and failure, which means that half a dozen very low (or very high) scores could be decisive. This isn't even roulette; it's like playing the lottery.

When the stakes are high, so are the incentives to game the system. One popular test, the National Assessment of Educational Progress, excludes the scores of students who are given extra time to take the test. Guess what? The states with the biggest improvements are frequently the same ones with the highest percentage of excluded students. Also, what-ever tests are used for accountability measures tend—big surprise—to get higher scores than any other test. In Ken-tucky, the improvement in the fourth-grade test used for high-stakes accountability was four times larger than the state's improvement in the NAEP, which their kids took, but without any consequences, good or bad.

And there's cheating. Schools from Atlanta to Baltimore to Phoenix to New York have been caught rejiggering test results. One elementary school teacher even placed different-colored M&Ms on the correct responses, which proved that her students could at least tell the difference between red and green.

All these bizarre reactions are results of being held ac-countable at the school level alone and being forced to "figure it out." This kind of accountability creates desperation and/or penalization for those schools and students that need the most guidance.

The accountability measures that emerged out of No Child

Left Behind were unfair. They held all schools accountable
for the same student outcomes despite students' very different
starting points. But even worse, they were insufficient. Knowing which schools are failing isn't the same as knowing what
to do about them. There's a famous story about the filming
of the movie *Jezebel,* during which supposedly the director,
William Wyler, made Bette Davis do forty-eight takes of the
same scene. Exasperated, she asked, "What do you want me
to do differently?" To which Wyler replied, "I'll know it when
I see it."

The bad news is that's the way a lot of accountability
measures work today. We expect that telling schools to get
better is enough.

The good news is that our research was developing the
same way. We would know a working system when we saw
it. And that's what happened. After clearing away the under-
brush, after examining all the false starts and dead ends, all
the half-solutions, what remained, like the health tenets of
sleeping eight hours a day, exercising regularly, and so on,
were the five keys to closing America's educational achievement gap.

NOTE

Let me acknowledge something before we continue. I'm aware there is a great confluence of pernicious factors that has brought our achievement gap into existence. I'm aware some of those factors include self-interested politicians, drug dealers, unhealthy foods, skewed value messages on television and everywhere, physical, emotional and sexual trauma, racism, and general disregard for the interests of poor people over those of the rich. These and countless more have contributed to the hole our inner-city low-income children are in. There are probably many ways we can attenuate the effects of the factors I've just listed. I don't know any of those. This book proceeds under the premise that those factors are not going to change. In this book we operate under the premise that the entire burden of closing the achievement gap sits on the shoulders of the school these children are attending. I feel I need to stress this because this is not fair to the schools and the administrators and teachers who work within those schools. I acknowledge this. To those people who are fighting to change those other antecedent factors, you have my admiration and support, but in the pages of this book we are going to imagine you don't exist. We are going to answer the question of whether those children walking in with all those things going against them can be brought to the same or higher achievement levels as their white suburban peers in a scalable way.

PART TWO

THE FIVE KEYS

THE FIRST KEY:
NO ROADBLOCK TEACHERS

4

MR. BRODINSKY, PLEASE SEE THE PRINCIPAL—AND BRING YOUR SUITCASE

Teachers.

There's no shortage of disagreement about the significance of standardized tests, or innovative curricula, or charter schools. I have friends who live to fight education unions, and others who would die to defend them. But there's no debate at all about the importance of teachers. Everyone understands that teachers are the engines that make schools run, the critical piece in any solution to the achievement gap. In Philadelphia, for example, I consider them the 11,000 most important people in a city of 1.5 million.

What most don't dwell on—what I didn't really dwell on myself when we began—is that not all teachers perform equally. Some are so good that their students get the equivalent of a year-and-a-half of progress every year; some are so bad that their students get less than half a year.

This is one of those counterintuitive-but-true facts that are everywhere in the world of education research. It's not that people aren't aware that some teachers are better than others;

it's that they don't really believe that you can find out who they are by looking at the performance of their students. After all, the argument goes, every class is different, with some made up of nothing but underachievers, and others full of future Rhodes Scholars. Some schools are in relatively affluent neighborhoods, with all their students from families with (at least) a couple of college degrees; others are 90 percent poor, or non-English-language speakers, or both. How is it reasonable or equitable to compare teachers from one school to the other, or one year to the next?

Well, for a long time, you couldn't. And no one really did. The performance evaluations that most schools have been using for decades (and that most still use today) are a joke. But no one is laughing. In one national study after another, teacher evaluations find fewer than 2 percent of teachers to be unsatisfactory. The Chicago Public Schools have four possible ratings for teachers: Superior, Excellent, Satisfactory, and Unsatisfactory. Over a four-year period, nearly 60 percent were rated Superior; another 25 percent were Excellent. The percentage rated Unsatisfactory? Four-tenths of 1 percent. In four years, 36,000 evaluations were able to find exactly 149 unsatisfactory teachers. Which is better than the city of Akron, Ohio. They had no unsatisfactory teachers at all. We should all just move to Akron.

In 2009, a group of researchers at the New Teacher Project named this "The Widget Effect"—the idea that all teachers were, like the kids in Lake Wobegon, above average.

The worst part of this notion isn't just that it provides no way of finding the most unsuccessful teachers; it's that there's no way of finding differences among *any* teachers. If you start out with the idea that student performance differences are entirely a function of their natural talents, or their family's income, or anything outside the schoolhouse doors, you'll never be able to identify the most unsuccessful teachers, or the superstars, or even the ones in the middle (which at the end of the day might be the most important in scaling the successes in individual schools to 50 million American students). When every teacher becomes a completely interchangeable part, then any differences in their students' achievement can't be their doing.

No more. It's true that you can't just collect every eighth-grader's score on a standardized test, total up the average for every one of their teachers, and see which ones are doing the best jobs. That would be like comparing the productivity of two farms in California's Central Valley and thinking that you discovered something about the skills of the two farmers. You'd have to compare their actual performance against their expected performance—compare the yields of the two farms against their prior yields. And, since rain and sun aren't the same every year, you'd have to do it for more than one growing season.

That was the big breakthrough in evaluating teachers. The key, it turns out, is not comparing test scores between teachers, or schools, or years, but comparing *growth,* by comparing a student's *actual* progress against that student's expected progress. If you know, for example, how well a hundred students were reading at the end of the third grade, and therefore how well you expected them to be reading at the end of the fourth grade, you can measure how much value their fourth-grade teachers added to the not-so-raw material they inherited.* This is called value-added measurement.

These kinds of growth measures are now being collected in dozens of American school districts every year. And every

---

* For more about value-added measurement and other measures of student growth, see Chapter 6.

year they collect critics. Every teacher who hits a home run in one year may not do the same in the following year. Or a teacher performing poorly one year may not be guaranteed to do the same the next time around. I wish they did; it would make the job of staffing America's classrooms a lot more straightforward, and make closing the achievement gap a lot easier. But we had promised to go only as far as the evidence could take us, and—so far—the evidence on growth measures isn't precise enough to make hiring and firing decisions, not all by itself. Which doesn't mean the evidence isn't there. Successful teachers aren't lucky. They're good.

And the good ones aren't just good; they're valuable. Dollars-and-cents valuable.

Economists have studied just how much a teacher is worth, using models that measure things like educational attainment and test scores to ask, "How much does an increase in the acquisition of cognitive skills (like analytical reading, or competency in math) add to someone's lifetime earnings?" And the answer is "a whole bunch." One year's improvement of a quarter of a standard deviation in overall educational achievement—an effect size of +.25—generates an average earnings increase of $5,300; and that means that a teacher who can consistently deliver that sort of improvement—that's the difference between a teacher smack in the middle of the pack, at the 50th percentile, and one at the 60th percentile—is generating about $106,000 in incremental income for every class of twenty students she teaches. Kick the teacher up to the 84th percentile—that's where the improvement is a full standard deviation, an effect size of +1.0—and the lifetime value is $400,000. One year with a great teacher is worth $20,000 for every student in that class. If they meet more great teachers, that increase in value just multiplies.

There are 3.5 million teachers in America. Just as a lark

and just to get your blood going, let's imagine something unrealistic. Let's imagine we can get all the students to the level occupied by the best 15 percent. That would be worth $14 trillion in future earnings for their students. That's trillion. With a *T*.

There's more: Students who spend a single year with a very effective teacher get up to 45 percent more out of that year than students who spend it with an average teacher.

Even small differences among teachers matter. One study shows that a typical student in the bottom quarter of the achievement spectrum, taking a typical test, taught by a typical teacher—that is, one in the middle 50 percent of the teacher pool—is likely to pass the test 38 percent of the time. When the teacher comes from the bottom quartile, the chances of the student's passing drop below 15 percent. But when the teacher is from the *top* quartile, the student's chances of passing the test zoom all the way to 60 percent.

That's pretty abstract. So imagine it this way. Picture three different fourth-grade classes, somewhere in an American inner city. Each one has twenty-one students, and—typically but sadly—their third-grade test scores put them in the bottom 25 percent of the whole country. At the end of the year, they all take the same test. In the class with a really good fourth-grade teacher—someone who, unlike the students, is in the top quartile—thirteen of them will pass the test. The class with an average teacher? Eight. But only three students in the class with a poor teacher will pass the same test. Three. That's it.

And that's a quarter—you read that right—of the classrooms in the country.

HIRING BETTER

Daunting as that was, this analysis put the problem into another box that I could get my arms around: We already knew that we were talking about "only" 25,000 schools, the bottom quarter of America's public schools. I can't say I thought this was going to be easy. But at least I thought it would be straightforward. The path was starting to clear. We just needed to hire the good teachers, and *only* the good teachers.

That's what I thought.

American elementary and secondary schools hire between 46,000 and 86,000 new teachers every year. All of them want to be good teachers. At least a quarter of them won't be. A single year with one of them can put dozens of kids months behind everyone else, so any system that could keep the poor teachers out of the classroom would be a giant step in the right direction. The costs of poor teachers outweigh the benefits provided by good ones. Every 10 percent drop in a class's math competency alone—which is the best you can expect from a teacher in the bottom quartile—can cost a class of twenty students as much as $500,000 in lifetime earnings. One teacher. Half a million dollars.

So if the costs of poor teachers aren't sufficient to cause us to evaluate teachers in such a way that we can cull the good from the bad, let's just pick the best people to be teachers to begin with. Let's hire better.

Unfortunately, though, for anyone who is deciding which teachers to hire out of a pool of applicants, they don't arrive with any identifying mark that shows which ones have what it takes to succeed and which don't. Once you get past a threshold—a very low threshold—there's no objective system that has been shown to improve the process of recruiting

United States. In Finland, typical families in the top 10 percent earn about 5.6 times as much as those in the bottom 10 percent. In this country, they earn nearly 16 times as much. And most significantly, there aren't any private school options in Finland. None. You can't buy your children a better education there.

So, if you can't rely on an education degree, or a teaching certificate, as a seal of quality when hiring a new teacher, what else might work? A cottage industry has tried to answer that question with better ways of predicting which teachers are actually going to be able to, you know, teach. Companies package sets of measurement tools including general IQ tests, personality inventories, and the Star Teacher Pre-Screener produced by the Haberman Foundation, fifty multiple-choice questions that the foundation claims can identify teachers who will succeed versus those who might fail (or, more likely, quit) 95 percent of the time.

Unfortunately, there's just no real evidence that any of these systems works any better than drawing names out of a hat. Hiring teachers based on some educational or psychological profile is a little like trying to draft an NFL team when all you know about the players is their height, weight, speed, and how much they can bench press. Until you see them play, you're picking blind.

For teachers, "seeing them play" can mean at least a year or two in the classroom. Sometimes three. Though some teachers who truly are unfit for classroom duty can be identified after observing a single lesson, it takes years before you have enough information to know whether most of them are any good. After three years, schools should know which teachers are going to be successful and which ones aren't. But then what do they do? What they do today in way too many

elementary and secondary teachers that's much bett[er]
throwing darts. From a carousel.*

Here's one way to understand the scope of the pr[oblem.]
Add up all the things that you can find on teachers' résur[nés:]
whether or not they have advanced degrees, or even cert[ifica-]
tion; whether they got a degree from a prestigious colleg[e or]
not; what their SAT scores were, or their grade-point avera[ge—]
even the number of years spent teaching—and turn all that [in-]
formation into a score. Then jump ahead five years, and co[m-]
pare student success in the classes taught by the teachers wi[th]
the lowest scores to those with the highest. All that informa[-]
tion you gathered before you hired them is almost completely
random, which means that someone who barely graduated
from Nowhere State is just as likely to be a great teacher as
someone with a summa cum laude from Harvard.

A lot of people—people I like and respect, including
James Richardson, our own lead researcher—will tell you,
even in the face of this, that the answer to America's educational achievement gap is getting the United States to be
more like Finland, or South Korea, or Singapore, or *somewhere* where teachers are paid better, have higher status,
and therefore attract the "best" college graduates. I've learned
a lot of things about the debate about closing America's
achievement gap over the last five years. One bit of advice
I'm ready to share is this: Whenever anyone brings up Finland, back away slowly. I have nothing against Finland. It
seems like a great country. But its experience is not ours. In
fact, it mystifies me that a country with fewer people than
Greater Philadelphia, no civil rights problem, and virtually no
significant income inequality is held up as a model for the

---

* There *are* subjective ways worth understanding. See Chapter 5.

school districts is give them tenure. Automatically. OK, let's take a deep breath and talk about this.

There are dozens of problems with the traditional system of tenure in American elementary and secondary schools. There's the fact that no one even pretends anymore that it's a way of protecting academic freedom, which was its original rationale. There's the fact that it's so widespread that nearly two-thirds of all the elementary and secondary teachers in the country now have tenure. (The percentage at colleges and universities? Thirty percent.) There's the fact that tenure has come to mean that no teacher can be fired, or even disciplined, before the completion of a long and complex, quasi-legal procedure that can take more than three hundred days, and more than $250,000, which is why more than 80 percent of school administrators admit that they keep poor teachers around: It's just too much trouble not to. There's the fact that tenure requires that the last teacher hired is the first one fired.

But the most tragic and inexcusable thing about tenure is that we have it completely upside down. We've built a system that makes it almost impossible to fire teachers *after* they've completed two or three years in the classroom, and that gives everyone an incentive to fire teachers *before* they've done so. And we did it despite overwhelming evidence that no one knows enough to make that decision until a teacher has been teaching for—you guessed it—two years.

After months of looking, we couldn't find much evidence that we can improve the overall quality of our teachers in the selection process. And even less evidence that we can know who the good ones are before they've been teaching for at least two years.

The most convincing example of this came from an unlikely source: a movement intended to do just the opposite.

The philosophy behind Teach For America, the nonprofit founded by Wendy Kopp in 1989, is the real-world version of an idea she first described in her senior thesis at Princeton. The idea—essentially that students in the country's under-achieving schools would get a big lift from a year or two being taught by some of the country's most overachieving college graduates—caught on pretty quickly. Wendy's organization has placed more than 24,000 TFA corps members in low-performing urban and rural schools throughout the United States since; nearly 6,000 in 2012 alone.

This is just a no-brainer on the surface: smart, engaged college seniors wanting to give back to society. And it's just as easy to predict that TFA corps members would generate some resentment among existing teachers, who see TFA as sponsoring a bunch of entitled twenty-two-year-olds on a two-year stint before going off to law or business school. A lot of the critics of Teach For America have been teachers with both self-interest and pride on the line; teachers don't like to think that the reason their students aren't perform-ing is that they're being taught by folks who didn't have the grades to get into Harvard or Stanford (in its first years, as many as one in eight of all Ivy League seniors applied for a TFA assignment).

I've met Wendy a few times, even heard her speak. She is aware of the critiques of her movement and is forthcom-ing about them. I like her. And I believe virtually directly her alumni are responsible for the incredible movement in infor-mation and examples for closing the achievement gap. When we look back on it, I believe Wendy and Teach For America will mark *the* turning point in the history of American educa-tion reform.

The first problem you'd expect with TFA corps members is that they are, by definition, always inexperienced, and almost all the research reminds us that first-year teachers, overall, are less effective than fifth-year teachers. By that standard, Teach For America does pretty well; students randomly assigned to TFA corps members do just as well in English as students assigned to their more experienced colleagues, better in math (though only a bit: an effect size of less than +.1) and even more so in science (an effect size of nearly +.2). To be fair, though, just as many studies show no, or even a negative, effect.

Can you preselect our teachers based on their academic records or achievements in other fields? This is such a powerful question, one I got to see firsthand when I volunteered to join a TFA Fellow and teach a class myself.

It began when the Social Genius, of course, put me in touch with Mike Wang, who was then the executive director of Teach For America's Mid-Atlantic Region (he's now the managing director of another organization: the Philadelphia School Partnership). The Social Genius asked if I'd like to teach an inner-city school English class.

I've always dreamed of being a teacher. No joke. Not giving up filmmaking, but in my fantasy, I would teach a once-a-week class to an auditorium full of curious and appreciative college students on a bucolic campus somewhere within a train ride of my house. On my weekly train ride, I'd take off my glasses to ponder a particularly perspicacious paragraph from a pupil as the scenery sped by. (I don't wear glasses and don't use alliteration unless it is embedded in a fantasy like this.)

Anyway, so I said yes to Teach For America.

I remember driving up to the gray stone building in north Philadelphia that housed Olney High School, one of the lowest-performing schools in Philadelphia. At the time, it had been split into two different schools with two different

principals,* both of whom met me in the lobby. I remember
that each of them seemed simultaneously resolute *and* overwhelmed.

After I met the principals came the school's teachers, and
a bunch of people associated with Teach For America, but I
have to confess that this part of the morning was kind of a
blur. Often when I enter a space for the first time, the new-
ness of the place overwhelms me; the sounds, the smells, the
lighting, the colors, and the endless signs of lives that I have
stepped into. So I don't remember much of the tour, but I do
recall being escorted to a corner classroom. Just outside, I
was introduced to the Teach For America teacher I would be
subbing for: a volunteer-for-the-Democratic-Party-in-my-spare-
time–looking guy. Superaffable. A do-gooder in every way.

He brought me into the classroom. There were about
thirty kids milling around; all African-American, all strato-
spherically cooler than I am. I was immediately intimidated. I
was once again a fifteen-year-old Indian with braces.

If that wasn't bad enough, half a dozen teachers filed into
the back of the classroom. I started to get that acid feeling in
my stomach. The students reluctantly took their seats. The
teacher said, "We are honored to have M. Night Shyamalan as
our teacher for today . . . Night, take it away." Then he walked
back and joined the other teachers.

Now here's the thing. In my mind, I was going to be a
guest speaker, like the times I visit my girls' school and the
first-graders ask me questions for five minutes. I didn't actually think I was going to teach anything.

---

* In 2011, the school was converted to a charter and taken over by Aspira,
Inc., a nonprofit devoted to Hispanic education; it's now known as Aspira
Olney High School.

Time stopped, similar to when you are on a plane with turbulence that's supposed to last thirty seconds, but it feels like much, much longer. The kids stared at me. I heard an announcement from the principal on the old wooden speaker in the classroom. I couldn't tell what he was saying. A couple of the kids decided I was a figurative douche and looked away.

So my mouth opened and I said something provocative: "Word for word, I am the highest-paid writer in the world."

That got their attention. "I'm smart, but there are a lot of people smarter than me. I'm a good writer, but there were better writers even in my English class in high school and there were only twenty kids in that class. How did this happen to me?"

There was a flurry of activity. Hands were raised throughout the classroom. Kids shouted ideas. One said, "You were lucky." I said, "I definitely am, but I don't know if that's a satisfactory explanation. I wrote and sold a screenplay when I was twenty-two for a really scary sum of money. I wrote an animated film that became one studio's highest-grossing film two years later. I wrote three other screenplays that each broke the record for screenplay sales. This happened at four different studios over a period of ten years." A really stylish kid said, "You work hard." I replied, "I do, but many people work harder than me." A girl yelled out from the back, "You know somebody." Everyone laughed at that one. I remember starting to feel connected to these kids at that very moment. I made sure I could see her in the back and said, "My parents are first-generation Indian doctors who spend all their time with their family and have no social skills. They don't know their neighbors' names."

When the kids finally gave up, I told them I had spent a

lot of time thinking about this, and believed I had come up with the answer: "I'm more me than they are them."

When you read a screenplay of mine, I told them, you see my fears, my limitations, my experiences, my beliefs, my hopes, my arrogance, my fragility, my sentimentality, and my complete inability to fit into any group. I told them, "No one on this planet can write me better than me. That permission to be OK with my flawed, misfit self in my scripts has made them stand out."

One last thing I remember about that day was a particular girl. She was sitting to the side. She was large and had clearly been excommunicated by the group. I chose to talk to her at that moment. Maybe it was the misfit connection. I said to her, "I can't write you. No one can. If you're truly honest with me, tell me why you have that look in your eyes, what it's like to choose those clothes today, what it's like to hear your principal through a broken speaker and not understand what he's saying. If you tell me what it's like to sit in your seat, just yours, the whole world will listen."

I have a photo of that day. The large girl chose not to be in the photo. I have a scrapbook they made for me of all their poetry.

Now here's the thing. I felt like a good teacher. I felt like I'd connected with them, but in reality you can't tell whether I'd be an effective teacher for a few years. I'm sure I would have done very little to help their learning in my first year. That's just what the data says.

The idea that great teachers are inspirational motivators, while true, isn't enough. Some teachers are great at connecting with kids, and some are just such terrific role models that the world is honored by their presence. We all remember the teacher who first showed us the magic in a piece of poetry, like the emotional intelligence when Emily Dickinson writes, "a Word that breathes distinctly / has not the power to die . . ."

But these wonderful teachers still need to teach. It's a great thing for kids to get juiced about being in the classroom, but they're actually there to learn. And a teacher who is a cold fish but can teach the binomial theorem successfully is actually a better friend to her students than a teacher who builds up a student's self-esteem but not his academics. The best teachers do both. But if I have to choose, I'll choose the one whose students learn the material over the one whose students don't. This is *especially* true for students in low-performing schools; affluent, suburban kids can afford to waste a year not learning how to solve for X.

TENURE

Even if 99 percent of teachers, whether they come from Teach For America or the most traditional school of education in the country, want to teach kids, that doesn't mean that 99 percent of them are *able* to teach kids, no matter how many Satisfactory ratings they get. Some teachers—OK, *a lot* of teachers—need to be told to seek alternate employment.

To Professor Hanushek at our lunch in Palo Alto, the logic was inescapable: Even though we can't do better at *hiring* teachers, we can be a lot more successful at *firing* them, or, more accurately, retaining the teachers that are good and great. If principals just made a point of firing (or, if you like, not rehiring) every fourth-grade teacher who fell into the bottom 5 to 8 percent on a scale that measured how well their students managed to acquire fourth-grade skills and knowledge, and replaced them with average teachers, that change would achieve effect sizes of somewhere between +.28 and

+.42 on students' overall performance. One of the most memorable moments in Davis Guggenheim's 2010 documentary *Waiting for Superman*—and at our lunch—was Eric Hanushek's calculation of the arithmetic of teacher evaluations: If all we did was replace between 5 and 8 percent of the least effective teachers in the United States with average ones, our students' overall achievement scores would rise to a level somewhere between those of Canada and Finland. Just 5 to 8 percent, *and nothing else.*

(Remember that scene in *Glengarry Glen Ross,* one of my favorite plays and movies, where the real-estate sales guys are told about the new contest? First prize is a Cadillac Eldorado; second prize is a set of steak knives. Third prize is you're fired.)

That, finally, was doable. We had spent months—years, really—finding out what we *can't* do. We can't hire teachers with a better chance of success. We can't improve the pool of potential teachers by recruiting from "better" colleges. There's no evidence that we can improve teachers' performance by giving them bonuses, or by sending them to graduate school.*

But you can improve the overall quality of classroom instruction using what academics describe as "selective retention" and ordinary people call "addition by subtraction": You have to cull the most unsuccessful teachers, the bottom few percent, the ones that are doing damage by their presence. You *have* to.

However, whether your goal is retaining only nine teachers in ten, or nineteen teachers out of twenty, you need to use a reliable tool, not just because you're talking about people's livelihoods, but because you don't want to lose good teachers any more than you want to keep bad ones.

* You can, however, improve their teaching skills. A lot. See Chapter 6.

MEASURING VALUE . . . ACCURATELY

The tools available for identifying both good and bad teachers by student outcomes are what you might call blunt instruments. Statisticians talk about two sorts of fudge factors in making sense of numbers; Type I errors are the sort that find false positives—a test that indicates prostate cancer in someone who doesn't really have it, for example. Type II are the opposite, the chance that a test won't find prostate cancer in someone who does have it. When you add the false positives to the false negatives in the best current tests of teacher impact on student achievement, you get a total error rate of 26 percent, which means that one teacher in four is either going to be a perfectly competent teacher who looks like a failure, or a failure that we didn't catch. And that's using three years' worth of data. To cut the error rate in half, we'd need nearly ten years' data.

This is obviously a problem. We can't afford to wait ten years—we can't even afford to wait three years—to find out which teachers can't cut it. If closing the achievement gap requires better teachers (and it does), we need to cut the error rate down to the point that we don't keep a lot of unsuccessful teachers in the classroom and a lot of successful ones out.

This is one of the most common arguments made against using student test scores to evaluate teachers. So far as I can tell, the argument comes down to this: Until someone comes up with a perfect tool for judging teachers, one that judges no teacher unfairly, there's no point in using anything.

The proper name for this kind of fuzzy thinking is "the nirvana fallacy." More than forty years ago, an economist named Harold Demsetz named this particular bit of logical malpractice (he called it a "nirvana approach"), describing it as what happens when people "seek to discover discrepancies between the ideal and the real, and . . . deduce that the real is inefficient" and try to summon what he called "perfection by incantation."

(If this sounds familiar, it's because it's pretty much the same thing Voltaire was talking about when he wrote that the perfect is the enemy of the good.)

Nirvana fallacies are pretty thick on the ground in any debate on education, partly because they align with self-interest—if no one can be fired without a "fair" evaluation, and a fair evaluation needs to be error-free, then no one can be fired. As a strategy, it's pretty formidable, waiting until that perfect test, that fail-safe system, appears.

But there's another way to cut the error rate down to the point that you wouldn't be making a mistake 26 percent of the time: using multiple tests, in which the results from one test multiply the reliability of another. Returning to the fact that in some alternate universe I should have been a doctor, doctors don't diagnose a cardiac condition based just on your blood pressure. They test your blood for triglycerides and C-reactive proteins. They give you an EKG. And a stress test. They might even stick a catheter with a couple of electrodes attached through a vein to check out your heart's electrical activity. No one of these tests is completely reliable. They might disagree with one another. But when they agree—when they're what statisticians call "positively correlated"—it's time to check into the hospital.

Teacher evaluations should be like that. If we had different tests that measured the same thing—in this case, competent teachers—not only would the results be more reliable, but teachers themselves would be a lot less hostile to the whole process.

That's the first objective of the Measures of Effective Teaching project that has been funded by the Bill and Melinda

Gates Foundation since 2009 and features the work of some of the biggest names in educational research: people like Ron Ferguson at Harvard's Kennedy School of Government, Doug Staiger from Dartmouth, and Drew Gitomer at the Educational Testing Service in Princeton. The MET researchers have figured out that the key isn't a better *single* test for finding good teachers, but *combining* data that is positively correlated with student improvement on standardized tests.

The first source of that data is observation, videotape. *Lots* of observation. For three years now, the MET researchers have been using very cool spy cams—panoramic digital video recorders that automatically record 360 degrees without a camera operator, which means that they capture everything that goes on in a classroom, from the lesson on a blackboard to the kid picking his nose in the back of the room—to film more than 20,000 different lessons.

I know what you're thinking: You might look at the same lesson as me and come to a completely different conclusion about it. The teacher I saw as a charismatic performer might look to you like a clown. Some of the teachers in the back of the TFA class might have thought I was a megalomaniac, and others might have thought I was concerned and connecting with the students. The MET folks thought about these discrepancies, too. To eliminate the danger of subjectivity, those lessons have been graded by some 500 different raters; and every one of them has been drilled in an observation rubric that is so precise that the scores for a particular lesson are usually within 5 percent of each other.

The key measures of any statistical test are reliability and validity. The rubrics made the videos reliable—in statistic-speak, they were measuring a phenomenon that appeared consistently. To give them validity, though, they had to measure a phenomenon that mattered, so the observation scores were then compared with the achievement growth of the students over the course of a year. Jackpot: The MET researchers found a consistent and positive correlation: Good lessons made for good students. And because the results were positively correlated, the error factors in evaluating teachers using either measure independently were lowered.*

I was surprised to learn that you could get a bunch of people to watch videos of classroom lessons and agree on which ones were good. But I was gobsmacked when I heard about the other way of separating the good teachers from the not-so-good: student surveys.

If you have kids in elementary or secondary school and have ever checked out websites like ratemyteachers.com, you know what I'm talking about. Students who rate teachers with comments like "Really nice, gives me a C no matter what; 2 Stars" would make anyone a little nervous.

Luckily, the student survey component of the MET project is more sophisticated. The key is asking students the right questions—the ones that really get at what matters inside the classroom. These questions get them to rank their teachers on criteria like "The teacher in this class encourages me to do my best," or "My teacher gives us time to explain our ideas," or "Our class stays busy and doesn't waste time," or "My teacher takes the time to summarize what we learn each day." Instead of asking students whether they like their teachers, or even if their teachers are any good, the MET survey asks students to evaluate the different parts of successful teaching. And, once again, the teachers who score highest on the student surveys—like the ones who get the best marks when their

---

* There's another reason to watch videos obsessively and identify best practices in the classroom, which is the chance to actually improve the quality of individual teachers. For more on this, see Chapter 5.

videos are rated—are the ones whose students show the most progress in any given year. Another positive correlation means another reduction in the error rate in teacher evaluations.

Add up all the different measures like video evaluations, student learning growth, and student surveys, and you have what you need to make decisions about teachers. The final report summarizing three years of MET research was issued in January of 2013, and it reinforced this conclusion big-time; as all the news stories that reported its publication put it, we finally "know how to identify good teachers." And, of course, not-so-good ones.

The MET researchers had been hoping for something like this since 2009. Their 2010 report, *Learning About Teaching,* substantiated the hypothesis that student perceptions were correlated with achievement; their 2012 report, *Gathering Feedback for Teaching,* did the same thing for classroom observations, wherever they were scored objectively and consistently. The final report didn't just assure that the "Culminating Findings from the MET Project's Three-Year Study" reflected a reliable and stable measure of teacher effectiveness by randomly assigning students to teachers. It also took special pains to make sure that the study wasn't just identifying teachers with some special talent for coaching students on high-stakes state-mandated tests; the research added a whole set of even more challenging assessments in math and English. And, since the same teachers who excelled (or didn't) at the state tests did so on the added ones, it seems a pretty good guess that their rankings weren't accidental. Put another way: The composite measures of effective teaching that the MET researchers collected and analyzed in 2009–10 accurately predicted real scores in 2010–11.

The final report also answered the question that really mattered: How much weight should we give to each of the three measures? Are last year's test scores more important than classroom observations? How about student surveys?

The answer turned out not to be simple. Not only did the researchers worry that giving too much emphasis to any one component would distort future teacher efforts (and not necessarily in the ways that would help to close the gap), but the decision involved trade-offs.

For example, the measure that was most *accurate* in forecasting scores on state exams gave a lot of weight to previous scores on similar tests: If all you wanted to do was predict next year's scores on a state test, as much as 81 percent of a total teacher evaluation would be based on last year's test scores, with 17 percent on student surveys, and only 2 percent on observation. However, this model—the MET researchers used four—was also the least *reliable* one, the one most likely to show gigantic swings from year to year. On the other hand, if 50 percent of the total score was taken from observation, the result was increased reliability, but at the expense of lower accuracy in predicting future scores.

There's no absolutely correct answer to this problem. It's like an NBA team deciding how much weight to give a player's college scoring average versus his performance in tryouts in predicting his pro potential. Different individual schools, or districts, will have to decide which is most important: reliability, accuracy predicting state test scores, or correlation with achievement on those higher-order tests. One good combination allocates 50 percent of teachers' total evaluation to their students' test scores, and 25 percent each to their standing in student surveys and observations. Another good model weights all three components equally: 33⅓ percent each.

No system is perfect, but any of them would provide a consistent and fair way of figuring out who belongs in the classroom and who doesn't, without waiting ten years.

Even better, each of them is an action plan. If your principal, or your local school board, or your state board of education can't tell you how they know who the best and worst teachers are (and if they don't, why they don't), and what happens to teachers whose students show less-than-average growth in achievement three years in a row, feel free to throw the book at them. This book. Anyone who says we don't know enough to get unsuccessful teachers out of the classroom is uninformed. We know. We didn't discover the philosopher's stone. We didn't find a one-size-fits-all answer. But we *did* find an answer. Or, part of one, anyway. The best estimates are that a student in an underperforming urban school who is fortunate enough to get a great teacher—one whose performance is one standard deviation higher than the mean, essentially one in the 80th percentile of all teachers—for four years in a row will close the gap separating her from her suburban counterpart, *without doing anything else.*

That was the good news. The bad news is that three good teachers—ones who are noticeably better than the average, scoring at about the 60th percentile in effectiveness—won't make up for one poor one. Again, Eric Hanushek has done the math: Assuming a class of twenty students, teachers in the 60th percentile are "worth" about $106,000 more in additional lifetime earnings than those at the 50th percentile. Three in a row? $320,000. But a single year with one teacher at the 8th percentile costs those same hypothetical twenty students $400,000.

This was so foreign to my own experience as a parent that I had to examine the numbers myself before I believed them. The reason is that—meaning no disrespect—the ratio of great teachers to poor ones in the schools I know best is nowhere near three-to-one. Even the most expensive private schools and the public schools in the most affluent suburbs have teachers whose skills, energies, and talents would place them in the very bottom percentile of the profession: teachers who have an effect size on student achievement of −.25 or worse. We don't know precisely how many there are; their shortcomings don't always show up in the growth measures for their students, because those students have families with the resources to make up for any deficiencies they're encountering in school.

It's sad and frustrating to say it, but we can afford these kind of "roadblock" teachers in schools where the students have help finding detours around them, mainly from their home environment. In schools on the wrong side of the achievement gap, we can't.

That's the bad news. The even worse news is that, even if great teachers were randomly assigned into America's public schools, the chance of getting one is only 20 percent in any given year. Getting a great one three years in a row is exponentially harder: not 20 percent, but .8 percent. And, teachers aren't assigned randomly, just the opposite. Partly because of the work rules demanded by collective-bargaining agreements in large urban school districts, the less skilled and more inexperienced the teacher, the greater the chance of his or her being assigned to an inner-city school.

This was depressing, but also promising. I knew that we'd found the first, and maybe the most important, key to closing the achievement gap: Increase the odds that kids receive great—or, at least, "good"—instruction for four years in a row by making sure that they don't hit a roadblock along the way. Every school that I visited that is closing the achievement gap lets go of a certain percentage of the lowest-performing teachers. These are charter schools that have the ability to do this. Some of the best schools we visited had rates of "nonrehiring" of 1 to 7 percent.

Eliminating those roadblocks is a necessary first step toward closing America's achievement gap. But it's not sufficient. One education expert put it this way: "You can't fire your way to Finland; you can't fire your way to excellence."

But the first key definitely gets you a passport to go there.

THE SECOND KEY:
THE RIGHT BALANCE
OF LEADERSHIP

MAKING CLARK KENT INTO SUPERMAN

NORTH STAR ACADEMY

I was late to visit North Star Academy in Newark, New Jersey. I was supposed to arrive at 7:30 A.M. I'm generally a very punctual guy, but I'll be candid and say I felt it hard to motivate myself to leave the house at 5:30 A.M. to drive all the way there. Yes, there was traffic, but if truth be told, I was dragging intentionally. This book was becoming a little bit of an obligation. I like to visit schools that are closing the achievement gap, and North Star, a school in the Uncommon Schools network of thirty-two charter schools located in Upstate New York, Brooklyn, and New Jersey, was considered one of the best on the East Coast. I was just being selfish and wasn't motivated to see it.

(By the way, that was the dramatic setup of a character who is about to encounter a life-changing experience. The best setups are the ones that make the character feel shortsighted and heading down the wrong path, thus highlighting the turn.)

So I arrived at around 7:45 A.M. A woman met me at the curb in front of the school. I said, "Hi, sorry I'm late."

She told me it's no problem. We walked to the stairs that led up to the glass doors of the school. There was another woman there. This one looked young, attractive, an urgency in her eyes. I stepped closer to say hi, but she cut me off and said, "Hurry. Morning circle is starting."

Actually, at that moment, I had no idea what she said. I knew there was a "circle" in it. She started speed-walking down the corridor. I had to move into a slight trot just to keep reasonably close to her. We trotted/speed-walked through the school and down a serpentine set of stairs. We were literally running down the stairs now. I have to tell you, I was pissed. I felt rushed and ignored and irrelevant. I didn't understand why we were doing this in this manner and felt my visit here was importunate. An ego-based anger flared inside me.

And then we hit the last stairs. I had to keep my eyes on the stairs so I didn't trip because we were moving so fast. So my eyes weren't looking up when I heard the sound. I'm a filmmaker, so one would think my main tool for storytelling is my eye, but really it's my ear. I can hear truth in a performance or in a silence or in a musical instrument or a sound effect. I heard this sound as I took the last flight of stairs. It was the sound of hundreds of students standing. That's all it was—the sound of students standing, but here's what I heard. I heard energy and precision, a military precision, and I heard strength, a collective strength. An entity had stood up. The first chill went through me.

As it turned out, at the bottom of the stairs was the entrance to North Star cafeteria. The children meet here every morning before school for breakfast and "brain food," which takes the form of a brain-teaser question. I missed all this because of my tardiness. What I saw was, to my eye, about a hundred kids in uniform marching to one end of the cafeteria. I was too late to be spoken to or greeted or advised as to what I saw, but my eye went immediately to a small attractive woman whose hair was pulled back. She strode down the aisle as the students marched past her. I say "strode" because that's what she was doing—huge powerful long steps. She was moving twice as fast as anyone in the cafeteria. She was yelling things I couldn't decipher yet. She turned on a dime and strode back the way she came. The kids were taking their seats in a big circle. In the center of the circle was a group of kids holding flags with university names on them. There were kids standing next to the flag-bearers in full costumes. Some were dressed like falcons, some like bobcats, some like alligators. The small woman with her hair pulled back, I found out later, was named Yasmin, and she was the principal. She continued speed-walking around the circle yelling to the kids. Then I heard what she was saying.

"What are we here for?"

The kids barked back, "Ed-u-ca-tion!"

She repeated this call over and over, challenging them, goading them. The kids barked back over and over. They yelled back these four syllables with power and fierceness, like a war cry. I got chills again. She proceeded to lead each class as they sang the alma mater of the college or university that their homeroom teacher attended. As they sang each teacher's school song, their respective mascot, whether falcon, bobcat, alligator, or any other creature, came running out from the center of the circle and whipped his or her respective class into a frothy mass of excitement. Did I mention it was 7:45 A.M.?

The mascots and flag-bearers joined their peers in the outer circle now. The small attractive woman with her hair tied back, Yasmin the principal, was the only one moving about the center of the circle. She continued speed-walking at all times.

"Yesterday I went to the store! Yes I did! Yes I did. I bought a ruler that cost sixty-one cents. I gave the man at the counter one dollar. How much change did he give me?! How much change did he give me?! How much change did he give me?!"

The entire cafeteria filled with the murmur of one hundred children counting and calculating under their breath. The principal picked a girl who answered in a full sentence.

"The man gave you thirty-nine cents."

"Very good, Tanya. Let's give Tanya the Spiderman cheer."

All one hundred kids, and the teachers and the principal, held their wrists out and made two spiderweb spraying sounds. Yasmin started speed-walking around the circle.

"What continent are we in? What continent are we in? What continent are we in?"

She pointed to the frailest boy in the cafeteria. He stood.

"The continent we are in is . . . The continent we are in is . . . The continent . . ."

He went silent. The principal stopped walking. She stood in the middle of the circle. She started raising her shoulders up and down. She whispered in a stage whisper.

"He's thinking. He's thinking. He's thinking."

One hundred students filled the cafeteria with their stage whispers as they moved their shoulders.

"He's thinking. He's thinking. He's thinking."

The boy didn't know the answer. The principal immediately jumped in.

"Who can help Clarence?"

A girl across the circle was chosen and stood.

"The continent we live on is North America."

The principal filled the cafeteria with her voice.

"I like that! I like that! That's teamwork. Let's give them the muscle cheer!"

The principal raised her arms as if she were making muscles and kissed each of her biceps. The throng of students and teachers kissed their own biceps.

I have been to many concerts. I have been to many plays. But no performer had command of a room like this woman did. Every set of eyes was on her. Every heartbeat was in sync with hers. She just gave a master class. The students and the teachers were the recipients.

This was clearly a Superman, the kind of rare person who can turn a whole school around and close the achievement gap by her sheer will and charisma and tenacity. This was a player like Michael Jordan that comes around so rarely you just get out of the way. There have been examples like this all over the country, superstars that are one in a million who lead inner-city children out of the achievement gap with their sub-urban peers, in fact make them *exceed* their white suburban counterparts. We have been in awe of these individuals in the past but knew wistfully that this was not a scalable solution to our educational problems; you can't find a Superman to run every school in the country.

Now here's the twist. The Superman I had watched was not found; she was created. The principal's name is Yasmin Vargas, and she was one of a string of principals that have been homegrown in the Uncommon Schools system. They all have been trained to walk, talk, and command in this manner. Yasmin Vargas is the thirty-three-year-old principal of North

Star Academy's elementary school in Vailsburg, a neighborhood in the West Ward of Newark, New Jersey. When I met her in September of 2012, she had been on the job less than two months.

How does North Star Academy do with this approach? For the last eight years, the State of New Jersey has given an annual test on literacy, math, and science—the NJ ASK, for "assessment of scholastic knowledge"—to students in the third through the eighth grades. Scores range from 100 to 300, with a score below 200 marked "partially proficient," 200 to 249 "proficient," and 250 to 300 "advanced proficient." Statewide, 63 percent of New Jersey's fourth-graders scored either proficient or advanced on the literacy portion of the NJ ASK; only 38 percent of those in urban districts did so. North Star's fourth-graders? *Ninety-eight percent.*

It's the same story for math. New Jersey's statewide percentage for fourth-graders scoring proficient and above was 79 percent. All of North Star's fourth-graders did: 100 percent. And it just goes on. By the time North Star's students hit eighth grade, 98 percent are at least proficient in literacy, and 79 percent in math, while the statewide numbers are, respectively, 82 percent and 72 percent. Only 29 percent of New Jersey students statewide pass the comprehensive test given at the end of first-year algebra; 76 percent of North Star's students do. It's pretty clear that they're doing something right. That's why we visited there. And this was clearly a leader-based environment.

This shouldn't have been a big surprise. One of the first papers James shared with me was from a task force of the American Educational Research Association entitled "Seven Strong Claims About School Leadership." The first claim was this: "School leadership is second only to classroom teaching as an influence on learning." So far, so good; I was pretty sure that a strong principal would be a huge asset to any school. Until I read the report, though, I didn't realize that the opposite also had to be true: Schools that don't have strong leadership, especially when they're asked to close the achievement gap, have an even bigger liability. From the same report: "There is not a single documented case of a school successfully turning around its achievement trajectory in the absence of strong leadership."

It's the same everywhere you look. In 2007, the consulting firm McKinsey & Company surveyed the world's most effective school systems and found a startlingly high correlation between strong leaders and successful schools. As an example, schools and principals in England—or, as they're sometimes known there, "headteachers"—were rated independently by national inspection teams. Ninety-seven percent of the schools that were independently rated as "good" or better also had leadership teams rated the same way. Only 8 percent of schools without a good leader managed to achieve a good rating. The U.K.'s Office for Standards in Education, which inspects and reports on 24,000 schools nationwide, found the same thing: 93 out of 100 schools *with* good leadership also achieve high scores on standardized tests, while only 1 out of 100 schools *without* it do.

This sounded pretty persuasive, but we'd spent a lot of time on ideas that looked good from a distance, not so good close-up. This theory about principals needed to be examined with a magnifying glass, not a telescope. Since we'd agreed that our magnifying glass—our standard for comparing strong tenets with weak ones—was measuring effect sizes, we still needed to figure out how much a successful leader is *really* worth. What was the effect size? And was it direct, or indirect?

WHAT LEADERS DO

Turns out there aren't nearly as many studies on the impact of principals as there are about teachers. I wondered whether some good starting points could be found in research about leadership generally. Were there differences between successful and unsuccessful managers working in situations that resembled the ones confronting elementary and secondary principals? Not the people who run really big organizations, like CEOs, but leaders who work further down the food chain? Sure enough, we found some intriguing results on the value of leaders who manage dozens of people instead of thousands.

First, leaders vary in large and consistent ways. The most · successful teams work under the most successful bosses. And the success is significant: If the team makes carburetors, they produce 10 percent more carburetors; if it analyzes blood work, it performs 10 percent more analyses. When the top managers moved on to new teams, the new teams increased *their* productivity.

Second: The boss's most important job isn't communicating strategy or even hiring and firing. It's "teaching skills that persist." Motivating a team of subordinates isn't nearly as important as improving their skills. Leaders don't achieve success by getting subordinates to work more hours—in the jargon of business-speak, by "reducing downtime"—but by increasing their productivity *while they work*. The effect size for increasing productivity per hour was nearly five times larger than the effect size for increasing the number of hours because, among other things, it reduced time away from the job, which is critical.

Interesting, like I said. But was research from the world

of business comparable to what goes on in an elementary or secondary school? There's a huge challenge in isolating the contribution of leadership to a school, rather than a business, since we can't measure easy-to-isolate things like profits, or widgets-per-hour. It's a challenge even to figure out how to design a study, much less make sense of the results.

One way, though, is to look at the year-to-year fluctuations in student achievement growth in the year after a new principal is hired. If you could hold the other effects constant, then maybe year-to-year variation in school achievement was a function of the principal's "added value."

That's just what three economists—Gregory Branch, Steven Rivkin, and the ever-present Eric Hanushek—did. Their source was a huge pile of data from the Texas Schools Project—and by huge, I mean *huge*. They compared student test data from 1993 to 2011 with personnel data on principals starting in 1990, which meant they had information on 7,420 different principals, who had been observed and evaluated 28,147 times, along with the annual achievement scores and demographic data—basically, poverty levels—for the schools they led.

The key was finding a large sample of schools, ideally schools with an achievement-gap problem, in their first years with new principals. This was the easy part. In Texas, three schools in ten lose their principals every year (the number nationally is one in five) and high-poverty and low-achieving schools are 40 percent more likely to have a first-year principal than an average school. The study then had to investigate whether these principals had a consistent impact—whether the same principal moved the needle in the same direction no matter where she landed—and whether that impact was correlated with student growth.

You can probably see where this one ended up: A principal that is one full standard deviation above the mean—that
is, one in the 80th percentile or so—has a positive effect
size on student achievement of +.11 for an entire school. A
principal in the lowest quartile—the 25th percentile—has an
effect size of −.15 for her school. And the effect is magni-
fied in the highest-poverty schools. The difference between
a good principal and a mediocre one is nearly as big as that
between great and poor teachers; and a principal's effect is on
hundreds of students, instead of a few dozen. Principals are
profoundly important. They matter a lot.

Which doesn't tell us the source of their impact. One
obvious question is whether principals work their magic by
changing the personnel at their schools or by improving the
staff they find. This is another answer that's hard to tease out;
remember that principal effect sizes are, almost by definition,
indirect. Principals affect student achievement through their
teachers—this is what statisticians call a *mediated effect*—and
trying to assign credit for success is a little like figuring out
whether a director hired actors who knew how to reach an
audience or guided the actors to reach the audience.

More clever research design. The economists behind the
Texas study calculated the turnover rate among teachers,
theorizing that one route to success was the principals' skill in
weeding out the underperforming teachers—those roadblocks
on the path to closing the achievement gap.

And, indeed, they found that the most effective principals
are also the ones engaging in the most "negative teacher selection," which is a euphemism for firing the lemons. But they
also did something more. They improved the instructional
success of existing teachers.

(Unfortunately, the study also found that some principals
are lemons as well, and the least effective principals are only

slightly more likely to leave the job than the most effective ones. Even worse: When they do, they usually just move to different schools, carrying their negative effect size of −.15 for the entire school with them, like a disease.)

I was intrigued. Just like teachers, principals matter. Good ones raise achievement and close the gap; mediocre ones do the opposite. But I still didn't know whether the difference between a good leader and the other kind was what they *are,* or what they *practice.*

I wanted to find out if there were some characteristics that could be used to identify the principals with the best chance for success. After all, this wasn't like hiring new teachers, who needed a few years in the classroom. Most principals have already been tested as teachers and have been good ones. Still, I wanted to see how school districts hire principals. Has it been thought out? As it turns out, very much so. They've done everything they can to find the Supermen.

In Chicago, for example, each teacher who wants to become a principal must first develop a portfolio that describes experience in half a dozen different competencies. This portfolio is then reviewed by a committee of retired principals, who are not exactly pushovers, since they fail two-thirds of the applicants. The remaining third are then given an exam and, if they pass *that,* are allowed to apply to a specific school. Then it gets really hard. Generally, five or six applicants compete for every position, and are interviewed by a school committee, which gives parents and teachers an effective veto on each candidate, in the hope that the final choice will at least have some support in place.

For the New York City Public Schools, it's even more elaborate. The system uses something called the APP, the Aspiring Principals Program, which includes fourteen months of training for the position. Candidates need both a master's degree and at least three years of classroom experience before they can even apply for the right license, which is called, accurately though confusingly, a certificate as a "School Building Leader." (When I first saw this, I thought it was describing a custodian.) Then they need an additional three years of experience as an administrator, with at least one under the supervision of another principal—I mean school building leader. They have to pass a special version of the New York State Teacher Certification Examination and then produce a résumé plus two essays that describe "leading a group of adults, and impacting student achievement." The next step is surviving a group interview; an individual interview (in which prospective principals are asked to review a school case study); another interview, in which candidates have to evaluate a video of a classroom lesson; and *another* interview, where they respond to three fictional-but-plausible scenarios that might be found in a principal's in-box.

It's hard to become a principal. It should be. Look up a description of an ideal principal, and you'll find a description of a superhero: Principals need to be able to work with both the school and larger communities. They have to mediate the conflicts and disagreements between teachers, parents, students, and other stakeholders. They assign teachers to grade levels and classes. They manage time and money. They're in charge of discipline, achievement, and performance on a huge number of standardized tests.

Which is why those auditions and interviews actually sounded really worthwhile. It's hard to succeed as a principal, and you want the very best people in the job. I had already heard from people who thought it was too easy to become a classroom teacher. But I sure didn't find anyone who thinks the same thing about principals. Only, here's the thing: The evidence was telling me that the performance of principals was just about as unpredictable as that of teachers. Remember that the top quarter of principals in that Texas study had a positive effect size of +.11, while the lowest quarter had a negative effect size of –.15. If the objective of those brutal application processes was to insure a consistent level of success, they weren't working all that well. I wanted to figure out why.

TRAITS VS. SKILLS

One possibility is that we're testing for the wrong things. The Future Leaders program now used in the U.K. (and based on work developed in the United States) selects and recruits school leaders using a thirteen-point competency model that includes, among other attributes, analytical thinking, ability to inspire others, a drive to collaborate, and a strong sense of moral purpose. New York wants candidates that can "foster a culture of excellence through personal leadership." These aren't competencies. They're traits. Relying on them to find successful principals is like nominating Mitt Romney for president because he looked presidential. He had presidential traits. And the evidence we had collected showed so much variability in the results that it made me think that all that care in finding principals with a particular set of "principal traits" might be irrelevant. It's not that the traits didn't matter; it's that they were needed for the wrong job.

According to Richard Elmore, we've been looking for some spectrum of superprincipal traits because of a long-standing historical mistake, which was the idea that teaching is such a mysterious activity that it couldn't be rationalized, or reproduced, or even evaluated. I remember nodding my head; not only did this gibe with what I had thought myself when we started the project—teaching was something some people can do and some can't—it would explain the variability among teachers. Principals can't figure out who has the magic touch until the teachers have been on the job for years.

The belief that we can identify the magic touch is everywhere. The Nobel Prize–winning psychologist and behavioral economist Daniel Kahneman, who practically invented the systematic study of those cognitive biases that mess up so much thinking about educational reform, tells a story about his service in the Israeli Army, when he was supposed to examine groups of officer candidates and score which ones had "the right stuff." Week after week, the young psych student would watch a bunch of potential officers go through a series of exercises and report which ones were good bets, which ones were losers, and which ones were going to be stars. And every month, he would receive updates on their actual performance, which was, inevitably, completely random. His highest-scoring candidates were just as likely to screw up at the next stage as his lowest-scoring ones, and vice versa. There was literally no relationship between the traits he saw on the examination course and future performance as an actual army officer. However, he continued to be convinced that his evaluations were valid. How could they not be? Every week, it was just so obvious which men were natural leaders. Not until years later did he realize that he had discovered his first cognitive bias: the "illusion of skill."

The illusion of skill (sometimes, the "illusion of validity") is bad news for the way most school districts pick principals. Not only does the illusion of skill fail to separate the good ones from the not-so-good: It also cuts the legs out from under all of them. If you believe that people either have the ability to throw a nine-inch basketball through an eighteen-inch hoop or they don't, you're going to be the kind of basketball coach who doesn't spend much time teaching players how to shoot. Principals are, most of the time, like that: If you believe that teaching talent is a trait—you either got it, or you ain't—you're left with managing buildings and salaries, not instruction. In Elmore's words, principals start to believe their most important function is serving as a buffer between instruction and outside interference.

Even worse news: If great principals are somehow born with the traits of leadership (just as great teachers are "born to be teachers," or Superman was born on Krypton), then there wasn't going to be any way of improving them systemically. Variability would be baked into the system. Like concrete.

Now we are getting to the real problem the research revealed to me. After a century of giving lip service to the idea that principals should be primarily responsible for instruction, it remains the activity that sucks up the fewest number of hours of every administrator. After all the testing, and interviews, and meetings, a typical urban principal spends *less than 20 percent* of the workday on instruction.

On the other hand, the principals in the top systems around the world surveyed by McKinsey & Company spend *80 percent* of the school day on improving instruction, most of it in the place instruction occurs: the classroom. Richard Elmore's Second Law reads: "The effect of professional development on practice and performance is inverse to the square of its distance from the classroom."*

Spending time in classrooms is something principals "do" and not something they "are." It's an activity, not a trait.

Classrooms are where Yasmin Vargas spends her day. She does so not because she has the spend-time-in-classrooms trait but because she was trained that way. Julie Jackson, a founding principal at Uncommon Schools and the regional

---

* His First Law: "Children generally do better on tests they can read than those they can't."

managing director for North Star, is an extraordinarily brilliant and successful educator. When I met her, I immediately knew I was in the presence of a preternaturally gifted leader. This was the definition of a Superman. She carried herself with confidence and strength. She both listened to others and spoke with authority. When I tried to compliment Yasmin, Yasmin just pointed to Julie. There were whisperings of the fact that a lot of what is taught to principals and teachers at the Uncommon Schools came from observing Julie. Uncommon decided to make more Julies by making others do what she did. Yasmin is the latest in a string of them.

Julie's a maniac for classroom observation and modeling, and so, therefore, are all the principals she's trained. It took me a day or two before I realized the value of all this observation, which was that it allowed Yasmin and all the principals like her to model the practices she wanted in her teachers, instead of publishing rules for them. Because the principals in Uncommon Schools visited every classroom, nearly every day, they could see what was working in one classroom and communicate it throughout an entire school.

So how do all these Clark Kents get to spend all this time on teacher instruction and modeling for teachers? We found that in school systems that are closing the gap, the management structure allows for this. Yasmin wasn't just trained to be like Julie; she was given the realistic opportunity to act like her. North Star, and all Uncommon Schools, handle school management for their principals. Every school has an operations manager, whose job is everything other than instruction: food service, discipline, and custodians of all varieties, and a whole lot of paperwork, leaving the principal to do one thing and one thing only: help teachers to help students learn. This is the exact opposite of a traditional school, where even the successful teachers become successful in isolation. No principal reinforces their success, because, well, that is not the principal's job.

In the school systems that are closing the achievement gap I visited in this country, that *is* the principal's job. A doable and scalable structure was in place.

CULTURE

After a day at North Star Academy, we were all struck speechless by what looked like an incredibly successful package of strategies. And then, right in the middle of our visit, Brett Peiser, one of the founders of the Uncommon Schools network, when asked about a great leader, said, "Great leaders know culture eats strategy for lunch."

He said this not like it was a nice thing teachers do, but like it was everything. Brett said we're facing an incredible force from these students' environments outside this school. Our force has to be louder and stronger and more consistent. By now, after a decade of No Child Left Behind, and thirty years of "A Nation at Risk," you won't have much trouble getting administrators or superintendents or principals to tell you about a school's "mission" or "values" or "core beliefs." Usually, they'll recite a mission statement even before you ask them, and all of them sound very good indeed.

I admit that "school culture" can be a pretty amorphous thing. And, given the amount of research that gets done on every aspect of educational practice, it wasn't a huge surprise that there were piles of studies on the subject, documenting everything from the way the kids dress for school—even how their teachers dress—to the look of individual classrooms to what teachers talk about in staff lounges. But most of the conclusions were so general that I started to wonder whether school culture was worth studying at all. Most of the principles you encounter are pretty uncontroversial—the kind of thing that no one ever objects to. Like "focusing on results" or "having high expectations." Both successful and ineffective schools claim to be driven by "honesty and professionalism" and are committed to "sustainable organizations." If there's a school in America that isn't in favor of "commitment," we haven't been able to find it. Or "collaboration." Or "empowerment."

Building a culture takes time: years of trial and error. That's one reason it's usually more prominent in advertising brochures than in the school itself. Most students have no idea of the core values of their school. The "force" of their culture wouldn't be very visceral. The first time I stepped into a school where the culture of the school slammed me in the face was also during my first visit to a school that was succeeding at closing the gap. It was incredibly poetic in retrospect, because the school was a part of the program that gave the country its first example of a culture with enough force to overwhelm its students' environments outside the school.

KIPP, the Knowledge Is Power Program, was founded in 1994 when two Teach For America alums, Mike Feinberg and Dave Levin, started the first KIPP school in Houston. The following year, Levin opened the second in New York. From those two middle schools, KIPP has since grown to 125 schools in twenty states and the District of Columbia—seventy middle schools, thirty-seven elementaries, and eighteen high schools, serving more than 40,000 students, nearly 90 percent of whom are eligible for free or reduced-price lunches.

Even so, KIPP graduation rates are stellar: Nine out of ten graduate, and eight out of ten continue on to college. Three years ago, I saw the system in action when I met with Marc Mannella, who had founded the KIPP Philadelphia Charter School in 2003. He has since become the CEO of the city's network of four KIPP schools—as of this writing, there are four—in Philadelphia. I remember being toured around Marc's original school. This was the first time I had seen the placards with the positive sayings. The first time I saw college banners everywhere. The first time I saw halls painted in bright, buoyant colors. I recall Marc telling us how they got the families to sign a contract in which everyone commits to the goals and culture of the school. They get everyone to buy in—every student, every member of the staff. I had never heard of this before that day—putting culture first, even if it seemed ahead of academic goals. But the result was I felt it with force. I felt the KIPP schools were onto something.

The numbers were impressive enough: A 2010 report from the Mathematica Policy Research think tank said it pretty clearly: "For the vast majority of KIPP schools studied, impacts on students' state assessment scores in mathematics and reading are positive, statistically significant, and educationally substantial." *Very* substantial. After three years at KIPP, the math improvement alone showed an effect size of +.48. Reading scores? An effect size of +.28. Put another way: In three years, KIPP students were receiving roughly 4.2 years' worth of math instruction, and 3.9 years of literacy improvement.

However, the KIPP secret actually reveals itself in a series of other numbers. The connective tissue that ties all 125 KIPP schools together is the "Five Pillars": high expectations; choice and commitment; more time (that is, a longer school day and year); power to lead (principals who manage instruction, budgets, and policies for their individual schools); and focus on results. Then there are the "Seven Keys for Implementing Character." A four-part "Framework for Effective Teaching" (including Self and Others; The Teaching Cycle; Knowledge; and Classroom Culture, the "countless tangible and intangible details in the space to create an environment where students are joyfully and meaningfully on-task"). They even have six different programs for developing leaders, not just principal preparation, but training for teacher leaders, and even administrators.

Marc Mannella is both the product of this devotion to leadership and one of its most vocal advocates. He not only hires and trains teachers and principals, but continues to review student performance every month, at what you might call a high level of granularity: not just overall grades on (for example) algebra exams, but how every student performed on every separate question. Want to know if a fourth-grader at KIPP Philadelphia Elementary Academy understands the commutative property? Marc Mannella does. And he knows the answer. This sort of instructional leadership percolates down to every classroom in the Philadelphia KIPP network: Students are assessed every six weeks. Those in kindergarten through fifth grade on their progress in literacy and math; everyone else on those subjects plus science.

And it resonates with every hiring decision KIPP makes. In Marc's words, "The number-one thing we're looking for is 'fit' . . . and, therefore, beliefs."

As it turns out, culture is more than a lot of apple pie aphorisms. It's little stuff as well as big stuff. If you wanted to distinguish French culture from Indian, you could (if you wanted to impress people) talk about how Marcel Proust and *Liberté, égalité, fraternité* are different from Rabindranath Tagore and *satyagraha*. But you could just as easily bring up baguettes and samosas, or Chanel dresses and saris. Culture is everything distinctive to a place. It's every way you know you're in an Uncommon School, for instance, instead of somewhere else.

Before evaluating teachers in a rigorous manner, or tasking principals and other leaders with observing and controlling the quality of instruction, closing the achievement gap means building a culture. And not just writing it down, but spending every day making sure that everyone involved in a kid's education, from the IT technician who maintains the school's computers to the analysts who review test scores to the classroom teachers to the playground aides, *buys off on the culture's norms.*

You can go into just about any school that's closing the gap and see how they are devoted to reinforcing a particular culture. Naming every class at North Star Academy after the alma mater of the teacher? A college-bound culture. The posters in every hallway announcing the highest scores on a recent test? A high-achieving culture. Uniforms. School colors. Fight songs. Mantras. Culture, culture, culture. A culture of high expectations seemed almost important enough to earn a place on the list of the keys to closing the achievement gap.

What *really* matters, though, is that whatever the school's high-expectation culture, everyone adopts it. If you were looking for a single reason why most schools have a few extraordinary teachers, a lot of average ones, and a few people who aren't cutting it at all, it isn't because the magic fairy dust wasn't given out uniformly—though it wasn't—or even that the strategies are deficient, but because no one has made certain that all teachers accepted a uniform culture in their bone marrow. "Culture eats strategy for lunch."

GOOD EDUCATION IS CONSISTENT EDUCATION

This brings us to the last thing we have found that great leaders "do." They create incredible consistency in their students' experience in their schools. There was something else in Richard Elmore's research that had to gestate for a while in my brain before I started to see its implications. Almost as an aside, he points out that the level of management that *really* matters in education isn't the individual classroom or the school district (and definitely not an entire state or country). It's the school. His reasoning was that the students don't just occupy a classroom for a year; they spend three or four years in a succession of classrooms in a single school.

We had already found the evidence for this when we calculated the importance of keeping a single poor year from derailing a student who would otherwise have closed a big part of the achievement gap. This was why the teachers with negative impact on student growth need to be weeded out.

But this was about something different, and maybe even more important. If the key to closing the gap was putting students in front of three or four good teachers in a row, then a principal isn't just a leader. She's a quality control officer.

Because traditional public schools for more than a century have treated teachers (especially experienced ones) as the custodians of a secret skill, they've allowed them a lot of leeway in the basics of classroom management. Some third-grade teachers are strict disciplinarians, and some are easygoing. Some give homework every night; others once a week. One teacher might stand by the blackboard for an entire lesson, and another wander through the classroom. I honestly don't know if this is good or bad, but I can tell you one thing it isn't: It isn't consistent. And all those third-graders (or most of them, anyway) are going to find themselves in fourth-grade classrooms with a mixture of kids from the strict and not-so-strict teachers and find that the homework schedule in the fourth grade is completely different from that in the third grade.

Or the eighth grade. The second half of my visit to North Star Academy was a tour of their middle school, with its principal, Serena Savarirayan, an Indian woman in her thirties.

She walked me down the halls as students walked silently along lines painted on the floor. (In North Star, the children walked along painted lines on the floor. Getting from class to class was an art form for them. North Star believed every second of the school day counted and didn't want students to lose any time in the hallways.) A child approached us with her mouth open and bloody. "My tooth fell out." Serena applauded the girl's bravery and guided her to the nurse to get cleaned up.

Somehow, Serena had struck a balance between unquestioned authority and humanity, and you could see this balance in every aspect of the middle school, especially in the classroom. One class we visited was taught by an Indian man in his late twenties with no more than a couple of years' experience (an Indian visitor escorted by an Indian principal while observing an Indian teacher was a coincidence, I believe). Serena and I stood against the wall as he conducted the class. The North Star way was on full display. When one student spoke, the entire class stood and faced him. When asked a question, each student responded in full sentences. The teacher moved continuously and spoke fast and loud. As he did, Serena offered me a whispered commentary about what was going on and then suddenly interrupted the class. "I believe you might want to acknowledge Sarah. She seems to have a question." The teacher moved his attention to a girl in the corner who had her hand up very sheepishly. Serena returned to whispering to me.

Two more times during the class, Serena interrupted with advice for her teacher, which struck me as astounding. Even more astounding: The teacher didn't seem to be taking any of this badly. I asked Serena, "He doesn't mind? How often do you go into classrooms and do this?" She looked at me. "That's all I do. I go from classroom to classroom and observe and instruct the teachers. I've been in this class three times this week."

I said, "What if you have a superstar teacher who doesn't want the intrusion?"

"Hasn't happened," she said.

When the class was finished, I took photos in the hall with the male teacher, who was getting ribbed by his fellow teachers for wearing a jacket because he knew I was visiting. I took a photo with the principal, who told me her Indian parents were very proud of me. There was great camaraderie there in the hall. The teachers there were secure, as if they couldn't fail. They weren't alone. I honestly felt that if I wanted to become a teacher, and with Serena's help, I probably would succeed, too.

THE CRAFT

At the North Star Academy, all teachers are taught to succeed. In the classrooms I visited with Yasmin and Serena, every teacher spoke to their class at about the same volume—loud—and at the same speed—fast. They moved forward and backward in a pattern that was familiar after the first two times I observed it. Each of them called kids in similar ways, and their tests are timed to appear at roughly the same time of day. They weren't robots, far from it. But they were a lot more alike than they were different, and they were different from any group of teachers I'd ever observed in my own kids' schools.

One reason for this is the message of one of the most influential books ever written about classroom teaching, *Teach Like a Champion,* by Doug Lemov. Not at all coincidentally, he was one of the guiding lights behind Uncommon Schools.

Nearly ten years ago, Doug, then a classroom teacher

himself, had one of those strokes of genius that are painfully obvious in retrospect but that had never occurred to anyone beforehand: Since he accepted that some teachers were performing at a higher level than others—he, at least, hadn't adopted the widget effect—why not find the teachers whose students were consistently achieving better-than-expected results on standardized tests and record what they actually did in their classrooms? He hired someone to operate a video (whose experience was mostly recording wedding videos), and the two of them started a five-year-long program to record what was going on in the country's most successful classrooms.

The result was what became known as Lemov's Taxonomy, collected in his book *Teach Like a Champion,* which describes forty-nine distinct techniques that are used by America's most effective teachers. Technique Number Six, for example, which Lemov calls "Begin with the End," reminds teachers to begin every lesson by circling back to anything that the class might have missed the day before. Number Twenty-eight, "Entry Routine," shows how to make a habit out of students picking up packets from a table, rather than having them handed to them at the door. Number Twenty-nine, "Do Now," requires that every classroom have an assignment that each student can start working on, without direction, as soon as he or she enters the room. Number Fifteen, called simply "Circulate," prompts teachers to move around the classroom in very specific ways: "breaking the plane" (an imaginary line that runs across the room, where the students in the front row sit) within five minutes of starting the lesson, always facing as much of the class as possible, and requiring that the aisles of every room be cleared of backpacks, chairs, or anything that impedes the teacher's systematic movement. There's even the "J-Factor," Number Forty-six, which is a list of specific techniques for injecting joy into the classroom: giving students nicknames, for example. (By the way, it was almost folklore that Julie Jackson was one of the superstar teachers that Doug Lemov videotaped to come up with his list in the first place.)

Just about every element of Lemov's Taxonomy was on view at North Star, in every classroom we visited. It took me a while to remember what all this reminded me of. It was something I'd noticed in a documentary on the legendary UCLA basketball coach John Wooden. The film, which interviewed players who had been on Wooden's teams in the 1950s, 1960s, and 1970s, made a lot out of the fact that Wooden's practices and plays were so consistent that someone who had played for him in 1960, for example, could have started for a team from ten years later without a single practice. The plays were the same, the technique for a bounce pass was the same, the lanes on the fast break were the same, and so were the assignments on defense. There was a "Wooden Way" for everything, up to and including the right way to smooth out your socks and tie your shoes.

The "North Star Way" was the same kind of thing. All teachers learn the same techniques, rhythms, and tactics for teaching these kids. It was a system that showed every teacher a way to be successful in every classroom—and, even better, it showed every student that the same work habits, demeanor, and study skills would be as rewarding in the fourth or fifth grade as they were in the second and third. New teachers even spend the summer before their first teaching assignments on lesson practice, and every one of them arrives with a clear idea of what they'll be teaching for the first weeks of school, kind of like a football team that calls its first twelve plays before the game even starts. It was a remarkable thing to see, and it was dependent on people like Yasmin and

Serena constantly observing and—there's no other word—coaching their teachers.

It's a two-way street. Yasmin and Serena were honoring what Elmore calls the principle of reciprocity. If a principal demands a particular performance from a teacher, she owes that teacher the tools to accomplish it. North Star's teachers were accountable for their class's performance, just like teachers in every school these days. But they were given a whole set of tools to get there, and because the teaching practice was so consistent across different grade levels, so were their students.

The principals are observed just as closely as their teachers. Every week, Yasmin and Serena meet individually with Julie Jackson. And, just as each principal's job is creating a consistent and successful environment for her teachers, Julie's is all about doing the same thing for her principals. This isn't just about a single school or a single year for her: Julie's responsibility extends beyond the students in the schools that are under her supervision. It's just as important that their teachers grow and that the right ones are identified, years before they're needed, as future principals. That's how they found Yasmin and thirty-one other principals like her.

The more I thought about this whole Clark Kent and Superman thing, the more I thought the analogy was all wrong. Superman had otherworldly skills that could not be copied, unless you were from Krypton, too. Batman would've been a better analogy; he just needed courage and fancy tools. We do all have the potential to be Batman.

THE THIRD KEY: FEEDBACK

6

YOU HAD ME AT "DATA"

Long before I visited North Star Academy, I already knew that one of the most powerful tools that schools have for improving instruction is getting the least effective teachers out of the classroom. The numbers didn't lie: Identifying low-performing teachers in underperforming schools—the *really* low performers, the ones whose effect size on student achievement was −.25 below the mean—and swapping them with even average replacements would go a long way toward closing the achievement gap.

A lot of reform arguments end there. But instructional leadership is more than just making the right staffing decisions. For one thing, it can take years to find out which teachers are in need of a new career, even using the best measurements there are. Principals like Yasmin and Serena need more in their tool kits than "selective retention" if they're going to close the gap. To make North Star's success scalable, the reality of the situation is they need some way to improve the performance of the teachers they retain.

And, if they're going to increase the value of existing teachers, they first need to measure it.

We'd already learned that "value-added measurement," or VAM (sometimes VAA, for "value-added assessment") is a catchall term for a family of complicated statistical techniques that use multiple years' worth of student test scores to estimate the various causes and effects of widely different teacher performance—which ones make the biggest and smallest contributions to student outcomes. The oldest and most commonly used is the Tennessee Value-Added Assessment System, but hundreds if not thousands of school districts now use some form of VAM to measure the performance of students, teachers, and entire schools.

As we'd learned, VAM is a lot subtler than the cartoon explanation that's usually used to describe it—the idea that test scores are the only measure of student achievement, or teacher quality. The statisticians who created it were well aware that students don't arrive in any classroom as blank slates, and that measuring their performance was a lot more complicated than just comparing their scores on standardized tests, or even their progress over the course of the school year. VAM (in its ideal form, anyway) compares students' *actual* progress to *predicted* progress, and assumes that any differences are due to the instruction they received.

Anyone who reads opinion pieces on the state of American educational reform knows that there are a few controversial assumptions baked into that definition of VAM. The first is the idea that actual progress is measurable by standardized tests at all. However, even though there's a kind of sentimental objection to the belief that kids can be "reduced to a test score," the alternative—subjective grading—is even worse: a flexible yardstick that may not have created the achievement gap, but definitely perpetuated it. Sooner or later, kids need to demonstrate mastery of sentence structure, the binomial theorem, and the U.S. Constitution, and the ones that can't are going to be at a giant disadvantage. The only way to make sure they know this stuff is to test them.

The second objection to comparing actual progress to predicted progress is to the idea that one can actually *predict* student achievement. To do this, you have to understand the method being used, which involves a bunch of statistical techniques known as "hierarchical linear modeling." (Boring-sounding, I know. Hang in there.)

To most people, including me, "hierarchical linear modeling" is the kind of social science jargon that sounds as if it were created so that academics would have a private language they could use to communicate with one another and intimidate everyone else. But the word "linear" just means that the phenomenon being examined can be plotted on a graph—in this case, a graph of student progress—that travels in only one direction. The simplest version of this kind of model, which is probably familiar to every parent, is the chart that pediatricians use to estimate the height of our kids at any given age. Those growth charts assume that if your son or daughter is in the 30th (or 70th) percentile for height at age seven, he or she will probably be in the 30th (or 70th) percentile at age twelve.

So, what's "hierarchical" linear modeling? Since progress in literacy isn't as by-the-numbers as height, it requires more information than just a kid's reading level at age seven. That information can include family circumstances like income, parents' educational background, geographic location (Vermont versus Mississippi; inner city versus suburbs), past performance by other kids in the same school, and past performance by the individual student. Deciding how much weight to give each one—where to rank them—is the "hierarchy" in "hierarchical linear modeling." It isn't perfect, but it does work, generally very well so long as good data are available, and—especially—when it's used to measure *growth* rather than *achievement*. In fact, most of the controversies around high-stakes testing arise because of confusing these two measures. The second one, achievement, measures where we want to end up: with all of America's eighth-graders, for example, reading at least at an eighth-grade level. But it's not very useful to reward teachers, schools, or school districts for their high-scoring eighth-graders if those same eighth-graders had already been high-scoring first-graders. That's why the most refined systems, and the most effective schools, are focused on growth. Did our eighth-graders do *better than predicted,* based on their scores in the first grade?

VAM is a lot more sophisticated than the early test comparisons that became so common after the passage of the No Child Left Behind law in 2001. Some of the country's biggest school districts have been using versions of VAMs to identify consistently underperforming schools and—sometimes—underperforming teachers. As it turned out, there were even more valuable ways to use all that value-added data. Data measurement—not just value-added measurement; *all* sorts of data—was the key to improving *teachers* and improving *instruction*. To making the practice of teaching data-driven.

In the world of education reform, the three words in this order, "data-driven instruction," usually have a specific, and pretty limited, definition: using objective assessments, like test scores, to identify the students in need of more, or different, classroom instruction. By that definition, some schools have been using data for a long time, or, at least, trying to. The original idea grew out of an unlikely place: the writings of a statistician named William Edwards Deming, whose theories about industry revolutionized the automobile business, first in Japan, then in America, and then pretty much everywhere.

Deming's ideas about what came to be known as Total Quality Management, or Continuous Improvement, are all refinements of the same concept: A successful organization is one that goes through cycles of what Deming called planning, doing, studying, and acting, over and over again. The idea was that continual repetition of the planning-then-doing-then-studying-then-acting cycle made everyone in the organization pay attention to data. And, the more they paid attention to it, the better they responded to it.

But it wasn't until the late 1990s that schools began to wonder whether they could benefit just as much as factories did from analyzing data. Following Deming, some educational reformers started thinking about a systematic way of collecting and using various kinds of data. They started collecting data on all kinds of things, not just test scores. Using the same model that had worked at Toyota and Ford, they broke down the types of data into inputs (like school expenditures; demographics), processes (the quality and quantity of instruction), and outcomes (test scores, graduation rates, including satisfaction surveys—both from students and their parents).

One key element in this process is defining "data" as "any kind of objective evidence." Back in 2000, the idea—which was then known as "Data-Based Decision-Making," or DBDM—was field-tested in six schools in Massachusetts by the New England Regional Alliance for Mathematics and Science Reform, whose researchers were careful to look not just at student test scores, but everything they thought might affect those scores, like the amount of time each student spent on-task: writing an essay, for example, or solving a problem. The goal was to figure out the *reasons* for failure and success. Were good outcomes correlated with more homework? Better attendance? How about the impact of taking other courses? Did students who took music do better in math? The results

were consistent enough to suggest that the relationships between certain practices and improved outcomes weren't random. As everyone who takes an introductory statistics course
is warned, correlation isn't causation; but it was encouraging
enough that a bunch of other studies followed.

There was Implementing Standards-Based Accountability,
which looked at data-driven instruction at selected schools in
California, Georgia, and Pennsylvania between 2002 and 2007.
More or less at the same time, the RAND Corporation visited
six school districts and one charter school in southwestern
Pennsylvania during the school years 2004 and 2005, and
surveyed twenty-six more. The Institute for Learning at the
University of Pittsburgh examined data-driven instructional efforts in three urban districts in the South and Northeast from
2002 to 2005. The nation's largest operator of for-profit public
schools, Edison Schools, did the same thing in its own classrooms during the same years.

In all these studies, the reason for looking at additional
sources of data was the same: The high-stakes tests that made
every school in America at least partly accountable when its
students failed to hit some acceptable threshold might have
been a good way to increase focus on achievement, but by
definition, their results arrived too late to affect ongoing instruction. An end-of-the-year assessment of math skills, or
reading ability, tells a school *whether* it was doing its job but
not *how to do it*.

One answer was more tests: Progress tests. District-level
midterms. "Benchmark tests," which were supposed to identify student progress and difficulties with any of the parts of
a class assignment. The benefits were quick turnaround, and,
because the consequences of doing poorly were a lot less
dire, more honest participation.

It wasn't just tests. In the Institute for Learning study, some of the principals and teachers systematically reviewed *all* student work: writing portfolios, worksheets, even homework. In two of the districts they studied, teachers and principals regularly took what they came to call "Learning Walks"—organized tours of halls and classrooms to acquire information on everything from student participation to teacher communication.

There's more. Richard Halverson, who studies educational leadership and policy analysis at the University of Wisconsin–Madison, developed and tested a "data-driven instructional systems" (DDIS) model in four midwestern elementary and middle schools as a way of connecting classroom practices with accountability measures like test scores. Halverson's notion is that two-way information flow is the key to closing the achievement gap in America's schools. The idea is to transform *summary* data—both the high-stakes test scores required by NCLB and, more recently, the Obama Administration's "Race to the Top" and all other end-of-year measures of student performance—into *formative* data: stuff that teachers can actually use in the classroom.

His system includes pretty much everything you'd want from data-based instruction: a rigorous way of acquiring and storing data—mostly standardized test scores, but also the kind of information collected by guidance counselors: household demographics, classroom grades, observations of students, discipline records, along with student writing samples and daily student assessments (usually assessments, in elementary schools, of literacy). The final step was a structure for reflecting on this data, aligning programs with it, and adapting curricula and teaching techniques in light of it. Like all the studies mentioned, the DDIS study sounds great.

But there was a problem with all of these studies. Outcomes didn't improve.

The problem was everywhere. One 2007 study surveyed

ninety-three different school districts in the state of Pennsylvania, forty-seven of which were using the Pennsylvania Value-Added Assessment System, or PVAAS, and forty-six that weren't. The study was a careful one, matching the control group with the experimental group on 100 different criteria, making them as identical as possible with the single exception that half of them were using a data-based system and half weren't. Using objective score results, plus surveys of more than 400 principals and nearly 2,400 teachers, it found no significant difference between the two groups of school districts.

Which was a disappointment, not just to them, but to me. It is a fact that the schools most effective at closing the education gap were obsessive about using data—all of them. But why wasn't data-driven instruction working in other schools?

One of the reasons that data wasn't influencing instruction was frequency. In Professor Halverson's schools, for example, data was assessed only four times a year—at most. Sometimes only once a year, at so-called data retreats. Another answer was variability of buy-in by the teachers. Even though everyone in these previously mentioned studies reported using some kind of data-based instruction, the variability of outcomes—test scores, graduation rates—was bigger *within* schools that were using data-based instruction than *between* schools that were using it and those that weren't. Short answer: The teachers who wanted to use it were using it. In almost all of these schools, the teachers who described themselves as "data-driven" were the ones who were being observed and videotaped. They were the ones who spent their summers reviewing data on their previous term's students. In one of Professor Halverson's elementary schools, a single teacher—one of the ones that really bought into the program—was a literacy specialist who spent six years redesigning a "Guided Reading" program to be used in kinder-garten through second grade. She instituted weekly meetings with classroom teachers and wrote a protocol for ongoing assessment of the progress kids made with the system. She even wrote an observation protocol that showed how incon-sistently teachers were communicating with their students: One teacher would say "sound it out" one day, "stretch it out" another, and "say it slowly" a third time, when they all meant the same thing.

There will always be rare examples of naturally analytical teachers who embrace data. If you like stories about hard-working, competent teachers using data to improve instruc-tion, such examples are hard to beat. But, if you want to turn an entire system around without depending on superteachers to do it, this kind of teaching is just as hard to replicate. It was the same story in the Pennsylvania study: Two-thirds or more of the principals who had access to all the PVAAS data made "minimal use of the information" provided. They didn't use it to identify students at risk, low-performing students, or even high-performing ones. Value-added data adds value only when someone actually uses it.

The evidence was clear, if depressing: If you want data-based instruction to work, it can't be voluntary. Teachers and principals who aren't "data-driven" can't opt out of the system, not unless you want the feedback loop between data and in-struction to have a giant hole in it.

The second reason that outcomes weren't improving was that value-added data only adds value if someone actually uses it.

The third answer was ubiquity. Data is collected every-where, but no one has taught teachers and principals how to analyze the data they're collecting. Richard Elmore, at Har-vard, put it into clear, discouraging, focus:

In our non-degree professional development programs at Harvard University, I have taken to routinely asking the assembled administrators and teachers how many of them have taken a basic course on educational measurement. In an audience of 50 to 100 participants, the usual count is two or three. These people are usually ringers—they are typically assistant superintendents for measurement and evaluation whose job is to run the testing operation in their school systems. Now, imagine what the state of healthcare would be if practicing physicians didn't know how to read ECGs, EEGs or chest x-rays, didn't know how to interpret a basic blood analysis, or didn't know anything about the test-retest reliability of these simple diagnostic measures. Imagine what it would be like if your basic family practitioner in a health maintenance organization didn't know how to interpret a piece of current medical research questioning the validity of the standard test for colorectal cancer.... The organization you are imagining is a school system.

To tell you the truth, the early evidence in support of data-based instruction wasn't especially persuasive. I wasn't against it. But it seemed a little like treating cancer by taking multivitamins—something that probably helps a little but not a lot. To figure out what to do was going to take someone more knowledgeable about data and its intricacies than me, since I spend *my* days thinking up horrors to inflict on unsuspecting suburban-type families. I needed someone like Professor Roland Fryer.

THE STUDY I WAS LOOKING FOR

As Michelle Rhee and I were leaving the restaurant after our dinner in 2009, she mentioned a young professor at Harvard who was doing a lot of innovative research on what worked and what didn't in education reform. She said his name was Roland Fryer.

Professor Fryer is an academic rock star, the youngest African-American to receive tenure at Harvard University. In 2009, when Bhavna, Jenn, and I met him and his fiancée at a Manhattan restaurant for brunch, he was one of *Time* magazine's "100 Most Influential People in the World." He has since received one of the MacArthur Foundation's "Genius Grants." He's even been on *The Colbert Report*.

And it was quite a brunch. We met in a cool Tribeca restaurant named Bread, the kind of restaurant where Hollywood families take their babies in strollers. Professor Fryer is a man who listens with his eyes, and he watched me meticulously as I spoke. I remember his attention wavering and then bursting forth with intensity and information. He listened to our early idea—that there were a few keys to closing the achievement gap, and that they needed to be implemented together. He nodded slightly. I felt this was a big endorsement from him. Professor Fryer, it turned out, was actually working on something similar to my list himself.

In 2007, he and Will Dobbie, a doctoral candidate and one of Professor Fryer's colleagues at Harvard's Educational Innovation Laboratory—EdLabs, as everyone calls it—completed a detailed study of thirty-five charter schools in New York City. And I do mean *detailed*. Not only did Fryer and Dobbie survey the principals, teachers, and students at the charters— twenty-two K–5 elementary schools, and thirteen grade 6–8 middle schools, representing a huge range of educational philosophies, from charters with a "relentless focus" on math and reading to the Bronx Charter School for the Arts—they observed and measured them like geneticists with a lab full of fruit flies.

They collected data, directly from principals, on teacher development, instructional time, parent involvement, and school culture. Every lesson plan in each testable grade level and subject received a score that showed how rigorous the lesson was. They visited every school, videotaping classrooms in at least one math and reading class and interviewing hundreds of randomly chosen teachers and students. They calculated how many hours teachers spent on instructional and noninstructional learning every week; determined the teacher salaries and turnover at each school, and the criteria used in hiring; and measured the number of times that each teacher received either formal or informal feedback from classroom visits. All that data was compared with student performance, school by school and classroom by classroom. These dudes were meticulous.

They were after the same thing I was looking for: a system of tenets that, together, worked to close the achievement gap. Fryer's own list was forming, but one of those tenets, clear as day, was feedback. Teachers at high-achieving elementary schools—those above the median in performance on standardized tests—got some kind of feedback from classroom visits and student achievement 16.41 times each semester. Those below the median? 11.31 times. At high-achieving middle schools, the difference was even bigger: Their teachers received feedback 13.42 times each semester, compared to 6.35 times elsewhere.

The frequency of feedback is critical, and also important is what it consists of; to be useful, it needs to incorporate a huge amount of data, which means lots of tests. So it wasn't surprising that high-achieving schools also test students more: 3.92 interim assessments of math and language arts every semester at high-achieving elementaries, vs. 2.42 times elsewhere. And, again, the difference got bigger as the kids got older: Middle schools whose students score above the median assess their students 4.00 times a semester; those below assess them 2.04 times.

High-achieving schools also had more strategies for using data to customize instruction for different students: Elementary schools on the top half of the achievement ladder used 4.62 different data-driven ways to create lesson plans that accommodated classroom differences, from modifying a writing lesson for a girl not yet fluent in English to creating an arithmetic unit for a boy with Asperger's (or for that matter, accelerating instruction for gifted students), while those on the lower half applied only 3.5 ways. In middle schools, the respective numbers were 4.67 vs. 4.00. The top-scoring elementaries produced more teacher reports, too, 4.27 vs. 3.5 elsewhere, and 3.00 at high-achieving middles vs. 2.86. They were also more likely to have plans for using data to differentiate instruction, and to track students using data.

The overall effect size found in the study's most successful schools was huge, too: +.48 in math, +.50 in English each year this data is being used. That's twice as big as the effect sizes for reducing class size in the Tennessee STAR experiment. It's even larger than the estimated effect size for replacing the lowest-performing 8 percent of teachers with average ones.

Of course, Dobbie and Fryer weren't just looking for evidence in support of feedback; there were actually five different practices that they tested in their New York study (and you'll be hearing about some of them in later chapters). They differentiated between feedback and data-driven instruction. This makes it hard to tease out which of the practices contributed to the overall effect. However, Professor Fryer did perform an analysis that suggests about a quarter of the total effect is traceable to the combination of teacher feedback and the use of value-added data in the classroom.*

Compelling stuff, I thought. But if there was one thing we were learning it was that the acid test wasn't whether something *worked,* but whether it could be *repeated.*

That's why Professor Fryer took the show on the road. During the 2010–11 school year, the Houston Independent School District implemented the New York City–tested practices in nine of the lowest-performing schools in the city—four "persistently low-achieving" high schools and five "academically unacceptable" middle schools—representing 7,000 students.

It was a pretty good place to test a new idea. More than 88 percent of the students in Houston Independent are black or Hispanic; 80 percent are eligible for free or reduced-price lunch, and 30 percent have only limited proficiency in English. Also—maybe most important—the nine schools selected for the experiment were all public schools, no charters. The one thing that was unarguably true of the students in all the New York schools—that their parents had chosen to put their kids in a particular school, usually by entering them in a lottery—didn't apply in Houston. If a practice worked in Houston, everyone's confidence that the reason was the practice itself and not something else would be a whole lot higher.

The test schools—those that implemented the Dobbie and Fryer practices—were compared to schools (fifteen high schools; nineteen middle schools) that resembled the test schools in racial, economic, and other characteristics. The biggest difference between the test schools and the "comparison group" schools was that thirteen of the comparison

---

* The other three-quarters included practices like intensive tutoring, a culture of high expectations, and more instructional time. More about this in Chapter 8.

308 619 478

group ranked as "academically acceptable" and the remaining twenty-one were rated even higher. These were solid schools. If the nine failing test schools that implemented the Dobbie and Fryer practices could catch up with them, the achievement gap might just be starting to close.

They didn't quite. But they made up a *lot* of ground, particularly in learning math. The effect size on math performance for the study's sixth-graders was between +.301 and +.484; and remember, that was after only one year. It wasn't quite as big for the seventh- and eighth-graders—"only" +.125—but the high school students showed big-time improvements, a combined effect size in math of +.363. The reading effects, on the other hand, were a lot smaller, with no significant results in the middle schools, and very modest improvements—effect sizes of about +.188—for the high schools, probably because language skills are usually acquired in lower grades. And even though we have only one year of data and despite some complicating and confounding factors—lots of new personnel, for example—the results are still impressive.

Once again, part of the credit goes to better, and more frequent, feedback. Schools were required to administer interim assessments every three to four weeks, and, based on those assessments, teachers were required to meet with students one on one to set individual performance goals. But, since so much else was going on in those schools—before the study began, all nine principals, 30 percent of the other administrators, and more than half of the teachers were removed and replaced*—it's almost impossible to know how much of the improvement was due to feedback and data alone.

---

* Interestingly, at least to me, the new principals were selected using the Haberman Star screener, and each of the new principals agreed to train the new teachers using the strategies in Lemov's *Teach Like a Champion*.

But when I saw the Houston figures, I took note. Not only was this the most powerful evidence yet for the importance of feedback loops to manage instruction; it was also a giant endorsement for the *systemic* approach. We already knew that another of those cognitive fallacies—this one sometimes known as the *modo hoc* (for "just this") fallacy—fools us into thinking that all of the properties of a system can be derived from the system's components looked at in isolation. Life doesn't work like that. Neither does school reform. You can't figure out how to close the achievement gap by examining *any* single practice. Using data and feedback to improve instruction is helpful all by itself. But it's far more valuable when it's part of a system of other practices that reinforce one another. Roland Fryer had demonstrated, in New York and Houston, how a bunch of practices reinforced themselves. I wasn't sure that he had tested the *right* bunch (though we would be hearing from him again), but I was absolutely certain that we were on the right track, and Dr. Fryer had given me another strong piece of evidence for the importance of frequent feedback.

THE BIG EASY

I had always dreamed of going to New Orleans. In this dream, I would go with family and friends and we would eat spicy Cajun food and drink and marvel at everyone's accents and then dance to an eclectic band as beads were passed all around us. In this dream, I would feel I was thrown back in time and experience the history and élan of the locals. When I did finally go to New Orleans, it was more than seven years after Katrina, and I visited a city recovering in every way from a major storm and a few centuries of neglect. It is one of the main cities where the chasm between how we treat the rich and how we treat the poor is on display. I flew there to go see the FirstLine Schools. They were founded by a man named Jay Altman. From all accounts, this was a man who knew everything about education; maybe one of the top ten on the subject of closing the achievement gap. I was anxious to learn from him and visit his school system. He invited me to visit the newly built Arthur Ashe Charter School. Now here's the important part: I made this visit after I had already seen the North Star Academy in Newark. I was expecting to see a version of that school, but with Creole accents. I waited in the sunny lobby and looked at the colorful banners of school mottoes: "100% all the time, every day" and "Ashe scholars are ACES, Achievement, Community, Excellence, Self." I was brought into their conference room and began talking with the codirectors of Arthur Ashe, Sabrina Pence and Sivi Domango. Sabrina was in charge of academics and curriculum and Sivi was in charge of school culture. They also share some duties. They were so incredibly generous with their time. I asked and asked questions. Now here's where my opinion came in. I felt they were tired. I felt these were two incredible women telling me their stories of persevering against almost impossible odds in the voucher-driven experiment that is New Orleans.

The public schools of New Orleans feature the highest percentage of students in charter schools of any city in the country. Layered onto that is citywide open enrollment, state-administered vouchers, and a huge number of other post-Katrina initiatives. The whole country will be looking to New Orleans for the results of these initiatives, and most eyes will look at FirstLine Schools as one of the harbingers of change. I shook off the feeling of enervation these two leaders were giving me.

Two youngish teachers were brought in to meet and

answer my questions. One was a man in his early twenties, John Bardes, who taught first- and second-grade math. The other teacher was a slightly older African-American woman, Monique Crockett, who taught sixth-grade English. They were both such lovely people. I am always in awe of these teachers that give themselves and their lives to help low-income children as if they were their own. After the usual questions, I asked them, "Can you tell me about your social lives?" This always gets a round of giggles before I say, "No, I'm serious." Now the reason I ask these questions of every teacher in every school I visit is to ascertain how sustainable their professional lives are. The young man went first and said he had a girlfriend. I was encouraged. I asked him importunately if he will marry one day. He said, "Whoa, whoa, I don't see the possibility of that anytime soon." Now this wasn't the usual guy, "Hey I'm too young to be tied down" braggadocio. "Why?" I asked, bordering on being a jackass. He said, "There's no time." The African-American teacher told me she had kids. This encouraged me again. "Do you think you can see yourself doing this job for ten years?" She looked down at her hands for a moment and then looked up and said, "No."

At this point I saw a man through the glass of the doorway. He had glasses and wore headphones as he listened to music on his iPod. He was trying to get into the conference room, which was locked. I rose to let him in. For whatever reason, I didn't think of who this might have been. It turned out to be Jay Altman, the founder I was scheduled to meet later. "Just thought I'd drop by to say hi." Jay turned out to be a brilliant and funny man. He immediately struck me as a Superman. I can see him being placed at the head of any school and eventually turning it around. Jay, an American, was asked to lecture and consult on education reform in England. He immediately peppered me with friendly questions about my book. He also told me he saw *The Sixth Sense* for the first time the night before and it was now one of his top five movies of all time. I thanked him. As I told him where I have traveled and whom I have met with, I realized he has been to all the places I have been to and more. He said, "So what are the tenets?" I listed them and he began to smile. I went through my reasoning, and the smile broadened. "I'm impressed," he said, and looked around the room at his colleagues. I have to admit that my heart soared a bit there. I felt like a student who got a good grade. He told me to stress school culture and that KIPP gave that to all of us. I agreed and promised I would.

Now we get to the part on feedback.

FirstLine is built around data. It is transparent about where every student is, and how much he or she has gained. The teachers are evaluated often, but they are not inculcated with the exact best practices from their peers as in North Star and they are not assigned curriculum that has been proven to work for teachers in other parts of their system. On the feedback scale, they were on one end of how to use data while Uncommon Schools (which North Star is a part of) are at the other end. I told Jay my feeling about this. Both Jay and the principals spoke almost reverently about Uncommon Schools. They pointed out they were newer and still finding their way. Jay told me in a very candid moment that he had completely changed his position on assigning curriculum. He doesn't feel it is sustainable for individual teachers to come up with best practices on top of the gargantuan workload they already have.

I knew what he was talking about. Back when James, Jenn, Bhavna, and I began our examination of all the potential additions to our list of gap-closing practices, I had thought that we'd find that changing the curriculum America's students are using would be a lot like reducing class size—maybe helping a little bit, not a lot—but the truth turned out to be more complicated.

One reason is that, to my surprise, the law—specifically the Department of Education Organization Act of 1979—prohibits the Department of Education from endorsing or sanctioning *any* curriculum. However, the law doesn't prevent the DOE from *evaluating* curriculum. And it does. The department's Institute of Education Sciences commissions studies to examine whether some textbooks are, in fact, better than others.

They are. Sometimes a *lot* better.

The effect size for choosing one curriculum over another can be huge. More than 90 percent of the entire K–2 student population in America uses one of seven different math curricula, defined as a sequence of textbooks plus supplementary materials. One IES study of the top four elementary school math curricula found effect sizes that were as high as +.30, the equivalent of a more than ten-point improvement in percentile rank versus the other curricula. Or, put another way, equivalent to the difference between having a teacher in the bottom third and one in the top. Another IES study, this one on the textbooks used to teach preschoolers the basics of early reading, had even larger effect sizes: After twelve research teams examined fourteen different preschool curricula used by largely low-income students—nearly 3,000 students in 315 classrooms, and more than 200 preschools, 88 percent of them either in Head Start or a local equivalent—the winning curriculum choice showed an effect size of +.76 in early reading and +.48 in vocabulary as compared to the average of the other choices, equivalent to a jump of 18 percentile points—from the 50th percentile to nearly the 70th—before entering kindergarten.

Effect sizes that big are hard to ignore. And the country's

best educators don't. Though some education professionals distinguish between "governance reformers" (those who want to get more and better teachers into the classroom, build more charters, and so on) and "curriculum reformers" (who think the way to improve schools is better teaching via improved materials and techniques), we found that the division is a false one. The men and women who select the curriculum at the schools that are actually closing the gap, including FirstLine, Uncommon, and KIPP, follow the What Works Clearinghouse, the website (http://ies.ed.gov/ncee/wwc/) set up to publish the results of IES studies, the way fantasy football players monitor espn.com.

"Better curricula," though, isn't one of the five keys to closing the achievement gap, not all by itself. For one thing, not every curriculum choice is so effective, or so obvious, as the math or early reading studies I just mentioned. For another, most of the hundreds of studies of different curricula produced by the What Works Clearinghouse are still too small to be easily generalizable. And those that aren't are heavily weighted toward early childhood reading and math, which are important, but only part of the entire elementary and secondary curriculum.

This doesn't mean that curriculum choices shouldn't be based on objective evidence. And it sure doesn't mean that creating and publishing that evidence is a waste of federal tax dollars. In fact, this might be the most useful thing that the Department of Education does, since the one thing that a local school district—even a large urban one, like New York or Philadelphia—can't do on its own is collect and evaluate data from everywhere in the country. It's just as valuable for the What Works Clearinghouse to let local schools know what works (and what doesn't) as it is for the National Institutes of Health to investigate and publish what works in medicine and health. The fact that we don't yet have as much evidence about curriculum as we do about vitamins and antibiotics doesn't mean we shouldn't be doing more studies. Actually, it means the opposite.

And it means that individual schools, and networks of schools like FirstLine, are collecting exactly the kind of data needed to make curriculum decisions. The choice of a particular textbook, or supplement, or educational software program, has to be made using the same kind of feedback loop that improves classroom instructional technique: Find out what's working (or not) in one classroom, and make sure that it's used (or not) in every classroom.

Jay Altman has figured it out. He admitted that a few years ago he was a vocal advocate of freedom for the teachers to customize and create their own teaching styles and curriculum (this freedom again has always been falsely tied to the charter school movement), but he has now come around to the opposite stance. I was very heartened by this. I told Jay I had the exact position he had about this subject of feedback until I started to visit schools and see the research. He told me in a few years FirstLine will have revamped the system and be much closer to Uncommon Schools in practice. I wondered whether if I visited here then and asked my importunate questions again, would I get different answers from a teaching staff that didn't have to figure out everything for themselves? "Yes, I'm getting married." "Sure I can see myself doing this for ten more years."

I got an intimate tour of the school. It turned out it was Wacky Tacky Day, where the teachers were supposed to dress up in the craziest outfits they had. Everyone apologized for teachers in pink wigs and leopard-pattern jackets and multi-colored suspenders. I found all of it incredibly endearing and wished I had worn something less appropriate. I remember distinctly being in a "Shout-Out" session, where teachers and students can shout out to anyone in the school for something they did well. A young boy raised his hand in the assembly. He was acknowledged by the ex-cop teacher in charge. "I want to give a shout-out to Daryl [not his real name] for doing so well on his test." Everyone looked to a boy seated two bleachers down in a gray hooded sweatshirt whose arms were crossed on his knees. The teacher said, "Way to go, Daryl . . . Wait: Are you crying?" I watched as the gray-sweatshirted boy wiped his eyes with his sweatshirt sleeve. He kept wiping his eyes over and over like a windshield wiper. Every wipe made my heart tear into pieces. As my hosts walked me out of the school, they told me the boy who shouted out to him was his brother, who doesn't live with him. Daryl had been the victim of abuse and injustice domestically. The boys got separated and Daryl got the short end of the deal. I felt the desperation to do everything we could for these kids.

Jay walked me out into the parking lot of his New Orleans school. I got the feeling again that Jay and I could be friends. As I drove to the airport, I reflected and felt like I saw a school system that was finding its way to great gains. I was anxious to see them in a year or two.

BROOKLYN HO!

It was freezing, East Coast freezing, on the day I visited Achievement First schools in Brooklyn. It reminded me of my NYU Film School days walking to class with my Discman. (I miss those things.)

Achievement First is the direct descendant of the Amistad Academy, a charter school opened in New Haven, Connecticut, in 1998. By 2005, when Joel Klein, the then Chancellor of the New York City Schools, invited them to bring their highly successful system to Brooklyn, they had grown into the Achievement First network, which, less than ten years later, is operating twenty schools in New York and Connecticut. Their Brooklyn Achievement First schools had been ranked in the top ten schools in all of NYC in 2012. They agreed graciously to allow me to visit their Endeavor Middle and Elementary schools.

When I arrived in the lobby at eight forty-five, I was struck by the similarity in style and approach among the highly successful charters. They were all cousins from the same family—with the oldest cousin being KIPP. Their core values and culture were splattered in primary colors on every wall and on every banner. I was toured around the elementary school by Devyn Humphrey, the director of admissions and community engagement.

I was struck by the similarity of every classroom's teaching style. It didn't matter whether I was observing a kindergarten class, a first-grade class, or third grade; the teachers had a distinctly similar style of talking, and the classroom children had an identical code of conduct. One of the things that struck me was the use of snaps. Teachers would snap their fingers and the kids would answer in a specific way. I couldn't quite gather the entire breadth of meaning of the snaps, but every class was using them. The teachers spoke in a clear and distinct way, posing questions in a provocative and engaging manner. They had clearly been trained. Part of the kids' code was this very cool thing called "shining." If a fellow student was answering a question and it impressed you, you could aim all your fingers of your hand at them and wiggle them so they looked like they were dancing. This was called shining, and it was done instead of applause to keep them on-task more efficiently without audible disruptions. It was moving to see a whole class of children shining a student who had done well. There was a great level of discipline on display. These kids were here to learn.

I was toured around the middle school and found the teachers had more variability in approach and pedagogy. As I walked around, I asked questions to see how many of the five tenets were being used. One by one, I saw all the tenets being employed. I was told the principals go through a yearlong Residency Program for School Leadership before getting the opportunity to open one of their own schools. The Achievement First schools teach 7,000 kids. Their goal is to grow until they are teaching 12,000 kids. They chose this number because it is larger than 95 percent of the public school systems in the United States and would serve as an example for the entire country that the achievement gap can be closed. They sold me.

The principals in the Achievement First schools spend the majority of their time in teacher instruction. They use observation and modeling constantly. I felt so encouraged to see the many tenets at work, including the management structure that gave principals the majority of time for teacher instruction. I was brought into a small room where I was to meet teachers and principals from the elementary and middle schools.

Two young ladies who taught English and math came to see me. I joked, at least I tried to, with them. They each had been teachers for more than five years and at Achievement First for three. When I got to my "How's your social life?" question, they both nodded and said, "Not bad." They told about trips to other cities with friends on weekends and dates and dinner parties. They both seemed like they had light and spunk in their eyes. I asked if they could see themselves doing this for five to ten years. They both answered they could. When I asked about marriage, they giggled. One said "Yes" and one said "No," but "No" in that charming "There are no guys worth it" kind of way. I relied on the fact that I'm Indian and people think I must have some deeply embedded Eastern wisdom and told her to keep looking, the right dude would roll up soon. Both teachers told me that in their first year at Achievement First they would have answered the social questions very differently. They were overwhelmed and didn't think they could continue at that pace for very long. "But now things have changed," they said. They were once working about eighty hours a week and now clocked around sixty. I met a third teacher. She was in her mid-twenties and had graduated from Duke. She had forsaken her law degree and joined Teach For America to teach in California. She had had a demoralizing couple of years and was about to quit when Achievement First recruited her and asked her to come to Brooklyn. She did and has had a wonderful first year. I started to get the feeling that Achievement First Endeavor Middle School had been on a learning curve and was seeing some real gains now.

At the end of the day, I met the principal of the lower school, Stephanie Blake. Stephanie was immediately a presence in the room. She was clearly extremely smart and not to be trifled with. She showed me her schedules and how she spends most of her time on feedback to the teachers in the form of modeling and instruction. She told me they spend Friday afternoons on teacher evaluations. She believes in assigning curriculum and in Doug Lemov's teaching styles. We discussed Uncommon Schools and she, too, spoke of them with a certain reverence. She looked me directly in the eye and said, "Come visit me in a couple years. We'll be better than Uncommon Schools." And I believed her.

My final meeting was with the principal of the middle school, Tom Kaiser. Tom had taken over four years ago. He has made Endeavor Middle School one of the top schools in

NYC. He has moved more and more to assigning curriculum and is moving more and more to a best-practices model for the teachers. "Achievement First just didn't have the wealth of knowledge then that it has now. We know so much more about what works for our teachers and we share it." Tom commented on the regimented culture and behavior of the students and said that some parents see this as a negative, but he doesn't. "We make the rules of behavior and conduct and expectation crystal clear and consistent. This gives the child power back. They now know everything that's expected of them. It never changes and they have the power to make a choice to excel in that environment or not, but they are very clear it is their choice." Seeing teachers in classroom after classroom teaching the same way with the same methods of evaluating gives power back to the children. I realized how much feedback means to everyone. Not just the teachers, but also to the students, who come from worlds where inconsistency and powerlessness are taken for granted.

I left the Achievement First schools feeling I was clearly seeing a continuum of feedback in schools that were closing the achievement gap. I would place the level of feedback usage in FirstLine schools second only to Uncommon, just above KIPP. What started to fascinate me on my drive back to Philly was how much their placement on that continuum of feedback determined the variability between schools in their respective systems. The variability among their own schools was highest in FirstLine and lowest in Uncommon Schools. More and more, I was seeing how the intense use of feedback—*all* forms of feedback, including data-driven instruction, promotion of best practices, and evaluation of curricula in light of every school's specific circumstances—determined sustainability.

The evidence on feedback was becoming clearer and

clearer. Whether the data concerned curriculum choice, teach-ing technique, or student progress, feedback had to be metic-ulous, frequent, and mandatory. And—maybe most important of all—it had to be produced in a form that was usable; there was absolutely no evidence that collecting data had any effect until it was understandable to every teacher in a school.

And this, I thought, was the obstacle to incorporat-ing Deming's cycle of planning-doing-studying-acting into schools. An idea that worked in a factory that employed 5,000 laborers was a lot harder to implement in a school with only a few dozen teachers for the obvious reason: No matter how good the leadership, no matter how high-quality the feed-back, if there wasn't enough time to analyze and act on it, it wasn't going to do the job. We'd already learned that closing the gap meant focusing every principal's time on instruction, but they needed enough time with each class for that focus to work. This is an intense amount of work for the principals. Again, to make this scalable and not just reliant on superhero principals, observational evidence suggested one way to make this intense approach workable: Keep the number of teachers that every principal was responsible for realistic.

Maybe the schools needed to be smaller.

THE FOURTH KEY: SMALLER SCHOOLS

7

THAT'S RIGHT, I SAID IT. SMALL SCHOOLS

The small-schools movement—advocacy for schools of no more than a particular number of students as a means for improving achievement—is now in its third decade, and not getting uniformly good press. Though dozens of studies supporting small schools appeared during the 1990s, for the last ten years, investigators have done their best to debunk them. Most famously, two statisticians at the University of Pennsylvania named Howard Wainer and Harris Zwerling showed that, while small schools were consistently overrepresented in any list of top performers, this was evidence of variability, not superiority. The smaller the school, the greater the probability that it will have a large percentage of students at either end of a statistical curve, just as the chance of getting heads three-quarters of the time is far greater after ten tosses than after a hundred. Theory debunked, and debunked so thoroughly that the Bill and Melinda Gates Foundation, which had spent more than $1.7 billion financing the building of smaller schools, decided to redeploy their money.

The variability problem is real. In any given year, a higher percentage of schools with 400 students will appear at the top of any ranking than those with 1,500 students. Also, a higher percentage will appear at the bottom. More variability means more outliers. The assumption is that those schools that appear at the top of rankings in one year will revert to the mean in the following one, that the performance improvement is a statistical artifact. There will be just as many high-performing small schools every year, but they'll be different schools. (Excluded from consideration here are large selective-admissions schools such as Masterman.)

It's what would happen if you divided twenty people into two groups of ten—let's call them the Red team and the Blue team—and told the Reds to flip a coin ten times, and the Blues a hundred times, with everyone who gets heads 60 percent of the time earning the title of "top-achiever." If you did this exercise every day for a month, most of the top-achievers would be Red, every time. They'll just be different Red team members.

But what if some of them were the same? What if some of those "top-achieving" Red coin-throwers got six heads out of ten every time?

Some of them do. Wainer and Zwerling, along with others, criticize the small-schools movement for misunderstanding the variability problem—in statistician-speak, the standard deviation from the mean. If their analysis is correct, then the small schools that showed up at the top of the performance list in Year 1 would be just as likely to be at the bottom in Year 5, and vice versa. That's just what the research shows— for schools whose only distinction is their small size. For those small schools, appearing in the top-performing segment is pure chance, as Wainer and Zwerling rightly concluded. But they were wrong in thinking size was an irrelevancy, because those aren't the only small schools that qualify as top-performers; they're not even most of them. Almost all of the small-school advantage appears only when small size is one part of an entire system; a system that includes, for example, teacher measurement, and instructional leaders, and lots and lots of feedback. When a system like that is in place, smaller size turbocharges each of the other practices. Chance disappears. The same small schools close the gap nearly every year.

This was definitely a powerful argument for making small school size part of the solution. But as the evidence on school size accumulated during our research process, the internal questions on whether it deserved a place as one of the five tenets got more pointed. There were some pretty obvious differences between size and the other tenets to which the country's most effective schools subscribed.

The first difference—maybe the most important one—is that the debate about school size is almost entirely focused on high schools: grades 9 through 12. The reason is simple: Even a large elementary school, one with four classes each of twenty-five students in each grade, is still going to top out at six hundred kids: big, but not crazy big. Only two states in the country—Florida and Georgia—have elementary schools that average more than 600 students. The national average is only 451. Even middle schools average only about 575 kids each. But eleven states average more than 1,000 students in their typical public high schools and nobody thinks twice when an urban high school has 1,500 kids or more. The *average* high school in Florida is bigger than that; in California, just a shade less. (Twenty-three high schools in Southern California alone have enrollments greater than 4,000.)

There are good historical reasons for this. In fact, these big high schools were the result of another stab at closing the achievement gap in America, a century ago. Before about 1920 or so, high schools, even when they didn't charge tuition, were still pretty hard to get into: Less than 20 percent of the country's kids attended them, and they typically had to take an exam to prove that they were high school material. Only half of the students graduated. Everyone else was expected to go to work. Starting in the twenties, a huge building boom in high schools changed that—but it changed it in a typically American way. European countries, even when they offered free high school, drew a very clear line between academic and vocational education, which took an already existing gap between social classes and built barbed wire around it. The American reformers (they're even known to historians as the "high school movement") weren't having any of this. They promoted "comprehensive high schools" that accepted everybody, and required everyone to take mostly the same courses. Everyone took English, math, some science, and history.

Schools that have to educate everybody tend to be big, and as the United States population doubled between 1910 and 1960, and doubled again between 1960 and today, the high schools got bigger and bigger. And, for a long time, they worked fairly well. By the 1960s, more than three-quarters of American eighteen-year-olds were graduating from an academic high school, while Germany and France were still putting more than half of their kids into vocational training programs.

This success—and it was a success—had two glaring weaknesses: One was built in from the beginning, and one appeared only a little more than thirty years ago. The problem that was there from the start was this: The comprehensive high schools, even when they were working, worked a whole lot better for some Americans than others. It isn't much of an exaggeration to say that the comprehensive high school helped everyone, but it helped white suburban families a lot more than nonwhite urban ones.

The problem that emerged in the 1970s and 1980s was even more fundamental: Big, comprehensive high schools were successful in an era when they were the terminal point for most Americans' education. When high school became a stop on the way to some kind of postsecondary education—college, usually, though not always—the measure of success changed, too. And, by that standard, high school is where the achievement gap got set in cement.

Secondary schools—middle schools, junior high schools, and high schools—have all of the same demands as elementary schools, but because they also need a lot of specialized instruction, in everything from French to chemistry to AP calculus, they typically require anywhere from five to eight teachers for every student, every day, which meant that every teacher was going to be responsible for the instruction of at least a hundred students. Simple arithmetic meant that high schools needed to be bigger than elementaries; but the same math increased the chances students would encounter one of those gap-widening roadblocks.

Having every teacher instruct a hundred or more kids every day also multiplies the amount of information each one generates. A thousand high school students taking one exam every week produce truckloads of potential data, all of which needs to be analyzed and returned to the instructors as feedback, even without any evaluation of classroom technique, student participation, or homework. And although everyone talks about the good and bad aspects of high-stakes testing in education, the stakes take a very different shape for high school students: The tests *they* take determine where they can attend college, or whether they'll attend college at all.

HOW SMALL IS SMALL?

There were other problems with figuring out whether school size belonged on the list.

We had hoped to find a system that could be implemented at the level closest to the ground in America's educational pyramid. My own dream was that readers of this book would be able to use it as ammunition in debates with teachers, principals, and (maybe) school boards. But while I could imagine them arguing that their schools needed more rigor in hiring and firing teachers, or to transform their principals into instructional leaders, or on behalf of improving instruction by using more data and evidence-based feedback, school size was different. Decisions about building a new high school are made a lot less frequently, and usually at much higher levels.

And even when those decisions are made, it's not obvious what reformers should argue for. Though it's still easy to find advocates for reducing the size of high schools, those advocates don't always agree on what constitutes "small": The Coalition of Small Preparatory Schools believes that the optimal size for schools that intend to send graduates on to college is between 3 (this is not a typo) and 230, and certainly no bigger than 350. Some places count a small high school as anything less than a thousand students.

This is one reason that truly effective schools like Uncommon, KIPP, FirstLine, Success Academy, and Harlem Children's Zone don't make much noise about keeping their schools to a particular size. For one thing, since almost all of them are schools of choice, they are understandably eager to find a place for every student they can.

But even when they don't make it explicit in their mission statements—even when they aren't completely aware of it—school size is a key part of any gap-closing strategy.

When I asked Brett Peiser, one of the founders of Uncommon Schools, how big was too big, he told me that if the combined enrollment at North Star's elementary and middle schools got to 750, he'd have to find a new school. His reason?

> It's a lot easier to find principals who can run schools with four hundred kids.

It was the same with Jay Altman at FirstLine:

> It's just not practical for principals to observe as aggressively as they need to when they have to visit twice as many classrooms. And even if it were, there are a lot more potential principals who can manage a secondary school with an enrollment of six hundred than ones who can manage one twice that size. You can build big schools. But you need Supermen to run them. [*That superhero problem again,* I thought.] And there just aren't very many of them around.

Even the Gates Foundation—after their evidence for the value of small schools was supposedly debunked—conceded that small school size is "a necessary but not sufficient condition for creating the desired learning environment."

If you're wondering what the "desired learning environment" is, so was I. The impact of small schools is hard to tease out of the data, because, even more than most of the practices we had found at schools like Achievement First/ Endeavor, Arthur Ashe, and North Star Academy, overall size has much larger mediated effects than direct ones. That is, whatever small schools accomplished, they probably did by affecting something else, like instructional technique. Or even by accelerating one thing, which improved another, which promoted a third, etc. Think about one of those Rube Goldberg drawings where a candle burns through a string, which drops a weight, which releases a ball down a chute, which closes a mousetrap. Small schools can do a lot to close the achievement gap—just as long as the string, ball, weight, and mousetrap are lined up beforehand.

Even with respect to direct effects, small high schools do have some clear advantages over larger ones. The biggest ones are that attendance and graduation rates tend to rise as school populations fall. One study of small high schools and Small Learning Communities (SLCs)—large high schools divided into distinct communities—commissioned by the RAND Corporation showed a clearly positive effect on attendance rates, graduation rates, and attitudes toward learning in Los Angeles, probably because of what are called "positive network effects." The smaller the school, the likelier that every student shared his or her classes with mostly familiar faces; and the more friends you have classes with, the less likely you are to skip class.

"Familiarity" is a little hard to quantify, though. Some enterprising researchers looked at a proxy for it: the average distance between home and school. It stands to reason that if the number of students in any district doesn't change, reducing the number of students in each school means more schools, and, therefore, less travel from a student's front door to a classroom. In 2012, an analysis of New York City's newest small high schools—"small" defined as fewer than 550 students—showed substantial effects just by examining the reduction in distance traveled to school, what social scientists call an "intermediate variable." Effect sizes on graduation alone were +.33 or more, which is equivalent to increasing graduation rates by more than 17 percent.

And the same phenomenon shows up elsewhere; the

Gates Foundation, having poured hundreds of millions into building new and redesigned schools, found that more than 80 percent of the small schools that the Foundation had created from scratch had attendance rates that were higher than the average of other schools in the same districts. The combination of more personal attention, higher expectations, and a smaller (and therefore more cohesive) team of teachers made for a more confident student body, with more interest in learning. Also, not a small thing, less fighting; small schools had significantly less violence, fewer episodes of students fighting with one another, or just disrupting classes. One study of Chicago's small-schools initiative found the same thing: Smaller schools had better attendance and higher high school graduation rates, though the same study couldn't find a causal link between school size and positive results. This is actually what you'd expect if school size were a mediating factor—something that provides a framework in which other practices, like classroom observation and frequent feedback, can flourish.

In 1992, a British anthropologist and evolutionary psychologist, then at University College London, published the results of more than a decade studying our closest cousins, the primates. After researching the behavior—and the brain sizes—of primate species from lemurs to chimps to humans, he found that there was a cognitive limit to the number of individuals with whom a social relationship can be sustained.

For humans, that number is somewhere between 100 and 230—best guess, around 150. The so-called Dunbar Number has been used to study everything from high-performing factory and office teams to online multiplayer video games and social-networking sites, like Facebook. It also, possibly coincidentally, is about the number of students in each grade in a high school with six hundred students. There seems to be an optimal number for all kinds of societies, and the society of sixteen-year-olds isn't any different.

The evidence that smaller schools promote higher achievement is thinner, but still there. In their own study, the Gates Foundation found that nearly six out of ten of their "new schools" scored higher than conventional schools in reading, though critics will question whether the phenomenon can be replicated in school systems throughout the country. Students in Chicago's small schools showed improved reading scores. Another study—of nearly two hundred high schools in thirty states that received grants from the Department of Education to create Small Learning Communities—showed improvement in standardized test scores, though the improvement was small, an effect size of +.06.

There's at least one study that examined not school size, but *changes* in school size. There, the results were much bigger. Looking at schools in the state of Indiana in the early 2000s, where some dramatic changes in school size occurred due to school closings and consolidations, an economist named Ilyana Kuziemko found that decreasing school sizes by 50 percent had the potential to have a huge impact on achievement. If extrapolated for two additional years, she calculated that math scores alone showed an effect size of +.25 within two years.

GOIN' BACK TO CALI

Probably because I grew up and still live in the eastern United States, most of the schools I've visited, both before and after starting this project, are housed in older buildings, some beautiful, some not. The Animo Leadership High School in Inglewood, California, is different.

When I visited, on a typical February day in Southern

California—sunny, seventy-one degrees—the first thing I noticed was that it looked like a modern museum, its outside walls covered in solar panels. Inside, clean design, lots of white. I'm a great believer in symbols, and the symbolism here wasn't subtle: Animo Leadership wanted to be a visionary school, a look at the future.

Animo Leadership is part of Green Dot Public Schools, one of a network of eighteen schools serving more than 10,000 students across Los Angeles. The first one was opened in August of 2000. Green Dot has its own version of the tenets, including some familiar ones, such as huge investments in data and knowledge management, and extending the school day to at least 5 P.M. daily. They are in the family of other successful charter systems that have been closing the gap.

In one important characteristic, though, they're different. Most of the other effective schools we found during our research, from KIPP to Uncommon to Achievement First, are heavily weighted toward lower grades: mostly elementary and middle schools. From its beginnings, however, Green Dot took a different path. In its first five years, Green Dot started five high schools from scratch in some of the highest-poverty areas of Los Angeles. All five would earn a spot on *Newsweek* magazine's list of the best high schools in the United States.

One reason is that Green Dot is obsessive about preparing students for college, and high school is the make-or-break installment in that particular drama. One hundred percent of Green Dot graduates—and that's more than 85 percent of all their students—complete the course of study required for admission to the University of California, one of the most selective public universities in the world. Ninety-one percent of graduates are accepted to college annually.

You can see this commitment clear as day at Animo Leadership (all of the Green Dot schools use the "Animo" prefix, Spanish for "strength," or, as the school's website puts it, "vigor, mind, spirit, valor, and the courage to overcome odds"). It was literally a perfect California day when I met Julio Murcia, the principal of Animo Leadership High School, and the director of development, Douglas Weston. Julio Murcia was a star principal in the Green Dot quiver of principals. He was wearing a sweatshirt. He immediately felt approachable. He felt (and looked) like one of my uncles. Julio had implemented an SAT tutoring element into his school as part of the standard curriculum. He told me his students get $1,000 Kaplan-like tutoring for $40. The students of Animo Leadership get exhaustive instructions on college applications and financial aid. He told me, with understandable pride, that every single senior applies for college at Animo Leadership. Or, rather, colleges, since they typically apply to between eight and twenty schools each, which is even more important than it sounds, since one of the biggest factors that make the achievement gap so durable is that even high-performing low-income students—those with SAT or ACT scores in the top 10 percent—don't apply to colleges the same way as kids from affluent families. Affluent kids carefully screen colleges, helped by parents and counselors who find schools whose student bodies have average test scores that match their own. Poor kids don't do this. One study, by Caroline Hoxby at Stanford University—one of the many scholars who showed just how little class size matters in student achievement—estimates that more than half of the highest-achieving low-income students fail to apply to any selective colleges at all; fewer than 8 percent actually apply to schools where their high school achievement would otherwise "fit."

But Green Dot's students do. And they get in. Not a surprise, since all that SAT prep has raised scores by an average of 200 points per student since it was implemented; some have raised their scores by 400 points. Now all of the Green Dot schools are implementing or are going to implement this practice.

The high school–centric mission of Green Dot makes for a different set of challenges than those faced by a school network focused on third- and fourth-graders. For one thing, it means that their teachers have to make up a lot of ground in a very short time; since students arrive at a Green Dot high school typically two or three grades behind their ninth-grade suburban peers, their instruction is accelerated to a scary pace: Animo Leadership's teachers are expected to give their students the equivalent of at least a grade-and-a-half's worth of teaching each year. Those teachers who can't are—another tenet in action—asked to leave. Julio and Douglas estimated that only 5 percent or less don't make the cut every year— some years no teachers are asked not to return. Which is pretty impressive on its own, and is especially notable since Green Dot is one of the only closing-the-gap networks that voluntarily operates under a collective-bargaining agreement with its teachers, a reform-oriented union contract, for sure, but one that still includes a variety of grievance procedures and obstacles to termination. Green Dot wants to offer the country a model that can be replicated, and there's little doubt that a union-friendly attitude is a big advantage in scaling up any program.

To get that big advantage, Green Dot has gone small, with a vengeance. Animo Leadership High School has no more than 170 students in each of its four grades, a total of a little less than 600. Green Dot is so focused on reducing the size of high schools to that magic number that when it was asked in 2008 to take over Locke High School, one of the biggest and least successful schools in the Los Angeles Unified School District, the first thing on the agenda was turning the 2,400-student school into four different schools, with 600 students each. Almost immediately, this change improved tenth-grade math and English scores by between 12 and 18 percent.* Green Dot describes its model for high-performance as "Small, Safe, Personalized Schools." After visiting Animo Leadership, it wasn't hard to see why.

THE BIG APPLE

I had heard that Robert Hughes, the president of New Visions for Public Schools, a not-for-profit that runs seventy-three public schools and four charter high schools serving more than 40,000 New York City students, was a foodie. This immediately endeared him to me. I told him I would meet him at his office and we would walk to a place I knew for lunch.

I arrived in his offices in Lower Manhattan fifteen minutes early. The offices of New Visions are beautiful and sleek. This was not what I was used to, visiting people for this book. I felt like I was waiting to meet a studio executive in L.A. The lobby was lined with weathered paperback books on education, and most of them centered around high school education reform. I was informed Mr. Hughes was in a conference behind a smoky glass wall. I nodded and took a seat. I was here to meet Robert Hughes because he was one of the most active people in the field of small schools. To be specific, he led the movement to decrease the size of high schools in NYC when he was funded by the Gates Foundation. In fact, his program in NYC delivered the most impressive results of the entire small-schools initiative.

"Hi." I torqued my neck and saw Hughes leaning over the sofa I was on. We shook hands. He said, "How much do you

---

* The goal is for no Green Dot school to exceed 560 students.

want to get into things? Should I bring propaganda?" I wasn't sure what he meant, but I shrugged my shoulders and said I just wanted to ask him questions on small schools. I got the feeling that he was in charge of a lot of things in NYC. Robert grabbed his coat and scarf; he's a very put-together dresser. He later confessed to me he was dressed up to see Geoffrey Canada, the founder of Harlem Children's Zone, who was featured in the documentary *Waiting for Superman*. Apparently, he wasn't dressed up for me.

We walked about six blocks to a restaurant called the Spotted Pig. This is a big film hang, whose celebrity co-owners include Bono, Mario Batali, and Jay-Z. When I mix my movies in NYC, I often eat here. He had heard of it. We took a booth by the window and I asked him straightaway about small schools. We both ordered Cubano sandwiches and an order of the house special gnudi with ricotta cheese in a brown butter sauce. Hughes began to tell me his theory on small schools and why they failed in most cities where they were implemented. He described how in New York, unlike the rest of the country where the Gates initiative played out, they took it one grade level at a time and grandfathered the teachers and faculty into a new set of behaviors and best practices to go along with the new culture of fewer students. They gradually implemented the small-schools idea over a period of time along with other things, and the outcomes, he says, "even by the Gates Foundation's assessments, were a success." Graduation rates went up significantly all across the city. The effect on the students was visible and lasting. As we ate, he described how the Gates Foundation pulled their funding for small schools. He seemed melancholy about it as he spoke. I led the witness when I asked him whether he believed he had proven that small schools alone have questionable effect but when combined with other proven tenets have a compound and measurable impact. Hughes said, "I one hundred percent agree with that."

I asked Robert at what number he would consider a high school to be small. He told me his small high schools were in the four hundreds. I asked him what number he would say was too large. Where was the tipping point? He ate slowly and thought about it. I was doing a Jedi mind trick on him to say six hundred because that is the number that has come up in the research for companies as well as schools. He looked up and said, "I don't know—six hundred." Either Robert Hughes had read the same research I had or my Jedi skills were improving.

As we contemplated ordering dessert (we both declined), I began to see how complicated all this has been for those on the front lines of education reform. Unlike the others I had met for this book, Hughes was in the system. He was bound by their judgments and bureaucracies. He wasn't trying to improve one school, and not even a group of schools, but a whole city. The gravity he was facing on a daily basis was unthinkable, the setbacks crushing. Even in the face of those challenges, he remained an advocate for the fourth key; he had demonstrated the value of small schools, and was ready to stand up for them.

As we were leaving the Spotted Pig, I asked him a last question, knowing he was in charge of managing nearly eighty schools in NYC. "If you saw a school system of, say, 10,000 kids or more closing the achievement gap, would you then consider mimicking their techniques wholesale and revamping the entire system?" I asked this imagining a very near future. Robert replied, "As long as the special ed kids are represented in those systems and those same schools are actually graduating the great majority of those kids they started with, yes. We have no ego here."

THE FIFTH KEY:
MORE TIME IN SCHOOL

8

DANNY, SEE ME AFTER SCHOOL . . . AND BEFORE . . . AND OVER THE SUMMER

One of the most beloved stock characters in movie history is the Extraordinary Teacher. The teacher who turns around the life of a student, sometimes an entire class, even a generation. The classic version is the retired Latin teacher in *Goodbye, Mr. Chips,* but more recent examples include Mark Thackeray in *To Sir, With Love, Stand and Deliver*'s Jaime Escalante, and my favorite, John Keating in *Dead Poets Society.* These characters appear so often because they have real-life analogues, usually in the memory of the writers who created them.* I still feel excited about history because of Mr. Hess. I had a wonderful biology teacher in Mr. Hill. Some class discussions on the brain and evolution I still quote today.

However, I had as many OK teachers in my life as extraordinary ones. Teachers who had trouble managing a classroom or communicating a concept. Teachers who played favorites

---

* Jaime Escalante, of course, was a real teacher at L.A.'s Garfield High long before Edward James Olmos played him in the movie.

or spent a class's "free reading" time studying for the GMAT. My experience is both typical and instructive. My mother and father were both first-generation immigrant doctors, and they had the drive, the expectation, and the example to compensate for any shortfalls in my classroom life, so I didn't suffer from the mediocre teachers.

It's the same with the next generation. Bhavna and I send our daughters to a fine school, whose students are expected to perform at the highest level and eventually to attend the country's most selective colleges. But this doesn't mean that the school employs only extraordinary teachers. What it means is that when my kids, and their classmates, encounter a not-so-great one, their home environment compensates. Sometimes the compensation is in the form of discussion with them. The vocabulary and ideas shared casually. Books on shelves. Trips. Lessons. Expectations. Either way, they don't suffer from a school with just as much difference between the top and bottom teachers as any struggling inner-city school.

That's the problem with stories of magical teachers. Believing that some teachers are touched by the education genie lets us write all those great stories about them, but it also means that no one is writing about below-average teachers. One thing that the evidence we'd spent years collecting showed is that ineffective teachers cost their students way more than effective teachers can pay back. The other thing we'd learned is that the costs aren't shared evenly. Children from affluent, educated families get just as many ineffective teachers as everyone else. They just don't pay for it. Kids from poor families do.

But they don't have to.

If you've read this far, you already know what dozens of schools are doing to close the achievement gap. They're identifying and removing teachers who are roadblocks to student progress. They're transforming principals from operations managers into instructional leaders, collecting data on everything from weekly test scores to classroom technique, and feeding it back to their teachers every week. And they're doing it in schools that are small enough to make all these systems practical. What these practices have in common is that each one offers a way for a school (or a network of schools) to guarantee consistent excellence among their teachers.

They have to be incredibly consistent because the environment outside the school that kids are facing is harsh and unpredictable. As a country, we have neglected an entire population. We have left low-income families in low-income neighborhoods few options and little support. We have not given them the tools. This book is written under the premise that society is going to make a decision to give the kids of low-income families the tools in the environment of school.

THIRTY MILLION WORDS

There *is* some question about when the compensation needs to happen. A lot of people believe that it should start even before kids enter kindergarten.

That's because kids really aren't competing on a level educational playing field before they start school, especially when it comes to vocabulary. Researchers Betty Hart and Todd Risley started studying the subject in the 1960s, but it wasn't until the 1990s that they were able to complete what is the most cited study on the subject. Hart and Risley identified forty-two families with young children and arranged to visit and observe them for an hour every month, beginning when the kids were seven-to-nine months old, and ending when they turned three. Simple demographic questionnaires on income and level of educational attainment sorted the families into three categories: thirteen of them with relatively high income and education, twenty-three in the middle, and six qualifying for some form of welfare. After two-and-a-half years, and more than 1,300 hours of recording the volume of conversation between parent and child, they found that the families in the top income and education tier spoke to their children more than those in the middle, who spoke to their kids more than those on welfare. A *lot* more. The upper-income families were recorded using an average of 2,153 words every hour; the middle-income families 1,251; and the welfare families 616. This meant that the average kid from an upper-income family hears 11.2 million words a year; one from a middle-income family 6.5 million; and from a family on welfare, 3.2 million words. By age four, that's a gap of some 30 million words.

Which wouldn't matter, except that the number of words that four-year-olds can understand and speak is directly related to the number of words they've heard. Typical kids from upper-class families visited by Hart and Risley had vocabularies that were more than twice as large as those from families on welfare. Not exactly a surprise, therefore, that by the time the poorer kids were in the third grade, they were already so far behind that it was virtually impossible to catch up.

The fact that kids enter America's school system at wildly different levels of readiness has been known for more than a century, way before the Coleman Report first popularized the phrase "inequality of opportunity." But the first hard evidence that schools could compensate for shortfalls in their home learning environments dates back to 1962, when the school district of Ypsilanti, Michigan, began a program targeted at its lowest-performing students: those who scored well below average on standardized, end-of-term tests. David Weikart, the district's director of special services, and Charles Eugene Beatty, then the principal at Perry Elementary School, hired four teachers to run an experimental preschool at Perry whose goal was to find out whether the school could improve the academic outcomes for its failing kids.

The Perry Preschool Experiment began with 123 three- and four-year-old kids, more or less evenly split between a control group and a treatment group, who were given a two-year-long program of "participatory learning"—not just the usual routines of preschool, like social and physical development, but language arts, math, and science for two-and-a-half hours a week, thirty weeks a year. The short-term benefits were pretty dramatic: The effect sizes for improvement in reading, math, and language ranged from +.5 to +.75. The effect size on vocabulary was even higher: +.91.

There were significant long-term benefits, too. The researchers—renamed, in 1970, the HighScope Educational Research Foundation—checked up on the same kids in 1985–86, when the original Perry students were twenty-seven years old. The fifty-eight kids who had been randomly assigned to the program had completed nearly a year more school, on average, than the sixty-five who had been in the control group—the ones who had never attended the preschool. The control group spent, on average, more than five years in various special education programs; the treatment group less than four. When the same group was visited at age forty, only about half as many of the treatment group had spent some time in prison as those in the control group, and they earned, on average, 40 percent more income. By any measure, the Perry Preschool was not only a success, but an unarguably good investment.

It wasn't the only one. Around the same time that Weikart and Beatty were testing their program in Michigan, Rick

Heber, the director of the Waisman Center on Mental Retardation and Human Development at the University of Wisconsin, organized the so-called Milwaukee Project, an intensive daycare program for children even younger than the Perry kids that Professor Heber's team had identified as in need of special help. The Milwaukee program began with six-month-old infants and continued through the first grade, with the intention of giving the participants reinforcement on language and development skills. The program was intensive: seven hours a day, with both regular education and medical and nutritional counseling for parents. And, once again, the initial gains were significant: effect sizes of +.75 in grades 1 through 4.

The Abecedarian Early Intervention Project, which operated in North Carolina from 1972 to 1977, did at least as well. Like the Milwaukee participants, the 111 children involved experienced a full-day intervention that began before they were six months old and lasted all year until they were five. The Abecedarian Project also provided homeschool teachers who met with parents once every two weeks, showing them how to educate their children at home for fifteen minutes daily. By the end of the program, participants in the treatment group were two years ahead of the control group in reading, and more than a year in math. When they were revisited at age twenty-one, two-thirds of the treatment group had graduated from high school, versus only half of the intervention group; and a third of the treatment group had attended college, as against only one in eight of the control group.

The Perry, Milwaukee, and Abecedarian projects are by far the most successful and most cited of all the studies used to promote the idea that early childhood education can close the achievement gap.

There are a few legitimate criticisms of the three studies. The first was that all three of the programs were targeted at *really* low-achieving kids, and the way they were targeted was by using their parents' IQ scores. The mothers of the Perry kids had mean IQs between 75 and 85; the mothers of the Milwaukee kids had IQ scores that were below 75. Only the Abecedarian Project accepted kids whose parents had IQ scores above 100, and even there, the best results occurred in kids whose mothers had IQ scores below 70, which is the level that the *Diagnostic and Statistical Manual of the American Psychiatric Association* classifies as mentally retarded.

I don't want to wade into the IQ wars. But these studies couldn't help but get my attention, especially since the project's leaders were very confident about the way that their preschool programs improved IQ scores: The control group for the Abecedarian Project scored 84 at age three; the treatment group averaged 101—which is staggering. By the time the kids were twenty-one, those who had been in the treatment group still scored 4.5 points higher than the control group. Heber's Milwaukee kids did even better: Those who had been through the program scored 110 at age five, versus 83 for the control group; and nine years after the program ended, the treatment group was still at 101, versus 91 for the control group. Unfortunately, a few years after publishing his study Professor Heber was accused of a whole series of frauds, convicted of diverting institutional funds into his own pocket, and sentenced to three years in prison, not the sort of thing that raises confidence in scientific conclusions or policy recommendations. (Oh well, an imprisoned murderer helped put together the first edition of the *Oxford English Dictionary*.)*

But even if there weren't an ongoing battle over whether IQ is a real, useful, and consistent measurement, and even if Professor Heber's claim that it could be raised significantly by

---

* *The Professor and the Madman* is a great book; you should read it!

early intervention weren't compromised by his ignoble ac-
tions, there are reasons for caution in extrapolating from the
game-changing results of the Perry Preschool studies and its
successors. No matter what you believe about the importance
or heritability of IQ, kids with scores that low are pretty far
out of the mainstream, and what works for the most at-risk
population may not work the same way for everyone. A diet
that helps adults weighing four hundred pounds each might
not get the same results in a group of slightly overweight
teenagers. It will definitely help, just not with such astounding
results.

The other criticism is that Perry, Milwaukee, and Abecedarian were small and local programs, hard to scale up to
something that could be used throughout the country. The
obvious large-scale analogue is Head Start.

THROWING THE BABY OUT WITH THE BATHWATER

Head Start has become one of those lightning-rod experiments. Like the Tennessee study, it is referenced everywhere—
but this time for its failings.

The success of the Head Start program, which started in
1965 as an eight-week-long summer school for kids about to
enter kindergarten and has since expanded into two or three
years of support for more than a million kids a year, has been
pretty spotty. One recent randomized trial of Head Start found
a decent effect size—+.24—on the ability of kids to name
letters, but no measurable effect on vocabulary—or, really,
much of anything else. In 2010, the Department of Health and
Human Services released the *Head Start Impact Study: Final
Report,* which found that while kids benefited from Head Start
(as opposed to being in a private program, or being cared for

at home) *while they were in the program,* there was virtually
no impact once they left.

For a lot of people, this is just confirmation that our inability to educate children from poor families is because of
some breakdown in their home lives rather than the educational system. If a multibillion-dollar program like Head Start
(or others, like Even Start, a Department of Education program that gives support to families who want to improve their
home learning environments) can't close the gap, maybe the
program isn't the solution.

The frustration is understandable. But we really shouldn't
overinterpret the Head Start results, which, if they demonstrate anything, show that the value of any preschool program
is determined by its quality more than the number of hours.
Even Head Start's most devoted defenders would agree that
quality was very uneven. One reason is that about half of
Head Start programs are only half-day; most operate far fewer
days than a typical school year. The typical Head Start student
spends about twenty-five hours a week in the HS program,
and another eighteen in some other form of child care.

As a result, the Head Start programs are wildly inconsistent. More than a quarter of them report an inability even to
maintain accurate attendance records. Some produce quantifiable and long-lasting benefits. Many don't. As Craig Ramey of
Virginia Tech Carilion Research Institute, one of the nation's
leading experts in early childhood education and the author
of the original Abecedarian study, puts it, Head Start isn't a
single program; it's a thousand different programs, run in a
thousand different ways. Ramey argues that successful pre-K
programs exhibit nine different hallmarks, including highly
knowledgeable and stable leaders; programs based on scientific evidence; high levels of staff training; and rigorous collec-

tion of data, and regular analysis of it. If there's a weak spot in Head Start, it's the last one: While exemplary Head Start programs collect, analyze, and utilize data effectively, no one would argue that this is true of the program as a whole.

Just as the Tennessee STAR analysis of school size was a classic false positive result, Head Start was a false negative.

Also, we had learned enough by this time about human nature to identify the roots of a lot of the hostility to Head Start, and to a lot of other old Great Society programs intended to level the playing field for all Americans. That component of the criticism was another example of the human talent for fallacious thinking—in this case, the bias known as the "fundamental attribution error." The fundamental attribution error (sometimes known as "correspondence bias") inclines us to blame the failures of others on something inside them, like a personality deficiency or character flaw, but their successes on luck. When it comes to ourselves, however, we reverse the process, attributing our successes to merit, and our failures to chance. It seems we want to believe in a world in which *our* missteps are the result of circumstances outside our control, but *other people* fall short because of something they've failed to do, like work hard enough (one reason this is an attribution *error* is that the same phenomenon makes us more likely to blame our own missteps on circumstances outside our control).

On the other hand, an analysis of the results of early interventions could be read a different way. Even without the Milwaukee results, all the programs we could research, from Head Start onward, showed *some* improvement, at least for a while. And some showed a lot.

Harlem Children's Zone is a ninety-seven-square-block neighborhood in Upper Manhattan, founded by a legend in the world of school reform, Geoffrey Canada. I got to meet him at a film ceremony once when he asked for a picture. He's so charismatic. He had me laughing the whole conversation. Harlem Children's Zone runs more than thirty programs aimed at increasing the school achievement and college attendance of Harlem residents, including a Head Start program and the Baby College, a nine-week-long parenting workshop for expectant parents and those with kids under the age of three. Its best-known institution might be the Promise Academy Charter Schools, and deservedly so: In (another) well-designed lottery experiment, Roland Fryer and Will Dobbie found that African-American students made up so much ground after three years at the Promise Academy middle school that they *completely eliminated the racial gap,* achieving scores identical to white students in New York City: Comparing lottery winners to losers revealed a huge effect size of +1.2 by eighth grade. By now, you know these numbers are head-scratching high.

But Harlem Children's Zone's intensive, all-day preschool might be even more impressive. Harlem Gems is the gold standard for such community programs. Or maybe the platinum standard. Gems is a kindergarten prep program with a four-to-one ratio of students to teachers that teaches three-year-olds not just preliteracy and language skills, but Spanish and French. And they teach them well: One hundred percent of Gems graduates were judged to be kindergarten-ready for six consecutive years. The program's quantitative results are equally impressive: Enrollment in Harlem Gems produces effect sizes of +.227 to .232 on the scores its graduates achieve in third-grade math, and +.238 to .318 in language arts.

Of course, it's worth mentioning that most of the Harlem Gems graduates become students in other HCZ schools—the Promise Academy charter schools—after scoring so well on their math and language arts assessments. And that high-quality preschools aren't filled with the kids who are furthest from the starting gate. One of the truly perverse things about the debate about pre-K education is that the American families that obsess about it the most are the ones that need it the least.

I expect that at least some of the people reading this book know exactly what I'm talking about. You know who you are. You're the ones who spent a year stressing out over whether the local Montessori preschool was the right place for your own four-year-old, or whether the local cooperative nursery school was too focused on academics.

Doesn't matter.

The evidence is pretty clear on this. A study that looked at four years' worth of assessment data on 2,297 Canadian kids, from the time they were less than eleven months old, demonstrated a huge effect size of +.58 in low-income families. Those families with even average incomes, however, experienced virtually no effect at all. To say nothing of those that can afford the "best" preschools. And this is just one among dozens of such studies. Elliot Tucker-Drob, a psychologist at the University of Texas, performed the classic nature-versus-nurture experiment as it applies to preschool by examining six hundred pairs of twins—divided between identical twins, with precisely the same genes, and fraternal twins, who share about half their genes—and did the regression analysis to reveal the impact of attending preschool. By isolating the socioeconomic status of the children from any natural talents they may have had, Drob found that income was decisive: "The very children who would benefit most from preschools are the least likely to be enrolled in them, [while] middle-class parents tend to be choosing between all very good options."

Now, not including the very low-IQ population—which we've seen is pretty significant and lasting for the general population of low-income kids—the benefits from even the best pre-K education aren't all that long-lasting. A huge meta-analysis of 117 studies of preschool programs, with nearly 2,000 estimated effect sizes—positive ones, averaging +.27 overall—showed that their full effects have disappeared by the third year after the program.

This doesn't mean that preschool doesn't matter. It's absolutely one of the practices needed for any realistic attempt at closing the achievement gap. The fact that its improvements tend to be temporary in most places doesn't indicate that preschool is unnecessary but that it's insufficient, since the challenge it's supposed to address doesn't go away when school starts. After all, if a five-year-old isn't ready for the first day of school because he didn't get prepared when he was three or four, his family isn't unexpectedly going to find the necessary resources when he's six or seven. High-quality preschools *can* get every kid to the kindergarten starting gate at the same time, but they can't keep a lot of them from falling behind by third grade.

WHAT I DIDN'T LEARN ON MY SUMMER VACATION

The researcher who has probably done more than anyone else to document the size and significance of the summer learning gap is Karl Alexander, the John Dewey Professor of Sociology at Johns Hopkins University, though when we discussed the subject with him, he was careful to remind us that the first real researcher of the summer achievement gap was Barbara Heyns, another sociologist at my alma mater, New York University.

Heyns studied nearly 3,000 middle school students in the Atlanta Public Schools during the 1970s and discovered that kids from lower-income and African-American families stayed more or less *even* with their upper-income, white, suburban classmates so long as school was in session, but fell behind by the equivalent of a month or more every summer. This was the gap!

As Professor Alexander describes it, the Heyns study inspired his own Baltimore Beginning School Study, which compared the test results achieved by ninth-grade kids to the scores of those same kids when they were in first grade, and all the grades in between. That study found that summer mattered far more than anyone had thought. The difference in the summer experiences of kids from families in different socioeconomic tiers—each kid's placement was determined by a combination of things, including parents' income, level of education, job status, and whether the student qualified for any kind of meal subsidy—accounted for more than half the difference in test scores by the time each kid entered high school.

The surprise wasn't that you could predict high school achievement from first-grade test scores, since achievement scores in one grade strongly predict scores in the next grade. Test scores strongly correlate from grade to grade; half of a fifth-grader's measured fluency in reading—or, for that matter, a tenth-grader's—is predicted by his score in the first grade. Students in the top math quartile in the fourth grade have a 64 percent chance of staying there through the eighth grade; those in the bottom quartile, a 62 percent chance of staying there as well. Since placement decisions are made based on the previous year's performance, this reinforces the early problems over and over again.

The surprise was that the scores were so powerfully changed by what happened to the students between June and

September. In Professor Alexander's study, the gap between families in the upper tier and those in the lowest doesn't emerge during the school year. In fact, the distance between a student from the bottom of the socioeconomic ladder and one from the top actually *shrinks* while school is in session. On a test of reading comprehension, those kids whose parents were more affluent and better educated started in the first grade with average scores of 298; the kids whose parents were poorer, and less likely to have attended college, started with scores of 272. At the end of the year, the average gain for kids from upper-tier families relative to lower-tier over five consecutive winters was −5.19. This isn't a misprint: These kids lost ground to their low-income classmates while school was in session. Is this blowing your mind? It blew mine when I first read it.

But, unfortunately, school doesn't run all year long. Every summer, on average, the high-tier students gained on the lower tier. The gap that was twenty-six points in the first grade turned into a forty-eight-point gap by the sixth grade, and a seventy-three-point gap by ninth grade. This was even worse than it sounded: *If the highest-quality preschool got everybody to the starting gate at the same time, a gap would still emerge during their first summer vacation, and grow every year thereafter.*

Even more unfortunately, studies that replicated this finding were depressingly easy to find. Harris Cooper, a professor of psychology and director of Duke University's Program in Education, examined nearly forty separate studies of the summer learning loss, and found that, on average, students from middle-class families improved their reading recognition every summer, while kids from families without those middle-class resources lost the equivalent of a three-month difference every summer.* It's like a marathon where everyone runs the first mile in about the same time, at which point half the runners walk for ten minutes, while half stop. Then they run for another mile, and half of them—the same half—walk for ten minutes, while the other half stops. And they do this for twenty-six miles.

There are a couple of conclusions that can be drawn from this, but one is that a coach can't show up at mile fifteen and do a whole lot of good. That's why quality pre-K programs are so essential. As Professor Alexander told us, you have to stop the cycle as early as possible; otherwise the gap is already too large.

He said something else, too: "Schools are episodic; families are all the time." Educational systems that want to close the achievement gap have to turn the usual relationship between families and schools upside down: Instead of affluent families compensating for deficits in school resources, schools need to compensate for shortfalls in home resources.

It's simple to calculate those deficits in terms of time. Time spent reading, or talking, or attending music lessons or religious school. Or days, weeks, or years spent in classrooms. Everyone's heard the popular argument that American students—not just low-achieving kids, but everyone—need more time in school. This is widely believed even though the current standard in most places, 180 days of school a year, each one between six and seven hours long, is, by historical standards, fairly short. One of those things "everyone knows" is that American schools in the twenty-first century are suffer-

---

* Interestingly, at least to me, *everyone*—middle class, upper class, lower class—lost a month in math computation during the summer. Parents apparently spend more time during the summer reading to their kids than doing algebra with them.

ing because they still run on a nineteenth-century, let's-get-the-kids-out-of-school-so-they-can-help-with-the-harvest schedule. But Philadelphia's schools were in session more than 250 days a year before the Civil War. New York's were open all year, except for a two-week break in August.

Even so, it's now nearly thirty years since the National Commission on Excellence in Education published the "Nation at Risk" report, which called for increasing the number of hours in the school day to at least 7 (and the number of days to between 200 and 220). There hasn't been a whole lot to show for it. As of 2008, thirty states still required 180 days; nineteen specify the number of hours, some as few as 990, which adds up to only 165 days of six hours each.

That was a pretty easy historical fact to research. Not so easy was finding great studies that showed how more hours improved student achievement. A compilation of fifteen empirical studies conducted between 1985 and 2009 found a consensus that there was *some* positive value in additional hours in school, especially when they could be connected to a particular subject: More hours spent on seventh-grade math produced—surprise!—higher algebra scores. Actually finding out how big the effect size was, though, not so easy.

One reason is that studies don't have a standardized way of distinguishing between time and "instructional time." Most researchers break school hours into a bunch of different overlapping categories: "Allocated school time" or "allocated class time" refers to the number of days or hours that students are required to attend annually. These, in turn, are broken into "instructional" and "noninstructional" time, with the noninstructional time devoted to administration, class management, and stuff like that. Instructional time, in turn, is divided into "engaged time" (sometimes "time on task") and "academic learning time." In some states, transportation, recess, and

lunch don't count, but assemblies and parent-teacher conferences do; other places, just the opposite. Just looking at
"allocated school time" as a measure of whether a school is
increasing its students' hours is a little like reviewing one of
my movies by calculating the number of days I spent shooting
it. Studies that tried to figure out the value of increased classroom "time" without knowing how much of it was spent on
instruction were probably doomed to be inconclusive.

Luckily, there were studies that didn't make this particular
mistake. The best one was part of our friend Roland Fryer's
survey of New York's high- and low-achieving charter schools.
That research, as you might have guessed from his careful
work, measured not only the length and number of days, but
the number of minutes spent on language arts and math in
each school, every day. The city's highest-achieving charter
elementary schools were definitely committed to a longer
year—about 191 days, of more than eight hours each—than
the lower-achievers, which averaged fewer than 184 days a
year, and a little more than seven hours a day. The difference
was smaller between high- and low-achieving middle schools,
but students in both spent significantly more time in class
than kids in typical public schools: 28 percent more for the
elementaries, and 21 percent more for the middle schools.

And the effect size? Though Professor Fryer would be
cautious about claiming certainty over which of the various
practices contributed to a particular school's success—like
us, he was evaluating a whole system of changes, including
more teacher feedback, and changes in a school's culture of
expectations—the increased instructional time in the high-
achieving schools correlated with effect sizes of +.15 in math,
and +.20 in language arts.

Most studies, though, not only fail to separate time learning from time spent staring at classroom walls; they also don't

do a great job separating trivial increases in classroom time from dramatic ones. It stands to reason that extending the number of hours in a school year by 10 percent isn't going to have the same impact as a 50 percent jump, and a lot of the less successful attempts to improve achievement by increasing hours were pretty modest: an additional fifteen minutes a day in some cases.

That's why just about every school that is succeeding in closing the achievement gap is adding a *lot* of hours to the school year, in just about every way they can think of. The Robert Treat Academy, a charter elementary school in Newark, New Jersey, a state where the annual requirement for school days is 180, holds classes up to 210 days a year— eleven months of school. In 2008, it was the highest-scoring urban public school in the state. At FirstLine Schools in New Orleans, not only is the school day eight hours long, but most students stay for another one-and-a-half hours daily. Not enough? After the Christmas and New Year's holidays, most of the schools in the FirstLine network offer school on Saturdays as well. Each of them also runs summer programs for about three to four weeks.

The KIPP network is even more focused on extending the hours their students spend in the classroom. A typical KIPP school runs from 7:30 to 5:00 daily (some until 5:30), along with a mandatory three-week summer program. Most of them require once-a-month Saturday classes as well. It all adds up to at least 60 percent more hours annually for KIPP's students.

At Uncommon Schools, not only is the school day longer, but the school year starts and stops at different times than more traditional public schools. A typical public school in the United States opens for business a day or two after Labor Day; when we visited North Star Academy, we learned that teachers reported for duty in 2012 on August 6. Typically, schools that recognize the dangers of summer (and holidays) have figured out how to modify the calendar to start earlier, and end later. Even when they offer the same number of instructional days each year—this is often a state requirement—they do so with more, and shorter, vacations from school. And they're not the only ones. One study of thirty-nine school districts in various parts of the country showed a significant (though modest) effect size of +.11 in schools that modified the instructional calendar to reduce the length of the summer gap.

And, if we needed more confirmation of the importance of extending the school year into the summer, we had it a lot closer to home.

THE KID IN THE BOW TIE

Alejandro Gac-Artigas was twelve when he published his memoir. He graduated from Harvard. He is an alum of Teach For America, where he taught bilingual first grade. He also worked as an analyst for McKinsey & Company. Alejandro is an extraordinary young man. The reason I had heard about him was through his work creating the Springboard Collaborative, a summer program in Philadelphia for low-income kids that—I heard through Bhavna and Jenn—was having surprising results. He was proving one of the tenets and documenting it in our back yard.

I was in intense preproduction on *After Earth,* the science-fiction film I was making with Jaden and Will Smith at Sony. We were building all kinds of sets—spaceships, caves, transport hangars—when Alejandro came to visit me. I am always preoccupied; you can ask Bhavna. (Actually, don't, she'll just get upset.) So visiting me while I am preparing for a movie that is going to start shooting in a few weeks is a waste of time for everyone involved. This didn't turn out to be a waste of time.

Alejandro was late. I believe he got lost. He was panicked. You could see this in the edges of his demeanor. But this is actually when you get to see someone for who they really are, and Alejandro Gac-Artigas is a good guy. He stood there in his bow tie and button-down sweater holding his briefcase and apologized over and over. We all laughed and told him to sit and eat with us. As you probably know by now, I love food. We had a beautiful lunch that day: a work of art made from pulled pork served over cornbread. Alejandro was overwhelmed. He told us his budget only allowed him to have peanut butter and jelly every single day. I felt like some slimy Hollywood type in his presence. A sellout. He gobbled down his food and pulled out charts. Alejandro has a chart fetish. He has graphed everything he has done. This is what all the colorful charts showed me.

Springboard runs its summer program, using an original proprietary curriculum, for four weeks each summer. Its teachers—Springboard Scholars—received intense professional development in April and May and started instruction in mid-June, while the parents of participating students were given effective strategies for reading to their children at home. There were learning bonuses (rewards) as well—books, school supplies, and, for those who achieved an incredible six-plus months in growth, laptops given directly to families.

The results: The forty-two students involved in the program had average reading gains of *2.8 months in 4 weeks*. They held these gains as they arrived at school in September. This happened during a summer when the expected reading loss is 3 months. The cost was about $900 per student, including fixed costs and incentives. Come September, the children in Alejandro's program, who had gains of 2.8 months from June, were almost 6 months ahead of their peers, who had slid 3 months.

I remember showing Alejandro around the spaceship sets and being dazzled by what he had just shown me. We agreed on the spot to give him seed money to expand his program. The MNS Foundation became the first foundation to award him a grant (after which he then received funding from reputable area foundations such as William Penn and the Samuel S. Fels Fund and also was awarded an Echoing Green Fellowship). A year later, I was lucky enough to be given an award by the Pennsylvania Society, a portion of which was a $50,000 donation to a Pennsylvania charity of my choice. I chose Springboard Collaborative with pretty much no hesitation. Alejandro expanded his pilot program from one to four schools with 340 low-income kids. He once again had gains of 2.8 months in 4 weeks against the expected losses of 3 months. Alejandro is working with the Philadelphia school system to expand throughout the city. As you can imagine, there is an intense and growing demand to be in Alejandro's program.

When I accepted the award that night and told the crowd of 1,000 in the Waldorf-Astoria about Alejandro, I spoke in hyperbole and pointed to him as one of the young men and women who will have changed the face of education in ten years. I was so happy to see him in his rented tuxedo shaking hands with potential donors, not eating peanut butter and jelly.

Once again, when we were able to clear away the fog, the evidence was clear, and inspiring: Suburban schools can—maybe—get away with a school year that is 180 days long, with every day no more than 7 hours long. Schools on the wrong side of the gap don't have that luxury. Whether they choose to keep students in school until 4:30 every day, or add Saturday classes, or modify the calendar to shorten the summer vacation, or mandate three or four weeks of summer school, a school that is serious about closing the gap needs more classroom hours—some say at *least* 1,700 hours every year, which is 500 more than the average school offers.

This doesn't mean that time is the only thing worth measuring. Five hundred additional low-quality hours taught by a teaching staff full of below-average instructors who are neither observed regularly by their principals nor given the quantitative and qualitative feedback they need is a waste, and a pretty expensive one at that.

But the message—from Alejandro Gac-Artigas's Springboard Collaborative; from KIPP, Uncommon, and FirstLine; from Karl Alexander and Roland Fryer—was unmistakable. Keep them in school and you won't need superheroes to close the gap. Most teachers can do the job just fine.

PART THREE

CONCLUSION

9

SOMETHING ELSE JOHN ADAMS SAID . . .

Although I started this project looking for a system of practices that could close America's achievement gap, I didn't really expect that some theme would necessarily tie all the practices together. After all, the inspiration for *I Got Schooled* was the model described by Kevin Fosnocht at that long-ago dinner, and the health habits he listed—eight hours of sleep, no smoking, exercise, a balanced diet, and managing stress—are largely independent of each other. Even though all of them reduce the strain on (for example) the cardiovascular system, that's not necessarily the reason for the huge impact they have on overall health. In fact, there doesn't even have to *be* a reason. The human body wants to be healthy. It's enough that these practices work.

But, after four years of research, travel, and interviews, I started to see a pattern in our five tenets. And it wasn't what anyone told me I'd find.

The clues should have been there from the beginning, though. One of the biggest wake-up calls in the entire project was recognizing that the problems with American education weren't evenly spread around; there's no real problem for students in the top quarter of America's schools. There are some ways in which they fall short, especially when you compare them to the top-performing students in other rich countries, but basically, they're doing just fine. The problem is the gap between them and the students in the bottom quarter. The problem isn't achievement; it's variability. We knew this going in but at first didn't see the implications.

And all of the traditional ways we organize education don't just ignore variability. They promote it.

MAKING THINGS BETTER, NOT WORSE

Sometimes they promote it in perverse ways. You might think that the widget effect, which rates teachers as interchangeable parts, 99 percent of them performing at a satisfactory level, would reduce variability. But it actually increases it. The widespread grade inflation in the schools of education that supply three-quarters of America's new teachers—education majors typically average at least half a grade higher than economics, physics, history, or literature majors—doesn't just tell aspiring teachers that they're all doing well, but that they're all doing *just as well as every other teacher.* It's the same thing that gets reinforced when 99 percent of teachers are rated as at least satisfactory. We've built a system that is designed to wish away any natural variability in teaching talent.

That's only the beginning. A lot of well-intentioned reform efforts promote teacher autonomy. The good intentions are real: to remove the bureaucratic barriers that keep the country's best teachers from practicing their profession at the highest levels of excellence. Unfortunately, autonomy doesn't just allow the best teachers to thrive; it also leaves alone the worst ones to mess up generations of students. Principals who spend their days on budgets and building management don't reduce variability in instruction; they nurture it. If classroom performance—as measured not just by improvement against expectation on tests, but weekly observation and annual surveys of students—isn't measured and communicated to the teacher, then, guess what? The evidence couldn't be clearer: Good teachers get better and poor teachers don't.

And, since analysis of test data, classroom observation, and student surveys demands huge amounts of time—from principals *and* teachers—schools that get too big don't get enough of it; a principal with eight fifth-grade classrooms can't visit them as frequently as a principal with three. More classrooms equals less feedback. And less feedback equals more variability.

But the biggest source of variability in student achievement in America isn't between *schools*. It's between *families*. To a great extent, this is the main issue causing the education gap in the first place. This was the discovery of the Coleman Report back in 1966, and it's still the favorite data point for reformers who argue that we can't fix America's achievement gap until we fix America's income gap, that it's wrong to expect schools and teachers to fix a problem they didn't create.

Except, they can. The last piece of our five-part puzzle showed me how the variability in educational achievement between families was really measured in time: the amount of time that higher-income families could use to supplement the education their children were receiving in school in a multitude of ways. Our most effective schools, like Uncommon, Achievement First, KIPP, and others, have proved that this bit of variability can be reduced, and even eliminated, by the obvious solution: more time in school.

Less variability. Smaller gap. It sure *felt* right. But did it hold up in the schools themselves? We had found dozens of schools that were, in every way we could measure it, closing the gap. I knew we had to return to them and see whether the five parts of the system were promoting a consistent—and consistently excellent—classroom experience.

The first tenet that we saw in practice wasn't so much a way of *promoting* consistency as it was eliminating something that *suppresses* it: poor teachers. The tenet with the most evidence for large-magnitude change demands an evaluation system that permits schools to terminate teachers who are just not up to the challenges of instruction. There's some disagreement about how deep the cuts should be, whether the worst-performing 5 percent, or 8 percent, or more. But there's none at all about the damage that students receive from even one substandard year in school, damage that *really* amplifies the achievement gap, since affluent, suburban families are so much better equipped than their inner-city counterparts to compensate for ineffective teachers.

And, outside the teaching profession itself, there's no real disagreement that a workable system for evaluating teachers can be implemented: one that can, at least, find the one teacher in ten or twenty who shouldn't be in the classroom at all. For too long, the main obstacle to this reform has been the argument that the only fair system is one that never makes a mistake; one that removes *all* poor teachers, and *only* poor teachers. But in the real world, the system doesn't have to be perfect. It just has to recognize that the needs of America's students have to come first, even if the cost is some unfairness. We can have a lively debate about how many mistakes we're willing to accept. By combining the best value-added growth measures with classroom performance scores calculated according to a consistent set of measurements, and adding *them* to the student evaluations on the questionnaires created by Ron Ferguson and his team at Harvard, we can reduce the error factor to fewer than one in ten using a single year's worth of data. Maybe even half that. Then use two years of data, or three, to make it defendably precise. Not perfectly precise; some unfairness is unavoidable. But we need a rigorous evaluation system in order to fix what ails America's poorest schools.

It doesn't have to be brutal. It doesn't have to find the "worst 5 percent." Sometimes, it doesn't have to find any failing teachers at all. When I visit schools run by KIPP, or Uncommon, or Achievement First, or FirstLine, I always ask them about turnover: the percentage of teachers who are asked not to return each year. And not one of them is regularly giving a thumbs-down to even 5 percent of their teaching staffs. Despite the fact that it's way easier for these schools to dismiss teachers—mostly because they aren't restricted by collective-bargaining agreements—than in traditional public schools, none of them seems to be especially eager to do so. They love and respect their teachers. They own them.

Julie Jackson of Uncommon Schools told me an interesting story of a young teacher who had gone to a prestigious university and was having grave trouble when she began teaching at the Uncommon Schools. She was not succeeding and gave up on herself. Julie fought hard with her. She told her she had just started teaching and not to give up. Julie told her she would succeed if she kept at it and worked at the skill they were espousing. She implored her to keep fighting and she would see results. As you would expect, the young woman turned things around and became a successful Uncommon Schools teacher. I asked Julie how she was so sure this woman was going to succeed when her first few salvos into teaching were very unsuccessful. Julie said, "We're making a system where almost everyone can succeed. We don't give up on teachers. We believe in them and show them how to improve." I asked the million-dollar question then. "What percentage of your teachers do you fire?" Including turnover from teachers just not returning, they believed it was somewhere between 2 and 5 percent depending on the year. This was jaw-dropping to me. Because I knew that the Uncommon Schools had closed the achievement gap, this meant that apparently 95 to 98 percent of the teachers in the Uncommon Schools had turned into Superman. Or were they made?

The reason they don't abuse the termination of teachers is simple. They don't have to discipline their teachers after they're hired because they are so good at disciplining themselves before. The most valuable aspect of having a coherent school culture might be that it gives the people doing the hiring a *cultural* template to go along with the skills-and-experience template that is used in most schools. When I asked Stephanie Blake, the principal at Achievement First's Endeavor Elementary School, about hiring teachers, she told me she first used to hire for skills alone and ignore that little voice that told her the teacher might not be 100 percent on board with the culture Stephanie wanted for the school. She soon discovered those individuals didn't last. Now, she says, she always goes for cultural fit. She may not have found a hiring trait—as Richard Elmore demonstrated, these don't seem to exist. But in her mind, she has found a weed-out trait—those who don't believe in the school's culture shouldn't be hired.

It's odd, but most schools don't really understand who they are, which is one reason they are so frequently surprised when the candidate that looks so good on paper turns out to be not so good in the classroom.

It's not that the teachers who disappoint in the classroom don't want to close the gap. They don't want *to want* to close the gap.

Confusing? One of the hazards of spending my professional life in the movie business is the number of lines from
memorable films that have taken up residence in my brain.
One of the most thought-provoking I know is in David Lean's
1962 masterpiece *Lawrence of Arabia*. The scene I have in
mind occurs after the title character's capture and torture by
the Turks, when Lawrence loses heart and tells his compan-
ion, Ali, that he will leave the Arab Revolt he started. He is not
the Arab Revolt. He is not, he tells Ali, even Arab; to which Ali
replies:

"A man can be whatever he wants, you said."
"He can. But he can't *want* what he wants."

Lawrence points to his fair skin:

"This is the stuff that decides what he wants."

When Lawrence points to his pasty white Peter O'Toole
chest, he isn't just talking about pigment. He's talking about
culture. A lot of what makes schools like North Star Academy
and Achievement First Endeavor work so brilliantly isn't that
their teachers want to close the achievement gap, but that
they want to want it. They're from the right culture.
    It carries over into every aspect of the principal's job.
When we visited North Star Academy, I was blown away by
how the principals and teachers so obviously had it together
on the knowledge and charisma front. But that morning meeting, when Yasmin Vargas did her Tony Robbins–level motivational routine for hundreds of elementary school students, was
important not just because it reinforced the school's cultural
norms, like "everyone here is headed for college," but in the
way it made clear that these norms were for the *entire school,*

not just one classroom or grade. One of the top entries on the list of "obvious things about education that never occurred to me before" has to be the realization that, from the standpoint of the guests of honor, school is not something that happens in one classroom, but in a succession of them. In elementary school, that succession is from second to third grade; in secondary school from fourth-period math to fifth-period English. But one of the key components of closing the achievement gap is remembering that it's the sequence that matters more than any one element. You can't make an effective education out of two or three superteachers any more than a great movie consists of two or three great highlight scenes.

There aren't a whole lot of ways that North Star Academy is like the U.S. Marine Corps, but there is at least one: Whether you get your recruit training in Alpha Company in Parris Island or Fox Company in San Diego, you're part of one big family at the end. The Marines have a cultural template. So does Uncommon Schools.

The first two keys of the system we found in dozens of effective schools were about finding the right people for the jobs: teachers who have bought into the project of closing the achievement gap, and principals who are committed to instructional leadership (and who are working in a system that allows them to do so—one that takes the burden of operations out of the hands of the instructional leaders). You have to answer the "who" questions before anything else.

The other practices are the "how" of educational reform: what those people do, where they do it, and for how long.

The "what" might be the most distinctive aspect of educational practice in schools that are successfully closing the gap. It's definitely the most obvious to outsiders. There are plenty of traditional elementary and secondary schools where principals are focused on instruction, and even ones where the teaching staffs are very skilled and enthusiastic. At least a third of America's high schools would qualify as "small" by our criteria already, just like most of the elementary and middle schools. And there are even traditional schools with extended days or even longer-than-average school years. But anyone who visits a classroom at a KIPP, Uncommon, Achievement First, or FirstLine school is going to be surprised by the sheer volume of supervision and observation that goes on. In almost every traditional school, a visit from the principal is an extraordinary event, one that usually means emergency, or at least trouble. In my own movie *The Happening*—yes: the same one whose location scouting brought me to Overbrook and Masterman—I even used a principal visit to signal the vast epidemic that occupies the rest of the film.

Of course, the constant visits from observers in gap-closing schools—constant enough that students don't even look up when other adults enter the room—are only the front end of the system. What really makes this kind of instructional practice successful is what happens to the information after it's collected; not just visits, but test-score data, often video observations, and surveys. That is when the data is analyzed, transformed into action plans, and fed back to classrooms on a weekly, if not daily, basis.

When I tell people outside my own team about the surprising results of our research, and I get to the part about constant observation and feedback (to say nothing of the demand that all teachers use similar techniques), I've gotten used to hearing how terrible it all sounds: "What kind of people want their bosses breathing down their necks every day?" This is one of the issues I completely switched position on during the years of research. I started with the artist's perspective, with freedom being paramount. Now I don't accept that the systems in place in schools like North Star Academy somehow deny teachers the freedom they want or need. For one thing, every teacher I've met in the effective schools you've been reading about feels like the information flow is reciprocal: that they are providing as much feedback to their principals as they are receiving. They also tell me that just as they receive guidance on the best way to teach math to fifth-graders based on the well-analyzed experiences of other teachers, so their experiences are providing guidance to their colleagues as well. In these schools, instructional leadership, like feedback itself, is a two-way street.

And there's something else, too. The teachers at North Star, or Arthur Ashe, or Achievement First Endeavor, get the biggest reward any teacher ever asks for. Their students reach their potential.

As to the "where" and "when" these practices work best, well, that was pretty obvious, too. It would be possible, I guess, to collect classroom data on a regular basis, analyze qualitative and quantitative data, and report back to teachers every week in a school with a thousand kids. All you'd need is the Time-Turner that Hermione Granger used to double up on her classes in *Harry Potter and the Prisoner of Azkaban*. If you aren't lucky enough to have one, though, it's going to be a lot more practical to keep enrollments under six hundred or so.

Then there's when, or, more accurately, how long all these tenets are practiced every year. You remember the *House, M.D.,* moment I had when Kevin Fosnocht first described the behaviors that made up a system for healthy living? I had another when I realized that America's achievement gap was also a symptom of a time gap; that from the time they're born, kids with more affluent and better-educated parents were receiving literally hundreds of additional hours in supplemental education every year that poorer families just can't supply. Sometimes just to describe the problem is to solve it, and that's why Robert Treat Academy in Newark is open more than two hundred days a year. It's why FirstLine Schools in New Orleans have Saturday classes starting every January. It's why a typical student in the KIPP network is in school from 7:30 to 5:00 every day, five days a week, along with one Saturday every month, without even counting the mandatory three-week program every summer.

Sounds like a lot, right? However, when I mention this subject to those same friends who are appalled by what they see as the rigidity of teaching practice in gap-closing schools, I tend to remind them that their own kids are spending the same hours a week in some kind of structured program, like after-school language classes, or music rehearsals, or math tutoring. That their kids spend their summers at computer and science camps. Parents who send their kids to schools like Uncommon and KIPP are just getting the biggest bargain in public schooling today: a strong middle-class education.

If you could flash back like a movie, you might recall that the real beginning of the search for the system that could close the achievement gap began with the dinner party thrown by my friend the Social Genius. If there was a consensus in that room (probably not), it was that any workable program would definitely include replacing traditional public schools with charters, and replacing teachers' unions with— well, anything but teachers' unions. Since just about all the success stories we found subsequently were charter schools, managed outside of union contracts, at least some of you might be wondering whether that consensus was right.

You can stop wondering. It turned out it wasn't.

It's not exactly coincidence that Arthur Ashe, and North Star, and Green Dot, and Achievement First Endeavor, and all the others, are charters. Or that management of their teaching staffs isn't subject to a collective-bargaining agreement. Charter school proponents do have a lot to be proud of, and union busters could, I guess, find some ammunition here. Without the ability to experiment with instruction, or the freedom from some of the work rules that have grown up around the profession of teaching like kudzu, schools like North Star wouldn't have found the space they needed to put their own system into practice.

But putting that system into practice doesn't require a charter. Or the death of teachers' unions. While most states permit collective bargaining with teachers' unions (thirty-one states and the District of Columbia require it, and fourteen allow it), the ones that forbid it—Georgia, North Carolina, South Carolina, Texas, and Virginia—don't have any improved achievement scores to show for it. And there is literally no correlation between how "union-friendly" a state's policies are and how well its students perform on any standardized tests. In fact, the opposite may be true: A strong union—one that can align its members' interests with student achievement—can be the best possible way to improve classroom instruction. After more than four years of visiting classrooms and schools, I can report that the thing that makes teachers happiest is their students' success in learning what they are being taught. A system that shows America's educators how to achieve that doesn't have to do anything else to get enormous support from the teaching community.

Since there are so many highly publicized schools that are using such a system, the real mystery is why that support hasn't been more forthcoming. Why aren't an avalanche of schools trying to use them?

It's not the obvious reason—fear of change, particularly change that reduces job security. Not exactly. However, fear of change has a close cousin: the natural conservatism of every institution. It's not a coincidence that so many of the closing-the-gap stories are taking place in schools that are *less than twenty years old, often less than ten*. It's hard enough to build a new culture from scratch; it's extremely difficult to replace an old way of doing things. And any school that was already going when the first TFA corps members graduated college or when KIPP opened its first charter school in Houston or when No Child Left Behind was signed into law—that's more than nine out of ten schools in the country—had an entrenched way of life in place, guarded by teachers, principals, alumni, and community members.

And not everything about the old public school way of life was a liability. In every failing school, there are still successful teachers, individuals who had figured out how to prosper even in a toxic environment. Since the kind of dramatic change in their schools that would result from implementing all five of the keys is going to catch them in its gears, it's not a big surprise that some very good teachers might not welcome them. I expect to hear a lot of "if it ain't broke, don't fix it," since, while a lot of American classrooms are broken, some aren't. It's hard to change habits. Even ones that aren't great for you.

However, the really unexpected thing we encountered, again and again, wasn't fear, or even conservatism, but skepticism that there was an answer. When my friend Kevin told the best and brightest medical residents about the simple health tenets and their collective power to heal, he was met with skepticism. Education is no different. Robert Hughes is the president of an organization, New Visions for Public Schools, that does a terrific job running dozens of public schools in New York City. But Visions has still established its own charter school as an incubator for new ideas, precisely because they don't believe that the practices being used by their neighbors at Achievement First and Success Academy and Harlem Children's Zone (to say nothing of KIPP and Uncommon Schools in their back yard) are necessarily relevant to the New York public schools.

There's nothing wrong with idea incubators or even a healthy dose of skepticism—until, that is, it becomes the paralysis of the "not invented here" syndrome. And we all fall into this trap. We need to own ideas, not be given them. Jay Altman, who has forgotten more about closing the achievement gap than someone like me will ever know, first started incubating his own ideas in New Orleans but eventually culled ideas from successful systems like KIPP and Uncommon and even the U.K's. ARK Schools—eleven academies run by Absolute Return for Kids, an international children's charity based in London. His turnaround on assigned curriculum is an example of this. So is one of the biggest revolutions in the history of medicine.

More than forty years ago, a group of physicians started the movement that became known as "evidence-based medicine," or EBM. Their reason wasn't that doctors hadn't been using evidence; it was that the evidence they were likeliest to believe was local and (often) personal experience instead of global data. One hospital might be three times likelier to perform cesarean deliveries than another, even in the exact same circumstances: age of mother, fetal heart rate, everything. The reasons were a whole encyclopedia of cognitive biases: availability errors made by doctors who miscalculated the probability of a diagnosis based on recent experience. Confirmation biases that persuaded them to use only data that supported a desired outcome. Most important, doctors turn out to be just as vulnerable to the "anchoring effect," which causes them to give too much value to a single trait in decision-making. In one hospital, the standard might be to perform a particular procedure because, well, that's what the head of obstetrics does when she encounters it, and she had delivered hundreds of babies, so she ought to know.

The proponents of evidence-based medicine, though, weren't persuaded that the experience of a single doctor who had delivered hundreds of babies was anywhere near as useful as the experience of thousands of doctors who had collectively delivered millions. With access to this kind of data, health care could be—is being—dramatically improved. More evidence, from more places, is better evidence in schools as well as hospitals.

And in traditional public schools as well as charters.

There's absolutely no reason why every public elementary and secondary school in New York, Los Angeles, Chicago, or Philadelphia couldn't take each of the five steps—some immediately; others, like building smaller high schools, over the next ten years—and expect similar results. I'll repeat myself: If we could convince America's educators that there was a magic potion that could transform students into learners, that could take students in America's most disadvantaged neighborhoods and allow them to compete with students in its richest ones, every teacher, principal, librarian, and playground aide in the country would be drinking it. We just have to convince them.

Which should be the best news of all. As of 2010, there were just short of 99,000 public elementary and secondary schools in the United States, with a combined enrollment of just under 49 million. The total number in public charters? A little more than a million, or barely 2 percent. Even if every charter school in the country performed at the level of North Star Academy, 98 percent of America's students wouldn't benefit. But, as Roland Fryer and others are demonstrating in big public systems, those 98 percent are just as capable of successfully implementing a new system of educational practices as any charter school in America.

Teachers and administrators in traditional public schools have the same desire to close the achievement gap as anyone at Uncommon, KIPP, or Achievement First. And their efforts haven't gone unrecognized. The Eli and Edythe Broad Foundation has been awarding the $1 million Broad Prize every year since 2002 to large urban school districts that have improved student achievement—state tests, graduation rates, SAT and ACT scores—while also closing the gap separating poor and minority students from their affluent, nonminority counterparts.

The Broad Prize is a very big deal indeed. Only seventy-five districts are eligible; but they represent virtually every large school system in the country with significant numbers of poor students. To be eligible, a school district must have more than 37,500 students, with 40 percent eligible for a free or reduced-price lunch, the traditional measure of low income. Prize winners have included the public school systems in Miami–Dade County, Norfolk, Charlotte-Mecklenburg, and the schools of the Houston Independent School District, where Roland Fryer tested and demonstrated his system of closing-the-gap practices.*

Another well-known prize for public schools that are showing success at closing the gap is the one awarded by the National Center for Urban School Transformation (NCUST) at San Diego State University, which has given out sixty-two $5,000 prizes to individual schools that have achieved success

---

* In 2012, the Broad Foundation also gave a prize of $250,000 to a Houston-based charter school network: the YES Prep Public Schools, which serves more than 5,000 low-income minority students in ten schools—and which you'll find on our list of the most effective schools at closing the gap in the entire country, in Appendix A.

by the same measures as those recognized by the Broad Prize committee.

These prizes are a starting point for anyone looking for evidence that public schools are actually turning the corner on student achievement. This is even more important than it sounds. As long as 98 out of a hundred students in American schools are attending traditional public schools, it is hugely important to see that there's some hope for improving them. Though we saw the miracles happening every day at places like Uncommon and Achievement First, unless the same phenomenon can be scaled up from thousands of kids to millions, we're only nibbling at the corners of the achievement gap. There will always be outliers in the public school system of 99,000 schools, but how are the best of those outliers doing without the five tenets—just with great teachers or one of the other tenets?

One of the winners of the NCUST's 2010 National Excellence in Urban Education Awards was the Branch Brook School, in Newark, New Jersey. Branch Brook is one of the most successful traditional public elementary schools in the state: In addition to the NCUST prize, it won the Blue Ribbon Award of Excellence from the U.S. Department of Education in 2005—the same award given to the Julia Masterman magnet school in Philadelphia—and a dozen others. It is consistently rated as the number-one public school in its region. Its students are doing well, too: In 2010, the year it was recognized for excellence, 60.7 percent of Branch Brook's third-graders achieved either proficient or advanced proficient scores in the language arts portion of the New Jersey Assessment of Skills and Knowledge, and an impressive 93 percent did so in math.

I just had to go visit there. As I drove to New Jersey again, I hoped for two things: I hoped that Branch Brook's success made sense in light of the things I'd learned, and secondly, I really hoped *I Got Schooled* wasn't going to be perceived as some simplistic, procharter book. This trip to Branch Brook was important to me. When I pulled up to Branch Brook School, I could see the worn and tattered award banners hanging along the front façade of the school. Principal Joseph Cullen gave me the tour. Joseph is a friendly, clean-cut man. He was knowledgeable in an unassuming way. He informed me that his school was small, about 176 students. I looked back to Jenn, who was on the tour. My eyes said, "Check." Joseph stressed as others did later that the small school size allowed them to know and monitor everyone personally. I immediately could tell everyone knew everyone here.

Later on the tour, I asked, "Do you have extended day?"

He said, "Yes, we do. Our kids start at eight with light work and breakfast and stay till between five and six P.M. They have a very successful after-school program of academic enrichment."

As we walked, I saw banners of colleges on all the walls. We learned this was mandated by their district superintendent.

The big kicker came when Joseph told me they have a pre-K program and that most of their kids had gone through it. They were solving the achievement gap early here at Branch Brook School.

I had a wonderful moment at Branch Brook when a third-grade class actually taught me about fables and what their purpose was. (Did you know in fables there are two characters, one character has a moral flaw and one has a moral asset?) Before our morning was over, I had spoken to teachers and visited most of the classrooms. All the teachers were used to Principal Cullen visiting them regularly to monitor them and their students. I saw "Exit Slips" on the walls that gave teachers immediate feedback at the end of classes as to what the student actually retained. They were using a certain amount of feedback at the student and teacher level.

As I said goodbye to teachers and then eventually to Principal Cullen, my heart was about to burst. The tenets were starting to be used here. Not all of them, but some, and they were seeing results that were starting not to surprise me.

There are similar traditional public school success stories. The Broad Foundation highlights these every year. In 2009, the million-dollar winner was the Aldine Independent School District in Harris County, near Houston. Aldine won because, in the words of the citation, it "outperformed other districts in Texas that serve students with similar family incomes in reading and math," and "a greater percentage of Aldine's Hispanic and low-income students performed at the highest achievement level on state reading and math assessments . . . than did their state counterparts." The objective data, as with Branch Brook, is good: On the Texas Assessment of Knowledge and Skills, between 80 and 90 percent of students from kindergarten to eleventh grade met state standards; the percentage that received a "commended" grade ranged from 7 percent (in Grade 10 Science) to 45 percent (in Grade 11 Social Studies). As it turns out, Aldine Independent School District uses some of the tenets. They have strong leaders with strong cultures. They have heavy amounts of feedback both from teachers' and students' performances, and they use tested curriculum.

And they're doing this educating 60,000 students.

I am the first one to stand up and cheer for what is going on at Aldine ISD and Branch Brook and all the dozens of schools and districts that are outdoing their peers in educating students on the wrong side of the achievement gap. We all should be applauding them. What we shouldn't be is surprised. These are systems that are using some of the tenets and seeing some of the results. And with nearly 100,000 schools in the United States, it's a good bet that you can find others using the tenets as well.

And there will be outliers. There have always been superior principals and teachers—superheroes—who have always had superhero-sized impacts on their students. Sometimes the stars align well enough that they meet one another. The communities where this occurs are lucky indeed. If you live in one of them, you probably should have put this book down by now. You're like the kind of person who smokes, drinks, has a high-stress job, sleeps three hours a night, and still dies in a skiing accident at the age of ninety-seven.

Most families, though, don't win that particular sweepstakes. That's why schools like Branch Brook are "outliers" in the first place. Unfortunately, giving them prizes and recognition, however well deserved, doesn't turn them into models that other schools can emulate. Success doesn't scale up all by itself. Unless and until American educators know as much about the *practices* of successful schools and school districts as they do about their *results,* it's hard to see how that success can be easily replicated. It's all very well to know that a particular hospital is winning prizes for improving patient outcomes, but not so helpful if no one knows how. And, while the Broad Foundation has been doing some good work at documenting the best practices of their winning school districts—winners of the Broad Prize have tended to offer a rigorous curriculum, aligned with quantifiable standards, evidence-based instruction, and a commitment to performance assessment and data analysis—and the NCUST has even published books like *Teaching Practices from America's Best Urban Schools,* neither program seems specific enough to be truly actionable in other schools.

The real value of what Mike Feinberg and his colleagues

do at KIPP Houston, what Julie Jackson and Yasmin Vargas do at Uncommon, and what Stephanie Blake and Tom Kaiser do at Achievement First is that their methods are specific; they know immediately if things are being done in the most effective way—and, even more important, so do their teachers. The kind of practices that are promoted by large national organizations like the Broad Foundation and the NCUST try not to be too prescriptive. Their practices are more imprecise. Advice that tells teachers to "express a genuine interest in each student's ideas" or "maintain a clean and attractive classroom" or "integrate material from other disciplines in teaching lesson objectives" is well intentioned, and a whole lot better than nothing. But it still leaves most teachers and administrators reinventing the wheel (or, at least most of it), figuring things out for themselves.

I'm pretty sure that the large urban school systems of America want to know *what* is successful, not just who is. That's the reason for the book you're reading—to put a lot of what we know in one place. To organize it. To acknowledge the grays. To dismiss the misconceptions. To make it real and make everyone believe that 98 percent of America's students are going to see some big-time improvements.

Now let's talk about the bill. How much would this cost to do nationally?

The United States spends a lot on education already: more than $610 billion in the 2008–09 school year, which is a little less than $11,000 per student. However, $66 billion of that is spent on capital outlays, mostly school-building, $17 billion is interest on school bonds, and $8.5 billion goes toward things like community service and adult education.

That still leaves "only" $518.5 billion, of which the largest share by far is instruction. The United States spends more than $300 billion a year on what the National Center for Education Statistics defines as "salaries and benefits for teachers and teacher aides, textbooks, supplies and purchased services [and] expenditures relating to extracurricular and cocurricular activities." Another $25 billion is for training, or "activities that include instructional staff training, educational media (library and audiovisual), and other instructional staff support services." (The rest is administration, operations, maintenance, transportation, and food services.)

So, given that, how much more is needed to implement the five keys—no roadblock teachers, leadership, feedback, manageable size, and more time—to closing the achievement gap?

An argument could be made that implementing some of what the evidence suggests would actually *save* money; we spend more than $19 billion every year on bonuses for teachers who earn graduate degrees, which have roughly the same impact on student achievement as painting classrooms a different color. However, since more than half of America's teachers, 52 percent, have either a master's, a Ph.D., or some other graduate degree, this is a way to pay underpaid teachers more. If we stopped paying these bonuses—and we absolutely should—the system would almost certainly just get gamed in a different way, probably by just moving the budget for graduate degree bonuses into the one for salary increases based on seniority. Since I'm not in the camp of reducing teacher income, let's just say this isn't a money-saver.

So, more money is going to be needed. How much? The honest answer is nobody knows, at least with any precision. But we can make some back-of-the-envelope estimates. The first key to closing the achievement gap, which is finding the teachers who are the biggest obstacles to student progress and removing them from classrooms, doesn't carry a huge price tag. Almost all of it could be easily paid for by using existing assessment funds and acting on them. However, the deluxe edition of a teacher evaluation package, which would combine the classroom observation scores with value-added test measures and student surveys—as mentioned before, to reduce the error factor in using value-added scoring alone— could cost between $500 million and $1 billion annually.

Then there's the second key, which is transforming principals into instructional leaders. The cost for this is personnel— someone to run a school's noninstructional operations. While I suspect that there are some fairly inexpensive ways to fund this, let's assume that every school in America will need an operations manager, along the lines of the administrative organization chart used by Uncommon and KIPP. If half the 99,000 schools in America needed to hire someone not already on staff, at a cost of $80,000 a year in salary and benefits, the cost would be in the neighborhood of $4 billion a year.

Luckily, that same $4 billion also frees the principals to execute the third key: providing feedback on the $1 billion worth of data collected in service of the first key. Annual net cost? Zero.

At a first approximation, reducing the size of America's schools looks like an expensive proposition. Then again, so is keeping them as big as they are. Building schools costs serious money. There are currently about 99,000 elementary, middle, and high schools in the United States. If, as predicted by the Census Bureau, the U.S. school-age population increases by 20 million or so over the next forty years (which is the average lifetime for a typical school) and 90 percent continue to attend public school, we're going to need space for some 18 million more students. If they were built to accommodate 600 kids each, that would translate into 750 new schools every year just for the additional growth. And if schools need to be replaced or renovated every forty years or so, then a quarter of 1 percent of the country's existing schools, just under 2,500 of them, will need to be rebuilt or renovated every year.

Just like the rest of America's infrastructure, schools aren't being built or rebuilt at anything like the speed needed to keep up with this schedule. Even so, in 2011, we still spent more than $12 billion on projects completed during the year (this is down from an average of $20 billion a year between 2000 and 2008) and about the same amount on projects that will be finished in 2012. But despite the economies-of-scale argument that high schools need to be as big as possible in order to make that budget go as far as possible, the "2012 Annual School Construction Report" admits "that the median cost per student in larger schools (with 1,600 to 2,500 students) was *more* than for smaller ones (fewer than 725 students), as was cost per square foot" (emphasis added). I don't expect the United States to build 10,000 new high schools over the next decade just to get average school size down to the point that principals and other instructional leaders can implement all the other gap-closing tenets. But, since it's actually even cheaper on a per-student basis to build a school for 700 kids than one for 2,000, why shouldn't we expect that new schools should be smaller than the ones they replace?

Still, there's going to be *some* incremental cost to reducing school size. However, if it's restricted to the places where it can help the most—the lowest-performing quartile of middle and high schools—that increment can't possibly be more than an additional 25 percent, since it would be for building schools that represent a quarter of potential construction. In current dollars, this is approximately $5.5 billion annually.

The final key—adding hours on-task to the school year—isn't free, either. Time is money, and increasing instructional hours by 40 percent—adding 500 hours to a school year that currently averages around 1,200—is going to cost. Not just in salaries for hourly employees, but operations and maintenance, too, since it costs more for the lights to be on for ten hours a day than it does for seven. The schools that are currently keeping their students in school for five hundred additional hours a year aren't generally paying their teachers significantly more for their time; but while the effect size seems to be scalable, the economics probably aren't. Existing teachers are going to want raises, and since their salaries currently represent more than $200 billion annually, paying them for a 40 percent increase in hours is going to run into the billions very quickly. Some cities have been able to institute a longer school day and year by increasing the total school budget by about 6 to 7 percent. The Massachusetts Expanded Learning Time Initiative increased school time by 30 percent and budgets by 20 percent. If that increase were applied to a quarter of the taxpayer-funded K–12 education in the United States, it would cost about an additional $10–20 billion a year, which is serious money no matter who's doing the counting.

And let's not forget summer. Alejandro Gac-Artigas's Springboard Collaborative is as cost-effective as any summer program in the country. Making it national might cut the per-student cost in half, but that would still mean that offering it to the 10 million elementary and secondary school students occupying the lowest achievement quintile would cost $4.5 billion annually.

Then there's preschool. In his 2013 State of the Union Address, President Obama called on Congress to fund universal pre-K education. Whatever you think of this particular priority (and I'm persuaded that it is likely to offer most of its benefits to the most disadvantaged families), it is definitely going to be expensive, especially if it's offered to everyone. The Center for American Progress estimates that the annual cost for offering a quality preschool education for every three- and four-year-old in the United States—free to every family at or under 200 percent of the poverty threshold, at a sliding scale for everyone above it—would be $12.3 billion a year in federal money alone, and probably another $7–8 billion in the state contributions that would qualify them for matching funds. Call it $20 billion a year if offered to everyone.

By my amateur calculations, the total for taking all of these practices nationally could, therefore, run into quite a tab: somewhere between $45 billion and $50 billion a year. This is applying the tenets to just those schools on the wrong side of the achievement gap.

I could minimize this by pointing out that it still represents an increase of less than 10 percent of America's existing education budget. Or less than 10 percent of the money we're spending on national defense. The opportunities for finding some money to offset the costs of the tenets by increasing class size look more promising. Increasing the average enrollment in a typical classroom would save more than $10 billion annually for each student added. This means that adding three more kids to each classroom—this is the difference between class sizes in the average elementary school in New York (18 per class) and Colorado (21.2)—would save some $30 billion annually. Most of the cost could be borne by allowing American class sizes to grow to the level they were at thirty years ago (with the added bonus that we could instigate this growth by removing the bottom-performing 8 percent of teachers and not replacing them at all). And this is exactly what I would recommend. This means the bill would be about $15 billion a year.

But there's a far better argument for spending the money. It isn't the amount of money it *costs* that matters. It's the amount of money it *generates*. Remember that fairly modest increases in performance—the equivalent of a twenty-five point improvement on the PISA assessment, which would raise the level currently occupied by America's lowest-achieving 20 percent of schools to the level of our second-lowest-achieving 20 percent—would add $130 billion a year to the country's GDP, every year of the working lives of the graduates of those schools. And that's the worst case; there are some compelling economic calculations that put the annual increase at close to a trillion dollars.

I have to think that, after three years of finding so many examples of irrational behavior, deciding not to invest $15 a year for twelve years in order to possibly generate between $115 and $1,000 a year for every year thereafter might be the most crazily irrational decision of all.

If you date the start of this investigation to that long-ago scholarship dinner, we began looking at education reform more than four years before Kevin Fosnocht and the Social Genius got me focused on a system. It was even longer before I started thinking about an evidence-based system for closing the achievement gap. While my thinking on the subject has evolved a lot since then, I can't really say high-profile policy-makers are inspiringly aware of the information.

There's some good news out of Washington. The Race to the Top initiative championed by President Obama and his Secretary of Education, Arne Duncan, is definitely one item. So is the Common Core curriculum, which was the brainchild of a combination of governors, corporate executives, and state superintendents of education, all of them believing that one of the necessary components of reforming American education generally, and closing the achievement gap specifically, was a national set of standards. When the standards for English Language Arts were issued in 2010, they included a lot of requirements: for example, that the schools teach a lot of writing, including practice in basic, five-paragraph essays. The

math standards were more specific: eight principles of math-
ematical practice; specific grade-by-grade content up through
grade 8, plus six more conceptual categories in high school.

Nonetheless, during the 2012 election, school reform was
talked about hardly at all, and when it was, it usually came
down to the old debate about "school choice." The GOP plat-
form was still built on the shaky bit of wishful thinking that
says if you give families vouchers, they'll somehow select the
schools that are best for their kids. They didn't offer much in
the way of real-world evidence that this would work, mostly
because it doesn't exist. Even if parents in inner-city Philadelphia actually had enough data to know whether one school
offered a better education than another, and even if they were
free to select the best from a menu that included every school
in the Greater Philadelphia region, that still isn't going to put
that school within a reasonable distance from their homes.
Market-based competition doesn't even put great supermar-
kets in inner cities; it sure isn't going to magically produce
great schools.

And they need them.

When I visited Green Dot's Animo Leadership High
School in February, it was the heat of college acceptance season. I stood in their seniors' college prep class and realized
I was seeing the endgame. From visiting Branch Brook Pre-K
to here, this was what it was about. I saw seniors in groups
of four huddled over college applications—above their heads,
paper stars hanging from the ceiling with each of their names.
Attached to each star, the names of the colleges that had offered them acceptance. The names of thirty to forty colleges
twirled above their heads. As Julio the principal told me, "If
we want them to be citizens and have a responsibility as
citizens, then they have to be educated as citizens." And that
means college.

My daughter was starting the college process, and there was no difference between her and these students, and that is the way it should be.

In the first chapter of this book, I quoted America's second president, John Adams, one of my heroes, on America's national obligation to spread "the opportunities and advantages of education." Seven years after he wrote those words, he put his thoughts even more precisely in a letter to a sympathetic English nobleman, Matthew Robinson-Morris, Baron Rokeby.

Rokeby was a notorious eccentric even in a country that makes a fetish of eccentricity. But he also wrote pamphlets supporting the American revolutionaries, and when Adams was posted to the Court of St. James's as the United States' first ambassador, he began a correspondence with him. On March 23, 1786, he wrote his new friend a letter that said, in part,

> There is room to hope that mankind will one day arrive at a great degree of perfection in the Sciences and art of Government, when it shall no longer be thought a divine science . . . But before any great things are accomplished, a memorable change must be made in the system of Education, and knowledge must become so general as to raise the lower ranks of Society nearer to the higher. The Education of a Nation, instead of being confined to a few schools & Universities, for the instruction of the few, must become the National Care and expense, for the information of the Many . . .

A memorable change. After meeting with dozens of men and women fighting for America's students, after reading hundreds of articles and books, and seeing, over and over again, how the practice of five tenets can close the country's educational achievement gap, I definitely experienced a memorable change in my own attitudes. But if that's all that this exercise changed, I'm going to be extremely disappointed.

I got schooled, for sure. My dream is that hundreds and thousands, even millions, of other people will, too. That's how Adams's memorable change can finally become a reality.

THE FIVE KEYS

No Roadblock Teachers

The Right Balance of Leadership

Feedback

Smaller Schools

More Time in School

FIFTY SCHOOLS THAT ARE CLOSING AMERICA'S ACHIEVEMENT GAP

Below is a list of fifty schools—elementary and secondary—that are closing the achievement gap. Every school on this list is there because:

- At least 65% of its students are from families poor enough to qualify for a free or reduced-price lunch.
- It admits students nonselectively, or by open enrollment.
- Its performance, as measured by academic outcomes, is above local and state averages.
- The five tenets are central to the success of these schools.

SCHOOL	LOCATION	CHARTER	AFFILIATION	ACADEMIC OUTCOMES
Achievement First Amistad High School	New Haven, CT	Y	Achievement First	On the Connecticut Academic Performance Test (CAPT), the school's 10th-graders outperform their peers in New Haven by 36 percentage points and their statewide peers by 9 percentage points.

SCHOOL	LOCATION	CHARTER	AFFILIATION	ACADEMIC OUTCOMES
Achievement First Brooklyn High School	New York, NY	Y	Achievement First	Students outperformed their district peers by 30 percentage points and their statewide peers by 18 percentage points on the 2012 New York Regents Exams in 10th and 11th grades.
Achievement First Crown Heights Middle School	New York, NY	Y	Achievement First	On the New York State tests, 8th-graders outperformed their district peers by 28 percentage points and their statewide peers by 12 percentage points.
Achievement First East New York Middle School	New York, NY	Y	Achievement First	77% of students scored Proficient or Above on the 7th-grade New York State test, compared with 35% in the district and 59% statewide.
Akili Academy	New Orleans, LA	Y	Independent	In 2012, 95% of Akili's 4th-graders passed the state's LEAP tests, outperforming the state average by 3% in math and 9% in ELA. In 2011, Akili's 3rd grade students achieved the highest scores in the Recovery School District (RSD).
Amistad Academy Elementary School	New Haven, CT	Y	Achievement First	At the beginning of the elementary school's first year of operation in 2006, only 4% of kindergarten scholars were reading at or above grade level; by the end of the year, the percentage had risen to 99%. On the 2012 Connecticut Mastery Test, the school's 4th-graders outperformed their New Haven peers by 20 percentage points.

SCHOOL	LOCATION	CHARTER	AFFILIATION	ACADEMIC OUTCOMES
Amistad Academy Middle School	New Haven, CT	Y	Achievement First	The school was named Connecticut's 2006 Title I Distinguished School after having the greatest performance gains of any middle school in the state. On the 2012 Connecticut Mastery Test, AA 8th-graders outperformed their New Haven peers by 40 percentage points and their statewide peers by 16 percentage points.
Animo Leadership Charter High School	Los Angeles, CA	Y	Green Dot	In 2011, the Growth Academic Performance Index score was 806; an improvement from 688 in 2007.
Animo Pat Brown Charter High School	Los Angeles, CA	Y	Green Dot	In 2011, the Growth Academic Performance Index score was 794, compared with a state score of 788. This places the school in the top third of all schools statewide for progress in spite of its economically disadvantaged student population.
Branch Brook Elementary School	Newark, NJ	N	District	In third grade, 85% of Branch Brook students achieved proficiency on New Jersey state reading tests compared with the state average of 81%. In math, 93% of Branch Brook students achieved proficiency in state tests, compared with the state average of 78%.
Burlington K–8 Campus	Los Angeles, CA	Y	Camino Nuevo	Burlington's outcomes place it in the top 10% of similar schools and in the top 30% of schools statewide. The API score is 824, reflecting the fact that the school outperforms the Los Angeles Unified School District (LAUSD) by 22% in math and 8% in ELA in 8th grade.

SCHOOL	LOCATION	CHARTER	AFFILIATION	ACADEMIC OUTCOMES
Camino Nuevo Charter High School	Los Angeles, CA	Y	Camino Nuevo	Camino Nuevo earned an API Similar Schools Rank of 10 for its K–8 and high school in 2009–10, placing it in the top 10% of all schools serving a similar demographic population. When comparing Camino Nuevo schools against all schools statewide, it places in the top 30th percentile. 99% of the class of 2012 graduated and 88% of 2012 graduates were accepted to four-year colleges. CNHS was recognized with the Title I Academic Achievement Award by the California Department of Education and ranks in the top 15% of all LAUSD high schools.
FirstLine Schools Arthur Ashe	New Orleans, LA	Y	FirstLine	In the 2012 state test (LEAP), Ashe 8th-graders outperformed the state average in three out of four subjects (ELA, math, and science). Ashe's 8th-graders had the highest math scores of any open-admissions school in New Orleans.
IDEA College Preparatory Donna	Donna, TX	Y	IDEA Public Schools	In the 2010–11 Texas Assessment of Knowledge and Skills (TAKS) test, these percentages of students performed at Proficient or Above: reading, 95%; math, 92%; writing, 96%. Donna is rated as Exemplary by the Texas Education Agency.

SCHOOL	LOCATION	CHARTER	AFFILIATION	ACADEMIC OUTCOMES
IDEA College Preparatory Mission	Mission, TX	Y	IDEA Public Schools	In the 2010–11 Texas Assessment of Knowledge and Skills (TAKS) test, these percentages of students performed at Proficient or Above: reading, 95%; math, 92%; writing, 97%. Mission is rated as Exemplary by the Texas Education Agency.
IDEA Frontier College Prep	Brownsville, TX	Y	IDEA Public Schools	In the 2010–11 Texas Assessment of Knowledge and Skills (TAKS) test, these percentages of students performed at Proficient or Above: reading, 98%; math, 97%; writing, 100%. Frontier College Prep is rated as Exemplary by the Texas Education Agency.
IDEA San Juan	San Juan, TX	Y	IDEA Public Schools	In the 2010–11 Texas Assessment of Knowledge and Skills (TAKS) test, these percentages of students performed at Proficient or Above: reading, 96%; math, 95%; writing, 99%. San Juan is rated as Exemplary by the Texas Education Agency.
IDEA Weslaco	Weslaco, TX	Y	IDEA Public Schools	In the 2010–11 Texas Assessment of Knowledge and Skills (TAKS) test, these percentages of students performed at Proficient or Above: reading, 92%; math, 94%; writing, 96%.

SCHOOL	LOCATION	CHARTER	AFFILIATION	ACADEMIC OUTCOMES
Jim Thorpe Elementary School	Santa Ana, CA	N	District	The percentage of students scoring at Proficient or Above is 76% in ELA and 86% in math compared with a district average of 43% and 47%, respectively. The school's API is 901, placing it in the highest 20% of schools in the state.
John F. Kennedy Elementary School	Houston, TX	N	District	In the 5th grade, students achieved 95% proficiency or above in math TAKS and 98% in reading. It is rated as Exemplary by the state.
Kearny International Business School	San Diego, CA	N	District	The school has improved its API by over 250 points in seven years to its 2012 score of 887. It has been nominated as a 2013 Blue Ribbon School, and listed as a California Distinguished School. Graduates have gone on to study at Harvard, Brandeis, UC Berkeley, and many others.
KIPP 3D Academy	Houston, TX	Y	KIPP	The school is rated as Exemplary by the state. Students enter KIPP 3D Academy in 5th grade with scores below the Houston Independent School District standards in reading, math, science, and social science. By the 6th grade, and continuing into the 7th and 8th grades, they have overtaken the HISD percentages of commended performance. They have also outperformed the number of students statewide who have achieved the standard or received commended performance.

SCHOOL	LOCATION	CHARTER	AFFILIATION	ACADEMIC OUTCOMES
KIPP Adelante Preparatory Academy	San Diego, CA	Y	KIPP	NCUST winner 2009. 63% of students make over one year of progress in math and 56% in reading in a single academic year. By the time the students reach 8th grade, they have overturned the 32% achievement gap in ELA from 5th grade, outperforming the school district by 7%.
KIPP Houston High School	Houston, TX	Y	KIPP	KHHS outperforms students from the Houston Independent School District in ELA, reading, math, social studies, and science in grades 9 through 11. It is rated as Exemplary by the State of Texas.
KIPP Infinity	New York, NY	Y	KIPP	64% of students make over one year of progress in math and 63% in reading in a single academic year. By the time the students reach 8th grade, the school has increased the percentage of Proficient or Above students by 21%. 86% of students achieve the same level in math; twice the number of the New York School District.
KIPP Tech Valley	Albany, NY	Y	KIPP	Students in KIPP Tech Valley outperform the school district students by 29% in ELA and 47% in math in the 8th grade. The percentage of students making 1+ years of academic progress in 2010–11: reading, 62%; math, 56%.

SCHOOL	LOCATION	CHARTER	AFFILIATION	ACADEMIC OUTCOMES
Lauderbach Elementary	Chula Vista, CA	N	District	Lauderbach's API is 860, compared with the state API of 788. The students beat the district performance in math and are comparable in reading despite a 35% difference in free and reduced-price lunch eligibility.
Leadership Prep Bedford Stuyvesant Elementary Academy	New York, NY	Y	Uncommon Schools	96% of students achieved Proficient or Advanced on the 2012 New York state assessments, compared with 78% statewide. In 2012, students closed the achievement gap in math by outperforming the city's and state's black and white students.
MC2 STEM High School	Cleveland, OH	N	District	MC2 STEM High School was a National Center for Urban School Transformation award winner in 2012. Over 80% of the students are proficient in science, mathematics, reading, and writing.
North Star Academy High School	Newark, NJ	Y	Uncommon Schools	100% of 11th-graders scored Proficient or Advanced on their ELA and math exams. The NSAHS Class of 2013 outperformed black and white students nationally on all sections of the SAT, and 100% of North Star's high school graduates have been accepted into a four-year college degree program.

SCHOOL	LOCATION	CHARTER	AFFILIATION	ACADEMIC OUTCOMES
North Star Academy Schools	Newark, NJ	Y	Uncommon Schools	The North Star schools in Newark reversed the achievement gap in math in 3rd, 4th, 7th, and 8th grades by an average of 12%. In ELA in grade 8, North Star schools outperformed the state average by 16% and New Jersey white students by 8%. North Star Academy was a winner of the 2011 National Blue Ribbon Award for Excellence.
North Star Vailsburg Elementary	Newark, NJ	Y	Uncommon Schools	The scores for ELA were 98% and 97%, respectively, outperforming every other student group in the city, district, and state.
Otay Elementary	Chula Vista, CA	N	District	A NCUST winner in 2012. Three-quarters of students are English learners from low-income families, yet nearly 70% of students are Proficient or Above in English-language arts, and over 80% have reached or exceeded grade-level standards in math, outperforming other schools from more affluent communities of the district. The school's API is 871.
Port Houston Elementary	Houston, TX	N	Houston Independent School District	The school is rated Exemplary by the TEA. 100% of its students achieve proficiency in ELA and math by the 6th grade.
Promise Academy, Harlem Children's Zone	New York, NY	Y	Harlem Children's Zone	100% of 3rd-graders at both Promise Academies scored at or above grade level on the math exam, outperforming their peers in the city and state. In 2008, 93% of Promise Academy High School 9th-graders passed the statewide algebra Regents exam.

SCHOOL	LOCATION	CHARTER	AFFILIATION	ACADEMIC OUTCOMES
Rochester Prep Middle School—West Campus & Brooks Campus	Rochester, NY	Y	Uncommon Schools	The longer the students are taught at Rochester Prep, the more significant the gains: In 2012, the math scores in grades 6, 7, and 8 reversed the statewide achievement gap by an average of 12 percentage points. By 6th grade, 75% of Rochester Prep students outperform the state in reading and continue to outperform the state in 7th and 8th grades.
Roxbury Preparatory	Boston, MA	Y	Uncommon Schools	In 2012, 80% of 8th-graders scored Advanced or Proficient in the state math exam, compared to a statewide score of 53%. In 2012, Roxbury Prep 8th-graders reversed the achievement gap by outperforming the state and white average on the state MCAS exams in math and ELA.
Solano Avenue Elementary School	Los Angeles, CA	N	District	A National Blue Ribbon Award winner in 2009. In 2011, it had an API of 922, outperforming all schools of similar characteristics in the state.
Success Academy Harlem 1	New York, NY	Y	Success Academies	96% of Success Academy scholars passed the 2012 state math exam. Success Academies rank in the top 1% of all schools in New York State. Students from Success Academy outperformed the state average by 31% in math and 33% in English. 91% scored Advanced in science compared to the city average of 43%. Recipient of the Blue Ribbon Award for academic excellence.

SCHOOL	LOCATION	CHARTER	AFFILIATION	ACADEMIC OUTCOMES
Trinidad Garza Early College High School	Dallas, TX	N	District	Garza ECHS was a NCUST award winner in 2012. Garza ECHS has a Recognized performance rating from the Texas Education Agency with Commended on reading/English language arts, mathematics, and social studies. 96% of students pass the Texas Assessment of Knowledge and Skills.
Troy Prep Middle School	Troy, NY	Y	Uncommon Schools	Students at TPMS reverse the achievement gap in grades 6 and 7. In 2010–11, 100% of students were Advanced or Proficient in math in grade 7 on state assessments, compared with 76% of New York's white students.
Uncommon Charter High School	New York, NY	Y	Uncommon Schools	In 2012, Uncommon Charter High School students outperformed city and state scores on all Regents exams. The school also succeeded in closing the achievement gap on the math and writing sections of the SAT.
Uplift Education Peak Preparatory	Dallas, TX	Y	Uplift Education	100% of this school's graduates are accepted and enrolled in college. In 2010–11, all three of the schools—primary, middle, and high—were rated as Exemplary by the Texas Education Agency. Peak Prep's alumni include two Dell Scholars and one Gates Millennium Scholar.

SCHOOL	LOCATION	CHARTER	AFFILIATION	ACADEMIC OUTCOMES
Uplift Education Summit International Preparatory	Arlington, TX	Y	Uplift Education	In the 2010–11 Texas Assessment of Knowledge and Skills (TAKS) test, these percentages of students performed at Proficient or Above: reading, 95%; math, 99%; science, 92%. It is rated as Exemplary by the TEA.
Uplift Education Williams Preparatory	Dallas, TX	Y	Uplift Education	In the 2010–11 Texas Assessment of Knowledge and Skills (TAKS) test, these percentages of students performed at Proficient or Above: reading, 97%; math, 97%; science, 95%. It is rated as Exemplary by the TEA.
Valor Academy	Los Angeles, CA	Y	Independent	Valor Academy's API for 2010–11 was 850, outperforming the average of all schools in the LAUSD by 122 points. On the Stanford 10 tests, which test students based on national standards, Valor Academy students, on average, made approximately two years of academic growth in one year.
Washington Heights Expeditionary Learning School	New York, NY	Y	Expeditionary Learning Schools	Most students enter the 6th grade at WHEELS significantly below grade level in reading. Students make on average five years of growth in three years of school. The NYC Department of Education rated this school as an A, reflecting its placement in the 96th percentile of NYC middle schools.

SCHOOL	LOCATION	CHARTER	AFFILIATION	ACADEMIC OUTCOMES
Williamsburg Collegiate	New York, NY	Y	Uncommon Schools	96% of Williamsburg Collegiate 8th-grade students scored Advanced or Proficient on the 2010 New York State math exam and 70% of the same cohort scored Advanced or Proficient on the 2009 New York State ELA exam. In 2009, the school's inaugural 8th-grade class scored Advanced or Proficient on the ELA exam, as compared to the 57% average in the city and the 51% average in the district. WCCS is one of four New York City charter schools that start in middle school where 100% of 8th-graders earned Advanced or Proficient scores on the NYS math exam in 2009.
YES Prep North Central	Houston, TX	Y	YES Prep	A National Blue Ribbon Award winner. The Department of Education awards the Blue Ribbon distinction to schools that serve as a national model and have dramatically increased student performance. TEA Rating: Exemplary (2004, 2006, 2007, 2008, 2009, 2010, 2011).
YES Prep South East	Houston, TX	Y	YES Prep	A National Blue Ribbon Award winner. TEA Rating: Exemplary (2007, 2008, 2009, 2010, 2011).

These schools are exemplary, and we know there are lots more like them. Since we're always looking to shine a light on the most effective schools, and the most successful practices, if you know of a school that should be on this list, please let us know by contacting us through our website: www.mnsfoundation.org.

A SHORT NOTE ON STATISTICAL SIGNIFICANCE, STANDARD DEVIATION, AND EFFECT SIZE

When we started the literature review under James Richardson, we considered a couple of different ways of scoring the results—different standards that could be used to compare the conclusions of one study with another. One candidate we considered using was a concept that shows up a lot in educational research but isn't usually explained very well: statistical significance.

Statistical significance is the probability that something didn't happen randomly. It works this way: Whenever a correlation is observed, such as getting heartburn after eating Thai food, you're not allowed to assume that the first event caused the second. Instead, you have to assume that the observed effect is random—statisticians call it the "null hypothesis"—and then you calculate the likelihood that it isn't. If you've "disproved the null hypothesis," you've found that the two phenomena are correlated: that you're more likely to get heartburn when you eat Thai food than when you don't.

This statistical association doesn't mean that eating Thai food *caused* the heartburn. Correlation isn't causation. It's just as likely, statistically speaking, that people who are about to get heartburn also develop a big appetite for pad thai. Even so, finding correlations is important in any kind of research, which means that scientists need a benchmark to understand when a correlation exists. The concept that is used to determine the significance of a correlation is another one of those terms that intimidate us nonmathematicians: standard deviation from the mean.

Standard deviation isn't all that complicated, once you understand what it's trying to measure, which is the distance between observed effects and the mean effect, which is just another word for the arithmetic average. For example, think about these three series of ten numbers:

$$1, 2, 3, 4, 5, 6, 7, 8, 9, 10$$

$$4, 4, 4, 5, 5, 6, 6, 6, 7, 8$$

$$1, 1, 1, 1, 1, 10, 10, 10, 10, 10$$

The average number for each group is exactly the same: 5.5. But it's clear that the three sets of numbers describe very different phenomena. In the first example, the numbers are evenly spread between one and ten; in the second, they are clustered together; and in the last one everything is at one end or the other of the series. Standard deviation quantifies this discrepancy by measuring the amount of dispersion among the numbers. To calculate the standard deviation (or SD) you measure the distance of each number from the average—which in each example is 5.5, as noted—square it (to avoid negative numbers), then calculate the average of all the numbers you have squared, and then take the square root of that figure.

For the first example this would be:

$$(1 - 5.5)^2 = (-4.5)^2 = 20.25$$

$$(2 - 5.5)^2 = (-3.5)^2 = 12.25$$

$$(3 - 5.5)^2 = (-2.5)^2 = 6.25$$

$$(4 - 5.5)^2 = (-1.5)^2 = 2.25$$

$$(5 - 5.5)^2 = (-.5)^2 = .25$$

$$(6 - 5.5)^2 = (.5)^2 = .25$$

$$(7 - 5.5)^2 = (1.5)^2 = 2.25$$

$$(8 - 5.5)^2 = (2.5)^2 = 6.25$$

$$(9 - 5.5)^2 = (3.5)^2 = 12.25$$

$$(10 - 5.5)^2 = (4.5)^2 = 20.25$$

The average of all those numbers is 8.25; and the standard deviation is 2.87. This is the standard deviation from the mean for this series of numbers.* Do the same thing to the third set of numbers, and the SD is 4.5. And the second set, the tightly clustered one? Its SD is only 1.28. The smaller the standard deviation, the more clustered the results; the bigger the standard deviation, the more dispersed. This means that the numbers in the second series have the least deviation from one another while those in the third series have the greatest deviation—something you could tell by looking at the series but that we have now quantified.

Most distributions aren't as tightly clustered as example number two, or as spread out as number three. A "normal" distribution, one that creates the bell-shaped curve that describes everything from IQ tests to SAT results, has about the same population at either end of the curve, with most results clustered around the middle. This kind of symmetrical distribution—one where a little more than two-thirds of all results fall within a single standard deviation (+/−1) on either side of the mean, another quarter or so within two SDs, and less than 5 percent more than two SDs away—is the key to understanding statistical significance. In order to conclude that a phenomenon—let's say, that the graduates of a particular charter school have higher SAT scores—isn't just a random event, statisticians have come to a consensus that if the event has an SD of 2.0 or greater, then it is statistically significant. Why 2.0? Because an event with an SD of 2.0 or greater could be expected to happen only one time in twenty by sheer happenstance. For example, the portion lying +/−2.0 SD represents 4.4 percent of the total.

---

* Technically, this is the *population* standard deviation.

Everyone's favorite example of this phenomenon is coin tossing. No one thinks twice about throwing heads six times out of ten; but if you get heads seven times out of ten, is it statistically significant? Is the coin rigged? No, because an easy calculation tells you to expect seven heads out of ten about 12 percent of the time.

Well, then, if seven heads out of ten is just coincidence, how about eight heads? The same arithmetic shows that this is likely to happen only a little more than 4 percent of the time. That, of course, is less than 5 percent, so you can confidently state that you have found a statistically significant result, one that occupies the far end of the bell curve. (Sometimes, you'll see a study in which the "confidence interval" is given as 99 percent, which represents three standard deviations from the mean. This is a higher level of statistical significance than is commonly used and than we use in this book.)

It's important to know whether a particular study found an effect that was just coincidental, like throwing heads seven times out of ten. You can get a statistically significant result just as easily with a big effect on a small sample as with a small effect on a big sample. It can be just as statistically significant when a class of 20 fifth-graders increase their math scores by ten points as when the 2,000 fifth-graders in a school district increase their scores by one point.

But statistical significance doesn't say diddly about the *size* of the effect you're measuring. All it does is tell you whether it occurred by chance. When a poll tells you that the candidate in one upcoming election has a twelve-point lead, and the candidate in another has a four-point lead, both estimates can be just as statistically significant—unlikely to have occurred by chance—but they're obviously reporting different things. Since I wasn't just interested in *whether* something moved the needle on achievement, but in *how far*, I needed to look beyond measuring statistical significance.

What I was looking for, James Richardson told me, was something called "effect size."

A quick trip to an elementary—a *very* elementary—statistics textbook told me that effect size is "the mean change in a variable divided by the standard deviation of that variable." Here's an example: Imagine that you wanted to know whether kids learn better in the morning or the afternoon. You decide to divide a class of twenty students in two, read half of them a story at 9 A.M., and the other half the same story at 3 P.M. Two hours after each group heard the story, you then give them a test of twenty questions to find out how well they remembered it.

Let's say the afternoon group averaged 17.8 correct answers, while the morning group got only 15.2 right. From this, you could say that the *effect* of afternoon instruction was +2.6.

And, you might think this was a clear argument for afternoon learning. But, just like those series of numbers above, you can get these averages two different ways. The first way, everyone in the afternoon group scored 17, 18, or 19 on the test, and all the morning kids got either 14, 15, or 16.

Morning group (average 15.2): 14, 14, 15, 15, 15, 15, 16, 16, 16, 16

Afternoon group (average 17.8): 17, 17, 17, 17, 18, 18, 18, 18, 19, 19

In this version, everyone who took the test after hearing the story at 3 o'clock did better than everyone who heard it at 9 o'clock. However, you can get exactly the same average scores if the afternoon group had some kids who scored 12 and 13, and some who scored 20. And that would mean something very different.

Morning group: 11, 12, 13, 13, 14, 14, 18, 19, 19, 19

Afternoon group: 12, 13, 14, 16, 16, 17, 17, 18, 19, 20

If your experiment got results like version number one, you'd probably think that the +2.6 improvement was entirely due to the time of day, since there was no overlap at all between the morning and afternoon groups: same story, similar kids, different results. Kids learn better in the afternoon. Slam dunk.

But what if your results looked more like version number two? In that one, four of the kids who heard the story in the morning actually did better than seven of the kids who heard it in the afternoon. In that case, it would be a lot harder to conclude that all kids learn better in the afternoon. Two versions, two different conclusions. What effect size does is assign a (relatively) simple score to the difference.

Effect size is calculated by subtracting the average score of one group—in this case, "morning listeners"—from the average score of another: "afternoon listeners"; and then dividing that figure by the standard deviation of the combined groups. In the example above, the standard deviation for version number one—the one where all the 3 o'clock kids did better than all the 9 o'clock kids—is small: only 1.5. No one in either group got a 12 or a 13; no one got a 20, either. In that case, the effect size is

$$(17.8 - 15.2)/1.5 = +1.73$$

Or, really, really big. It's the kind of effect size you get when your recipe works on almost everyone in almost exactly the same way. In this case, *just by hearing the story in the afternoon,* everyone did better when asked to recall it.

However, real-life experiments are never that clear-cut, mostly because there's almost always some other factor involved in addition to the one you're testing for. Some kids might actually do better in the morning, while others—the ones who skip breakfast, maybe—don't. Some kids do worse in the afternoon, especially if they're worn out from recess. Since there are always reasons for variations like these in test results, you're almost always going to see more scattered numbers—more deviation. In version number two, the standard deviation is 2.67, which translates to an effect size of

$$(17.8 - 15.2)/2.67 = +.97$$

Or a lot smaller—though still larger than what most research finds in the real world, where, as I learned, effect sizes tend to be more like +.2 or +.3 (and, a lot of the time, nonexistent).

But here's another way of understanding effect size: The difference in educational achievement between America's lowest-performing students and the students who are performing right in the middle is roughly one SD; sometimes lower, more frequently higher, depending on the particular skill being tested for, the students' age, and so on. The bigger the effect size of a particular practice, as revealed in well-designed and repeatable tests, the more it is narrowing the size of the standard deviation from the mean. The practices that do the most to shrink the size of the SD—the ones that show the largest results in populations of students who use that practice when compared to a control group that doesn't use it—make up the five keys.

ACKNOWLEDGMENTS

Many thanks to Eric Simonoff and Ari Emanuel for their representation. A particular thanks to Bill Rosen. Bill's fluency with research helped me get over my phobia of all things academic. His deep practicality (cynicism) was the perfect foil for my untested theories. I want to acknowledge the M. Night Shyamalan Foundation for funding the research for this book over five years, and I'd like to thank all the people who work at the foundation for their support and hard work. I want to thank Jenn Walters-Michalec, who helps run our foundation. She was constantly giving this book CPR and bringing it back to life. Jenn even titled the book. And thanks to James Richardson, my Hugh Grant–looking friend. His research and the countless times we talked made the book real. To Emily Zubernis and Elizabeth Soslau for contributing to the research. To Dom, Joanna, and China in my office for helping me with all the less glamorous aspects of writing a book. I want to thank Claire Robertson-Kraft for proofreading so meticulously. And to my attorneys, Marc H. Glick and Stephen Breimer, for watching over me.

Thank you so much to Bob Bender and Jon Karp at Simon & Schuster.

Also thanks go out to Kevin Fosnocht, Eric Hanushek, Richard Elmore, Karl Alexander, Jonah Rockoff, Robert Hughes, Ted Hershberg, Michelle Rhee, Wendy Kopp, Roland Fryer, Kate Walsh, Mike Wang, Marc Mannella, Jay Altman, Douglas Weston, Marjorie Rendell, and Susan and Bob Burch.

And finally to Dr. Bhavna Shyamalan. She was the one who brought public school education to my attention. Her training in research and statistics guided the book's academic standard. She probably should have been the one to write this book; it would have been much better. I got A's in college to impress her, and I think I wrote this book so she'd still think I am smart.

NOTES

CHAPTER ONE: AS JOHN ADAMS SAID . . .

PAGE

7 *the highest they've ever been:* Farhi, 2012.

7 *have improved every single time:* National Center for Education Statistics, 2011.

8 *the United States would lead the world:* Riddle, 2010.

9 *as students whose families have never fallen:* Hernandez, 2011.

9 *Every ten points is approximately equal:* National Center for Education Statistics, 2011.

9 *an almost unbelievable 32 percent:* Hernandez, 2011.

10 *as opposed to 91 percent everywhere else:* National Center for Education Statistics, 2011.

10 *Latino students four times more likely:* National Center for Education Statistics, 2011.

14 *"greater resources would be spent":* Rawls, 1971.

15 *". . . the preservation of [the people's] rights":* McCullough, 2002.

15 *"partly but not wholly paid by the public":* Smith, 1991.

15 *will not be able to exist without education:* de Tocqueville, 2011.

16 *"watch what happens to them after they leave school":*
Schleicher, 2010.
17 *Twenty-five points raises the score:* Ibid.

CHAPTER TWO: I'M NOT A DOCTOR,
BUT I WATCH A LOT OF *HOUSE, M.D.*

PAGE

23 *a few hundred have even been run:* Manzi, 2012.
23 *only one of them was a randomized field trial:* Boruch et al.,
2002.
27 *The overall effect size of charter schools:* CREDO, 2009.
28 *and 12 percent worse:* CREDO, 2010.
31 *an "insensitivity to numbers":* Finucane, 2000.
32 *95 percent of all educational interventions:* Hattie, 2009.
41 The effects most worth knowing about: Elmore, 2008.

CHAPTER THREE: WHY ISN'T *THAT* ON THE LIST?

PAGE

43 *the number-one choice for a change:* Rockoff, 2009. It was actually the first choice among people with children. It was the
second choice for people without children. They chose "more
discipline."
44 *so small that they were insignificant:* Rockoff, 2009.
44 might *have some small effects:* Hoxby, 2000.
45 *reducing class size has any noticeable impact:* Hoxby, 2000.
45 *In 1960, the average class size:* Krueger, 2002.
45 *(Private schools have lowered):* National Center for Education
Statistics, 2011. Worth noting is that these numbers include students in various special education programs, and that the average class size for other students may be higher.
45 *and 20 percent neutral:* Krueger, 2002. Only about a third of
the studies were even statistically significant. That is, of the
40 percent that were positive, only 14 percent were probably
more than just random noise.
46 *improvement in their subsequent educational achievement:*
Krueger, 2000.

47 *about twelve weeks' worth of additional schooling:* Mosteller, 1995. The tests used were the Stanford Achievement Test and the Tennessee Basic Skills First (BSF) test.

47 *more likely to take college prep tests:* Krueger, 2000.

50 *it didn't raise it, either:* Staiger, 2010.

51 *about $12 billion annually:* Chingos, 2011.

52 *nearly nine hundred times between them:* Mosteller, 1995, and Krueger, 2000. Just as a standard for comparison, the most cited article ever in the journal *Review of Research in Education* is a 1977 article by the statistician Gene Glass, which carries the stirring title "Integrating Findings: The Meta-Analysis of Research" and has been cited fewer than eight hundred times in more than thirty years.

56 *But the cost of that better year:* Hanushek, 2003.

56 *People have been taking potshots:* A good collection can be found in Baker, 2012.

56 *but there is literally no relationship:* Hanushek, 2009.

56 *real expenditures per pupil:* Hanushek, 2009.

57 *Special education explains only 20 percent:* Hanushek, 2003.

58 *no statistically significant impact at all:* Hanushek, 2003.

58 *spent more than $19 billion on them:* Hanushek, 2010.

58 *Virtually undetectable:* Goldhaber, 1997.

58 *There are studies showing that teacher performance:* Hanushek, 2010. Master's degrees in science and math had a positive effect. But 90 percent of master's degrees awarded to teachers are in Education programs.

59 *"extrinsic incentives bias":* Heath, 1999.

59 *about how much they were paid:* Buckingham, 1999.

62 *good public schools than a desire for choice:* Gutmann, 2003.

62 *but the vouchers have made:* Hoxby, 2002.

63 *the biggest "benefit":* Wolf, 2008.

64 *44th to 50th percentile after three to four years:* Wolf, 2008.

64 *as likely to be negative as positive:* Rouse, 2009.

64 *"not statistically different from zero":* Rouse, 2009.

64 *the less likely they were to take advantage:* Davies, 2011.

65 *the Woodside School Foundation raised $10 million:* Reich, 2005.

65 *Half of Ravenswood schools earn:* Reich, 2005.

66 *what Elmore calls the "overflow":* Elmore, 2000.

68 *even more than that of their* families: Rumberger, 2005.

68 *study's 600,000 students:* Borman, 2010, cited in Kahlenberg, 2013.

68 *attending a school with more affluent classmates:* Schwartz, 2010.

68 *pursuing some sort of socioeconomic integration:* Kahlenberg, 2013.

70 *or patterns of enrollment:* Hanushek, 2002.

71 *students do well on just about any test:* Elmore, 2008.

71 *fluctuations from one year to the next:* Kane, 2002.

72 *the state's improvement in the NAEP:* Kane, 2002.

CHAPTER FOUR:
MR. BRODINSKY, PLEASE SEE THE PRINCIPAL—
AND BRING YOUR SUITCASE

80 *exactly 149 unsatisfactory teachers:* Gates Foundation, 2010.

80 *named this "The Widget Effect":* Weisberg, 2009.

82 *the evidence on growth measures:* Rothstein et al., 2010, actually finds, in a meta-analysis, that only a third of the teachers who appeared in the top fifth in one year appeared there in the following year.

82 *about $106,000 in incremental income:* Staiger, 2010.

82 *One year with a great teacher:* Hanushek, 2010. The current average lifetime earnings in the U.S. have a present value of $1.16M, which means that improving one SD = between $12K and $24K. Obviously, the number is larger for larger classes.

83 *students who spend it with an average teacher:* Aaronson, 2007.

83 *zoom all the way to 60 percent:* Sanders, 1996.

84 *46,000 and 86,000 new teachers:* Hanushek, 2010, says that in 2000 some 86,000 recent graduates entered teaching, out of 107,000 graduating from ed school the year before. The BLS predicts that, from 2010 to 2020, the U.S. will hire 71,900 new high school teachers, 281,500 K–5th grade teachers, and 108,300 middle school teachers, for a total of 461,700. (They also predict 113,600 new pre-K hires, but these are jobs requiring only an associate's degree.)

84 *as $500,000 in lifetime earnings:* Staiger, 2010.

85 *almost completely random:* Aaronson, 2007. The total difference amounts to about 8 percent.

86 *95 percent of the time:* Haberman, 1995. Martin Haberman, Professor of Education at the University of Wisconsin–Milwaukee, and the eponymous founder of the Haberman Foundation, is an advocate of alternative certification for teachers and has written extensively about how to identify "star" teachers for urban schools. Haberman argues that alternative certification may be the most effective means of recruiting such teachers, based on their characteristics. His research indicates that the most effective teachers for urban schools share some common characteristics: Often they did not decide to teach until after college graduation, are between thirty and fifty years old, are parents themselves, and live in urban areas. Haberman argues that because alternative certification programs tend to offer abbreviated training, often cater to career changers, and are typically less expensive than traditional training, they are more likely to appeal to potential teachers who meet his criteria than are traditional programs. Even with all that, the impact is modest. Students of teachers who score a full standard deviation above the mean on the Haberman test tend to score only about .02 SD above the mean on their own tests. Rockoff, 2008.

87 *80 percent of school administrators:* Weisberg, 2009.

87 *we couldn't find much evidence:* Rockoff et al., 2008, does state that while "no single factor can predict success in teaching, using a broad set of measures can help schools improve the quality of their teachers."

89 *TFA corps members do just as well:* Decker, 2004, and Kane, 2008.

89 *or even a negative, effect:* Darling-Hammond et al., 2005; Laczko-Kerr, 2002.

93 *that change would achieve effect sizes:* Hanushek, 2010.

95 *or a failure that we didn't catch:* Schochet, 2010.

96 *"perfection by incantation":* Demsetz, 1969.

99 *assessments in math and English:* Kane, 2013. Specifically, the SAT 9 Open-Ended Reading Assessment and the Balanced Assessment in Mathematics developed at the Harvard Graduate School of Education.

100 *Another good model:* Kane, 2013.

103 *"You can't fire your way":* Darling-Hammond, 2011.

CHAPTER FIVE:
MAKING CLARK KENT INTO SUPERMAN

PAGE

113 *"in the absence of strong leadership":* Leithwood, 2008.

113 *managed to achieve a good rating:* McKinsey, 2007.

114 *the new teams increased their productivity:* Lazear, 2012.

114 *"teaching skills that persist":* Ibid.

114 *it reduced time away from the job:* Ibid.

116 *A principal in the lowest quartile:* Branch, 2012.

116 *"negative teacher selection":* Ibid.

117 *negative effect size of –.15:* Ibid.

117 *fourteen months of training for the position:* Clark, 2009.

118 *three fictional-but-plausible scenarios:* From the NYC Department of Education: http://schools.nyc.gov/Offices/DHR/Career Opportunities/Principal+Candidate+Pool.htm.

120 *the "illusion of skill":* Kahneman, 2011.

121 *buffer between instruction and outside interference:* Elmore, 2000.

121 *fewest number of hours of every administrator:* Ibid.

121 *"The effect of professional development":* Elmore, 2008.

123 *even how their teachers dress:* Peterson, 1998.

123 *teachers talk about in staff lounges:* Kottler, 1997.

125 *KIPP students were receiving:* Tuttle, 2010.

132 *giving students nicknames, for example:* Lemov, 2010.

CHAPTER SIX: YOU HAD ME AT "DATA"

PAGE

141 *but everything they thought might affect:* Feldman, 2001.

142 *surveyed twenty-six more:* Dembosky et al., 2006.

142 *Edison Schools, did the same:* Marsh, 2006. Only the RAND Pennsylvania study was focused entirely on data-driven instruction. The Institute for Learning study, for example, examined

four different areas, including curriculum, leadership, and coaching, as well as data-driven instruction.

144 *found no significant difference:* McCaffrey, 2007.

145 *"minimal use of the information":* Ibid.

145 *not unless you want the feedback loop:* Marsh, 2006.

146 *The organization you are imagining:* Elmore, 2008.

148 *how rigorous the lesson was:* Dobbie, 2011. Just to show how committed they were to objectivity, the lessons were coded using "Bloom's Taxonomy," a classification of curricular rigor originally developed more than fifty years ago.

149 *to track students:* Dobbie, 2011.

149 *about a quarter of the total effect:* Dobbie, 2011; see Table 7 for the regression analysis.

150 *nine of the lowest-performing schools in the city:* Fryer, 2012.

156 *textbooks plus supplementary materials:* Whitehurst, 2009.

156 *rank versus the other curricula:* Agodini et al., 2009.

156 *the winning curriculum choice:* Preschool Curriculum Evaluation Research Consortium, 2008.

CHAPTER SEVEN:
THAT'S RIGHT, I SAID IT. SMALL SCHOOLS

PAGE

167 *evidence of variability, not superiority:* Wainer and Zwerling, 2006; Wainer, 2007.

169 *more than 600 students:* NCES, 2011.

170 *the "high school movement":* Goldin, 2008.

170 *into vocational training programs:* Ibid.

172 *no bigger than 350:* CSPS, 2012.

173 *"a necessary but not sufficient condition":* Evan et al., 2006.

174 *the less likely you are to skip class:* Bowman, 2011.

174 *increasing graduation rates by more than 17 percent:* Schwartz, 2012.

175 *the average of other schools in the same districts:* Evan et al., 2006.

175 *though the same study couldn't find a causal link:* Wasley, 2000.

175 *a social relationship can be sustained:* Dunbar, 2010.

176 *whether the phenomenon can be replicated:* Evan et al., 2006. The actual numbers were 57 percent of students in small schools scoring better than their conventional counterparts in "English Language Arts," though only 24 percent did better in math.

176 *though the improvement was small:* Lee, 2007. Other research suggests that the relationship between high school size and math gain is curvilinear; that is, one that looks a little like a "U." In one study, students attending very small (< 674) or very large (> 2592) schools showed the largest improvement in their standardized math scores; the students in the middle showed the smallest. Werblow, 2009.

176 *an effect size of +.25 within two years:* Kuziemko, 2006.

178 *fewer than 8 percent actually apply:* Hoxby, 2012.

CHAPTER EIGHT:
DANNY, SEE ME AFTER SCHOOL . . . AND BEFORE . . .
AND OVER THE SUMMER

PAGE

188 *virtually impossible to catch up:* Hart, 1995.

189 *The effect size on vocabulary:* Schweinhart et al., 2005.

190 *effect sizes of +.75 in grades 1 through 4:* Garber, 1988.

190 *one in eight of the control group:* Campbell, 2002; Knudsen et al., 2006.

191 *versus 91 for the control group:* Garber, 1988.

192 *but no measurable effect on vocabulary:* Whitehurst, 2009.

193 *virtually no impact once they left:* Puma et al., 2010.

194 *true of the program as a whole:* Ramey, 2010.

195 *effect size of +1.2 by eighth grade:* Dobbie, 2009.

195 *Enrollment in Harlem Gems:* Ibid.

196 *can afford the "best" preschools:* Geoffroy et al., 2007.

196 *among dozens of such studies:* Doyle, 2009; Geoffroy et al., 2010.

196 *"choosing between all very good options":* Tucker-Drob, 2012; Wenner Moyer, 2013.

197 *by the third year after the program:* Leak et al., 2010.

198 *a month or more every summer:* Heyns, 1978; Heyns, 1987.

198 *accounted for more than half the difference:* Alexander, 2007.

198 *predicted by his score in the first grade:* Ibid.

198 *a 62 percent chance of staying there:* McKinsey, 2009.

199 *seventy-three-point gap by ninth grade:* Alexander, 2007.

199 *three-month difference, every summer:* Cooper, 1996.

201 *New York's were open all year:* Patall, 2010.

201 *only 165 days of six hours each:* The Chalkboard Project, 2008.

201 *"academic learning time":* Patall, 2010.

202 *other places, just the opposite:* The Chalkboard Project, 2008.

202 *21 percent more for the middle schools:* Dobbie, 2011.

202 *the increased instructional time:* Ibid.

204 *effect size of +.11 in schools:* Cooper, 2003. It should be noted that the authors of this study were critical of the overall quality of the data collection in these programs. Not really rigorous enough and, in any case, a modest effect size.

CHAPTER NINE:
SOMETHING ELSE JOHN ADAMS SAID . . .

PAGE

212 *education majors typically average:* Koedel, 2011.

222 *how well its students perform on any standardized tests:* Winkler, 2012.

232 *we spend more than $19 billion every year:* Hanushek, 2010.

233 *between $500 million and $1 billion annually:* West, 2013; Greene, 2013. This assumes paying professional scorers to evaluate four classroom sessions for approximately 3 million teachers annually, at a rate of $40 an hour.

234 *"that the median cost per student":* Abramson, 2012.

235 *budgets by 20 percent:* Patall, 2010.

236 *$10 billion annually for each student added:* Chingos, 2011.

237 *$130 billion a year to the country's GDP:* Schleicher, 2010.

239 *"the opportunities and advantages of education":* McCullough, 2002.

239 *for the information of the Many:* Adams, 1856.

APPENDIX B:
A SHORT NOTE ON STATISTICAL SIGNIFICANCE, STANDARD DEVIATION, AND EFFECT SIZE

PAGE

260 *"the mean change in a variable"*: Coe, 2002.

261 *find out how well they remembered it:* This is actually a simplified version of a real experiment, conducted in 1999, that involved 38 seven- and eight-year-olds in a Newcastle prep school. Dowson, 2000.

tion and Development of Middle School Teachers and Administrators. Charlotte, NC: Information Age Publishing.

Baker, B. 2012. *Revisiting That Age-Old Question: Does Money Matter in Education?* Albert Shanker Institute. Washington, DC: Albert Shanker Institute.

Ballou, D., and Michael Podgursky. 1997. *Teacher Pay and Teacher Quality*. Kalamazoo, MI: W. E. Upjohn Institute for Employment Research.

Bernatek, B. C. 2012. *Blended Learning in Practice: Case Studies from Leading Schools*. Michael and Susan Dell Foundation.

Booker, K., et al. 2007. The Impact of Charter School Attendance on Student Performance. *Journal of Public Economics* 91 (5–6), 849–76.

Booker, K. 2008. *Going Beyond Test Scores: Evaluating Charter School Impact on Educational Attainment in Chicago and Florida*. Santa Monica, CA: RAND Corporation.

Borman, G., et al. 2010. Schools and Inequality: A Multilevel Analysis of Coleman's Equality of Educational Opportunity Data. *Teacher's College Record* 112 (5), 1201–46.

Boruch, R., et al. 2002. The Importance of Randomized Field Trials. In R. Boruch and F. Mosteller, *Evidence Matters: Randomized Trials in Education Research*. Washington, DC: Brookings Institution Press.

Bowman, R. 2011. *Student Achievement, School Structure, and the Effects of Small Learning Community Implementation in Los Angeles: A Network Approach*. Pardee RAND Graduate School. Santa Monica, CA: RAND Corporation.

Boyd, D. G. 2005. *How Reduced Barriers to Entry Into Teaching Changes the Teacher Workforce and Affects Student Achievement*. Cambridge: National Bureau of Economic Research.

Bradley, R. H., & B. M. Caldwell. 1980. The Relation of Home Environment, Cognitive Competence, and IQ Among Males and Females. *Child Development* 51 (4), 1140–48.

Braeden, M. 2008. Teacher-Quality Gap Examined Worldwide. *Education Week* 27 (23), p. 5.

Branch, G. H. 2012. *Estimating the Effect of Leaders on Productivity: The Case of School Principals*. Cambridge: National Bureau of Economic Research.

BIBLIOGRAPHY

Aaronson, D. B. 2007. Teachers and Student Achievement in the Chicago Public High Schools. *Journal of Labor Economics* 25, 95–135.

Abramson, P. 2012. It's Still Billions of Dollars: The 2012 Annual School Construction Report. *School Planning & Management*.

Adams, J. 1856. *The Works of John Adams, Second President of the United States: With a Life of the Author, Notes and Illustrations.* Vol. 1. Boston: Little, Brown.

Agodini, R., et al. 2009. *Achievement Effects of Four Early Elementary School Math Curricula: Findings from First Graders in 39 Schools.* Institute for Education Sciences/National Center for Education Evaluation and Regional Assistance. Washington, DC: Department of Education.

Alexander, K. E. 2007. Lasting Consequences of the Summer Learning Gap. *American Sociological Review* 72, 167–180.

Allen, J. P. 2011. An Interaction-Based Approach to Enhancing Secondary School Instruction and Student Achievement. *Science* 333 (6045), 1034–37.

Alterman, E. 2008. *Why We're Liberals: A Political Handbook for Post-Bush America.* New York: Viking.

Andrews, P. G. 2000. *Leaders for a Movement: Professional Prepara-*

Braun, H. J. 2006. *Comparing Private Schools and Public Schools Using Hierarchical Linear Modeling*. National Center for Education Statistics.

Bryk, T. 2010. *Organizing Schools for Improvement: Lessons from Chicago*. Chicago: University of Chicago Press.

Buckingham, Marcus, and Curt Coffman. 1999. *First, Break All the Rules: What the World's Greatest Managers Do Differently*. New York: Simon & Schuster.

Campbell, F. A.-J. 2002. Early Childhood Education: Young Adult Outcomes from the Abecedarian Project. *Applied Developmental Science* 6 (1), 42–57.

The Chalkboard Project. 2008. *A Review of Research on Extended Learning Time in K–12 Schools*. Eugene, OR: The Chalkboard Project.

Chetty, R., et al. 2011. How Does Your Kindergarten Classroom Affect Your Income? Evidence from Project STAR. *Quarterly Journal of Economics* 126 (4), 1593–1660.

Chin, T. &. 2004. Social Reproduction and Childrearing Practices: Social Class, Children's Agency, and the Summer Activity Gap. *Sociology of Education* 77, 185–210.

Chingos, Matthew, & Grover J. "Russ" Whitehurst. 2011. *Class Size: What Research Says and What it Means for State Policy*. Washington, DC: Brookings Institution.

Clark, C. M. 2009. *School Principals and School Performance*. CALDER.

Coe, R. 2002. *It's the Effect Size, Stupid*. University of Durham, School of Education. Exeter: British Education Research Association.

Cooper, H. N. 1996. The Effects of Summer Vacation on Achievement Test Scores: A Narrative and Meta-Analytic Review. *Review of Educational Research* 66 (3), 227–68.

Cooper, H., et al. 2003. The Effects of Modified School Calendars on Student Achievement and on School and Community Attitudes. *Review of Educational Research* 73 (1), 1–52.

CREDO. 2009. *Multiple Choice: Charter School Performance in 16 States*. Palo Alto, CA: Stanford University.

CREDO. 2010. *Charter School Performance in New York City*. Palo Alto, CA: Hoover Institution/Stanford University.

CSPS. 2012. *Coalition of Small Preparatory Schools.* Retrieved Jan. 5, 2013, from http://smallschoolscoalition.com/?page_id=15.

Darling-Hammond, L., & P. Youngs. 2002. "Defining Highly Qualified Teachers": What Does Scientifically-Based Research Actually Tell Us? *Educational Researcher* 31 (9), 13–25.

Darling-Hammond, L., et al. 2005. Does Teacher Preparation Matter? Evidence About Teacher Certification, Teach for America, and Teacher Effectiveness. *Education Policy Analysis Archives* 13 (42), 1–48.

Darling-Hammond, L. 2011. *An Education Exchange Exploring How Teachers and Communities Work Together to Improve Teaching and Learning.* SCOPE—Stanford Center on Opportunity Policy and Education. Palo Alto, CA: SCOPE.

Davies, S., & J. Aurini. 2011. Exploring School Choice in Canada: Who Chooses What and Why? *Canadian Public Policy* 37 (4), 459–77.

de Tocqueville, A. 2011. *Democracy in America.* (H. Mansfield, ed.) Chicago: University of Chicago Press.

Deal, T., & K. D. Peterson. 1990. *Shaping School Culture: The Heart of Leadership.* San Francisco, CA: Jossey-Bass.

Decker, P. M. 2004. The Effects of Teach for America on Students: Findings from a National Evaluation. *Mathematics Policy Research Report*, 8792–750, pp. 1–51.

Dembosky, J. W., et al. 2006. *Data-Driven Decisionmaking in Southwestern Pennsylvania School Districts.* Santa Monica, CA: RAND Corporation.

Demsetz, H. 1969. Information and Efficiency: Another Viewpoint. *Journal of Law and Economics* 12, 1–22.

Dewey, J. 2000. *Liberalism and Social Action.* New York: Prometheus Books.

Dobbie, W., & R. G. Fryer. 2009. *Are High-Quality Schools Enough to Close the Achievement Gap? Evidence from a Bold Social Experiment in Harlem.* Harvard University. Cambridge, MA: National Bureau of Economic Research.

Dobbie, W. 2011. *Getting Beneath the Veil of Effective Schools: Evidence from New York City.* Cambridge, MA: National Bureau of Economic Research.

Dowson, V. 2000. *Time-of-Day Effects in School-Children's Imme-*

diate and Delayed Recall of Meaningful Material. Centre for Evaluation and Monitoring, Durham University. Durham: TERSE.

Doyle, O., et al. 2009. Investing in Early Human Development: Timing and Economic Efficiency. *Economics and Human Biology* 7 (1), 1–6.

Dunbar, R. 2010. *How Many Friends Does One Person Need?: Dunbar's Number and Other Evolutionary Quirks.* Cambridge, MA: Harvard University Press.

Durando, J. 2009, June 11. Kids Reap Benefits of Long School Year. *USA Today.*

Ehrenberg, R., and D. J. Brewer. 1994. Do School and Teacher Characteristics Matter? Evidence from High School and Beyond. *Economics of Education Review* 13 (1), 1–17.

Elmore, R. F. 2000. *Building a New Structure for School Leadership.* Washington, DC: Albert Shanker Institute.

Elmore, R. F. 2008. Leadership as the Practice of Improvement. In B. N. Pont, *Improving School Leadership.* Vol. 2: *Case Studies on System Leadership* (pp. 37–68). Geneva: OECD.

Evan, A., et al. 2006. *Evaluation of the Bill & Melinda Gates Foundation's High School Grants Initiative, 2001–2005 Final Report.* American Institutes for Research.

Farhi, P. 2012, April/May. Flunking the Test. *American Journalism Review.*

Feldman, J., & R. Tung. 2001. *Whole School Reform: How Schools Use the Data-Based Inquiry and Decision Making Process.* Center for Collaborative Education. American Educational Research Association.

Fetler, M. 1999. High School Staff Characteristics and Mathematics Test Results. *Education Policy Analysis Archives* 7 (9).

Finn, C. E. 2012, April. Why Principals Need More Authority. *The Atlantic.*

Finucane, M. A. 2000. The Affect Heuristic in Judgments of Risks and Benefits. *Journal of Behavioral Decision Making* 13, 1–17.

Fryer, R. G. 2010. Racial Inequality in the 21st Century: The Declining Significance of Urban Discrimination. In O. Ashenfelter and D. Card, *Handbook of Labor Economics.* Vol. 4. Orlando: Elsevier North-Holland.

Fryer, R. G. 2012. *Injecting Successful Charter School Strategies into*

Traditional Public Schools: Early Results from an Experiment in Houston. Harvard University, EdLabs, and NBER. Cambridge, MA: National Bureau of Economic Research.

Garber, H. 1988. *The Milwaukee Project.* Washington, DC: American Association on Mental Retardation.

Garet et al. 2010. *Middle School Mathematics Professional Development Study: Findings After the First Year of Implementation.* Washington, DC: Institute of Education Sciences.

Gates Foundation. 2010. *Learning About Teaching: Initial Findings from the Measures of Effective Teaching Project.* Bill & Melinda Gates Foundation.

Geoffroy, M.-C., et al. 2007. Association Between Nonmaternal Care in the First Year of Life and Children's Receptive Language Skills Prior to School Entry: The Moderating Role of Socioeconomic Status. *Journal of Child Psychology and Psychiatry* 48 (5), 490–97.

Geoffroy, M.-C., et al. 2010. Closing the Gap in Academic Readiness and Achievement: The Role of Early Childcare. *Journal of Child Psychology and Psychiatry* 51 (12), 1359–67.

Giffin, J. H.-K. 2009. Value-Added as a Classroom Diagnostic. In T. Hershberg and C. Robertson-Kraft, eds., *A Grand Bargain for Education Reform.* Cambridge, MA: Harvard Education Press.

Goldhaber, D., & D. Brewer. 1997. Why Don't Schools and Teachers Seem to Matter? Assessing the Impact of Unobservables on Educational Productivity. *Journal of Human Resources* 32 (3), 505–23.

Goldhaber, D., & Y. H. Lui. 2003. Occupational Choices and the Academic Proficiency of the Teacher Workforce. In Fowler, W., ed., *Developments in School Finance, 2001–2002* (pp. 53–75). Washington, DC: National Center for Education Statistics.

Goldhaber, D. 2004. Why Do We License Teachers? In F. R. Hess, *A Qualified Teacher in Every Classroom: Appraising Old Answers and New Ideas.* Cambridge, MA: Harvard Education Press.

Goldin, C. 2008. *The Race Between Education and Technology.* Cambridge, MA: Harvard University Press.

Gormley, W. G., et al. 2004. *The Effects of Oklahoma's Universal Pre-Kindergarten Program on School Readiness.* Georgetown University. Center for Research on Children in the United States.

Green, E. 2010, March 2. Building a Better Teacher. *New York Times.*

Greene, J. P. 2013, Jan. 10. *Understanding the Gates Foundation's Measures of Effective Teaching Project.* Retrieved Jan. 28, 2013, from Jay P. Greene's Blog: http://jaypgreene.com/2013/01/09 /understanding-the-gates-foundations-measuring-effective-teachers -project/.

Greenwald, R. H. 1996. The Effect of School Resources on Student Achievement. *Review of Educational Research* 66, 361–96.

Grissmer, D. F. 1998. Why Did the Black-White Score Gap Narrow in the 1970s and 1980s? In C. Jencks and M. Phillips, eds. *The Black-White Test Score Gap* (pp. 181–226). Washington, DC: Brookings Institution Press.

Gutmann, A. 2003. Assessing Arguments for School Choice: Pluralism, Parental Choice, or Educational Results. In A. Wolfe, ed. *School Choice: The Moral Debate* (pp. 126–48). Princeton, NJ: Princeton University Press.

Haberman, M. 1995. *Star Teachers of Children in Poverty.* West Lafayette, IN: Kappa Delta Pi.

Halverson, R. G. 2005. *The New Instructional Leadership: Creating Data-Driven Instructional Systems in Schools.* University of Wisconsin-Madison, School of Education, Department of Educational Leadership and Policy Analysis. Washington, DC: National Council of Professors of Educational Administration.

Hanushek, E. 1986. The Impact of Differential Expenditures on School Performance. *Educational Researcher* 18, 45–51.

Hanushek, E. A. 1997. Assessing the Effects of School Resources on Student Performance. *Educational Evaluation and Policy Analysis* 19 (2), 141–64.

Hanushek, E. 1999. Some Findings from an Independent Investigation of the Tennessee STAR Experiment and from Other Investigations of Class Size Effects. *Education Evaluation and Policy Analysis* 21 (2), 143–63.

Hanushek, E. A. 2002. Sorting Out Accountability Systems. In W. M. Evers and H. Walberg, eds. *School Accountability* (pp. 75–104). Palo Alto, CA: Hoover Institution Press.

Hanushek, E. A. 2003. The Failure of Input-Based Schooling Policies. *Economic Journal* 113, F64–F98.

Hanushek, E. A. 2004. Why Public Schools Lose Teachers. *Journal of Human Resources* 39 (2), 326–54.

Hanushek, E., & M Raymond. 2005. Does School Accountability Lead to Improved Student Performance? *Journal of Policy Analysis and Management* 2, 297–327.

Hanushek, E. A. 2009. *Schoolhouses, Courthouses, and Statehouses: Solving the Funding-Achievement Puzzle in America's Public Schools.* Princeton: Princeton University Press.

Hanushek, E. 2010. *The Economic Value of Higher Teacher Quality.* National Center for Analysis of Longitudinal Data in Education Research. Washington, DC: CALDER, Urban Institute.

Hart, B., & T. R. Risley. 1995. *Meaningful Differences in the Everyday Experience of Young American Children.* Baltimore: Brookes Publishing Co.

Hattie, J. 2009. *Visible Learning: A Synthesis of Over 800 Meta-Analyses Relating to Achievement.* Abingdon: Routledge.

Heath, C. 1999. On the Social Psychology of Agency Relationships: Lay Theories of Motivation Overemphasize Extrinsic Incentives. *Organizational Behavior and Human Decision Processes* 78 (1), 25–62.

Hernandez, D. J. 2011. *Double Jeopardy: How Third-Grade Reading Skills and Poverty Influence High School Graduation.* Center for Demographic Analysis, SUNY Albany. Annie E. Casey Foundation.

Heyns, B. 1978. *Summer Learning and the Effects of Schooling.* Orlando, FL: Academic Press.

Heyns, B. 1987. Schooling and Cognitive Development: Is There a Season for Learning? *Child Development* 58, 1151–60.

Hill, H. C. 2008. *Validating the Ecological Assumption: The Relationship of Measure Scores to Classroom Teaching and Student Learning.* Ann Arbor: Learning Mathematics for Teaching Project.

Hoxby, C. 2000. The Effects of Class Size on Student Achievement: New Evidence from Population Variation. *Quarterly Journal of Economics* 115 (4), 1239–85.

Hoxby, C. M. 2002. *School Choice and School Productivity: Could School Choice Be a Tide That Lifts All Boats?* Cambridge, MA: National Bureau of Economic Research.

Hoxby, C., & C. Avery. 2012. *The Missing "One-Offs": The Hidden Supply of High-Achieving, Low-Income Students*. Cambridge, MA: National Bureau of Economic Research.

Jacob, B. 2007. The Challenges of Staffing Urban Schools with Effective Teachers. *Future of Children* 17 (1), 129–83.

Jesson, D. 2008. *Using Data, Improving Schools*. Office for Standards in Education, Children's Services, and Skills. London: Ofsted.

Kahlenberg, R. D. 2013, Winter. From All Walks of Life: New Hope for School Integration. *American Educator*, 2–40.

Kahneman, D. 2011. *Thinking Fast and Slow*. New York: Farrar, Straus & Giroux.

Kane, T. J. 2002. The Promise and Pitfalls of Using Imprecise School Accountability Measures. *Journal of Economic Perspectives* 16 (4), 91–114.

Kane, T. J. 2008. What Does Certification Tell Us About Teacher Effectiveness. *Economics of Education Review*, vol. 27, no. 6, pp. 615–31.

Kane, T. J. 2012. *Gathering Feedback for Teaching: Combining High-Quality Observations with Student Surveys and Achievement Gains*. Bill & Melinda Gates Foundation.

Kane, T. J. 2013. *Ensuring Fair and Reliable Measures of Effective Teaching: Culminating Findings from the MET Project's Three-Year Study*. Seattle: Bill & Melinda Gates Foundation.

Kane, T. J. 2013. *Have We Identified Effective Teachers? Validating Measures of Effective Teaching Using Random Assignment*. Seattle: Bill & Melinda Gates Foundation.

Knudsen, E. I., J. J. Heckman, J. L. Cameron, and J. P. Shonkoff. "Economic, neurobiological, and behavioral perspectives on building America's future workforce," *Proceedings of the National Academy of Science*, v. 103, no. 27, pp. 10155–62.

Koedel, C. 2011, Aug. Grade Inflation for Education Majors and Low Standards for Teachers: When Everyone Makes the Grade. *AEI Education Outlook*, vol. 7, August 22, 2011.

Kottler, J. A. 1997. *What's Really Said in the Teachers' Lounge: Provocative Ideas About Cultures and Classrooms*. Newbury Park, CA: Corwin Press.

Krueger, A. B. 2000. *The Effect of Attending a Small Class in the Early Grades on College-Test Taking and Middle School Test Results:*

Evidence from Project STAR. Cambridge, MA: National Bureau of Economic Research.

Krueger, A. B. 2002. *The Class Size Debate.* Washington, DC: Economic Policy Institute.

Krueger, A. B., & D Whitman. 2002. "Would Smaller Classes Help Close the Black-White Achievement Gap?" In J. E. Chubb and T. Loveless, eds. *Bridging the Achievement Gap.* Washington, DC: Brookings Institution Press.

Krueger, A. B. 2003. Economic Considerations and Class Size. *Economic Journal* 113 (485), F34–F63.

Kruger, M. W. 2007. The Impact of School Leadership on School Level Factors: Validation of a Causal Model. *School Effectiveness and School Improvement* 18 (1), 1–20.

Kuziemko, I. 2006. Using Shocks to School Enrollment to Estimate the Effect of School Size on Student Achievement. *Economics of Education Review* 25 (1), 63–75.

Laczko-Kerr, I., & D. Berliner. 2002. The Effectiveness of "Teach for America" and Other Under-Certified Teachers on Student Academic Achievement: A Case of Harmful Public Policy Education. *Education Policy Analysis Archives* 10 (37), 1–53.

Lazear, E. S. 2012. *The Value of Bosses.* Cambridge, MA: National Bureau of Economic Research.

Leak, J., et al. 2010. Is Timing Everything? How Early Childhood Education Program Impacts Vary by Starting Age, Program Duration, and Time Since the End of the Program. Paper prepared for the Association for Policy Analysis and Management meetings (pp. 1–25). Boston.

Lee, M., and T. Friedrich. 2007. The "Smaller" the School, the Better? The Smaller Learning Communities (SLC) Program in US High Schools. *Improving Schools* 10 (3), 261–82.

Lee, V., and J. B. Smith. 1997. High School Size: Which Works Best, and for Whom? *Education Evaluation and Policy Analysis* 19, 205–27.

Leithwood, K., & D. Jantzi. 1990. Transformational Leadership: How Principals Help Reform School Cultures. *School Effectiveness and School Improvement: An International Journal of Research, Policy, and Practice* 1 (4), 249–80.

Leithwood, K. A. 1998. *Organizational Learning in Schools.* San Francisco, CA: Jossey-Bass.

Leithwood, K., & C. Riehl. 2003. *What We Know About Successful School Leadership*. Temple University, Laboratory for Student Success. AERA.

Leithwood, K. A. 2008. Seven Strong Claims About Successful School Leadership. *School Leadership and Management* 28 (1), 27–42.

Lemov, D. 2010. *Teach Like a Champion: 49 Techniques That Put Students on the Path to College*. San Francisco, CA: Jossey-Bass.

Ludwig, J., & D. Phillips. 2007. The Benefits and Costs of Head Start. *Social Policy Report* 21 (3), 3–19.

Manzi, J. 2012. *Uncontrolled: The Surprising Payoff of Trial-and-Error for Business, Politics, and Society*. New York: Basic Books.

Marsh, J. A. 2006. *Making Sense of Data-Driven Decision-Making: Evidence from Recent RAND Research*. Santa Monica, CA: RAND Corporation.

McCaffrey, D. F. 2007. *Value-Added Assessment in Practice: Lessons from the Pennsylvania Value-Added Assessment System Pilot Project*. Santa Monica, CA: RAND Corporation.

McCullough, D. 2002. *John Adams*. New York: Simon & Schuster.

McKinsey. 2007. *How the World's Best-Performing School Systems Come Out on Top*. McKinsey & Co.

McKinsey. 2009. *Detailed Findings on the Economic Impact of the Achievement Gap in America's Schools*. McKinsey & Company.

Melhuish, E., et al. 2008. Effects of the Home Learning Environment and Preschool Center Experience Upon Literacy and Numeracy Development in Early Primary School. *Journal of Social Issues* 64 (1), 95–114.

Mosteller, F. 1995. The Tennessee Study of Class Size in the Early School Grades. *The Future of Children: Critical Issues for Children and Youths* 5 (2), 113–127.

National Center for Education Statistics. 2011. *Condition of Education–2011*. Washington, DC: Department of Education.

NCES. 2011. *Numbers and Types of Public Elementary and Secondary Schools from the Common Core of Data: School Year 2009–2010*. Retrieved Jan. 5, 2013, from Institute for Education Sciences/National Center for Education Statistics: http://nces.ed .gov/pubs2011/pesschools09/index.asp.

Olen, H. 2011, Nov. 10. *What Happens When Petulant Parents Won't Share*. Retrieved Aug. 27, 2012, from Slate.com: http://www

.slate.com/blogs/xx_factor/2011/11/10/school_funding_equality
_what_happens_when_well_off_parents_won_t_share_.html.

Ouchi, W. 2003. *Making Schools Work: A Revolutionary Plan to Get Your Children the Education They Need*. New York: Simon & Schuster.

Patall, E. A. 2010. Extending the School Day or School Year: A Systematic Review of Research (1985–2009). *Review of Educational Research* 3, 401–36.

Peterson, K. D. 1998. How Leaders Influence the Culture of Schools. *Educational Leadership* 56 (1), 28–30.

Phi Delta Kappa/Gallup. 2011. *43rd Annual 2011 PDK/Gallup Poll of the Public's Attitudes Toward the Public Schools*. Princeton, NJ: Gallup Organization.

Pittman, R., & P. Haughwout. 1987. Influence of High School Size on Dropout Rate. *Educational Evaluation and Policy Analysis* 9, 337–43.

Preschool Curriculum Evaluation Research Consortium. 2008. *Effects of Preschool Curriculum Programs on School Readiness*. Institute of Education Sciences/National Center for Education Research. Washington, DC: Department of Education.

Puma, M., et al. 2010. *Head Start Impact Study Final Report*. Washington, DC: Department of Health and Human Services Administration for Children and Families.

Ramey, C. T., & S. L. Ramey. 2010. Head Start: Strategies to Improve Outcomes for Children Living in Poverty. In R. Haskins and W. S. Barnett, eds. *Investing in Young Children: New Directions in Federal and Early Childhood Policy* (pp. 59–67). Washington, DC: Brookings Institution Press.

Rawls, J. 1971. *A Theory of Justice*. Cambridge, MA: Belknap Press of Harvard University Press.

Raymond, M. F. 2001. *Teach for America: An Evaluation of Teacher Differences and Student Outcomes in Houston, Texas*. Palo Alto, CA: Hoover Institution/Stanford University.

Reich, R. http://www.ssireview.org/articles/entry/a_failure_of_philan thropy.

Riddle, M. http://nasspblogs.org/principaldifference/2010/12/pisa_its _poverty_not_stupid_1.html.

Rivkin, S. H. 2000. *Teachers, Schools, and Academic Achievement*. Cambridge.

Rivkin, S. H. 2005. Teachers, Schools, and Academic Achievement. *Econometrica* 73, 417–58.

Rockoff, J. E., et al. 2008. *Can You Recognize an Effective Teacher When You Recruit One?* Cambridge, MA: National Bureau of Economic Research.

Rockoff, J. 2008. *Does Mentoring Reduce Turnover and Improve Skills of New Employees? Evidence from Teachers in New York City.* National Bureau of Economic Research. Cambridge, MA: National Bureau of Economic Research.

Rockoff, J. 2009. *Field Experiments in Class Size from the Early Twentieth Century.*

Rockoff, J., & L. J. Truner. 2010. Short-Run Impacts of Accountability on School Quality. *American Economic Journal: Economic Policy* 2 (4), 119–147.

Rockoff, J., & C. Speroni. 2010. Subjective and Objective Evaluations of Teacher Effectiveness: Evidence from New York City. *Labour Economics* 94 (11–12), 687–96.

Rockoff, J. E., et al. 2012. Information and Employee Evaluation: Evidence from a Randomized Intervention in Public Schools. *American Economic Review* 102 (7), 3184–3213.

Rothstein, R., et al. 2010. *Problems with the Use of Student Test Scores to Evaluate Teachers.* Washington, DC: Economic Policy Institute.

Rouse, C. E. 2009. School Vouchers and Student Achievement: Recent Evidence, Remaining Questions. *Annual Review of Economics,* vol. 1, 17–42.

Rumberger, R. W. 2005. Does Segregation Still Matter? The Impact of Student Composition on Academic Achievement in High School. *Teacher's College Record* 107 (9), 1999–2045.

Sammons, P., et al. 2005. Investigating the Effects of Preschool Provision: Using Mixed Methods in the EPPE Research. *International Journal of Social Research Methodology* 8, 207–44.

Sammons, P., et al. 2007. *Effective Pre-School and Primary Education 3-11 Project.* Illinois Department of Child and Family Services.

Sanders, W. L. 1996. *Cumulative and Residual Effects of Teachers on Future Student Academic Achievement.* Knoxville, TN: University of Tennessee Value-Added Research and Assessment Center.

Schleicher, A. 2010. Globalization and the Challenge for Education Improvement. *Council on Foundations Annual Conference— Social Change: Education.* Denver.

Schochet, P. Z. 2010. *Error Rates in Measuring Teacher and School Performance Based on Student Test Score Gains.* Mathematica Policy Research, Institute of Education Sciences. Washington, DC: Department of Education.

Schwartz, A. E., et al. 2012. *Do Small Schools Improve Performance in Large, Urban Districts? Causal Evidence from New York City.* New York: New York University, Institute for Education and Social Policy. Social Science Research Network.

Schwartz, H. 2010. *Housing Policy Is School Policy: Economically Integrative Housing Promotes Academic Success in Montgomery County, Maryland.* New York: Century Foundation.

Schweinhart, L. J., et al. 2005. *Lifetime Effects: The HighScope Perry Preschool Study Through Age 40: Summary, Conclusions, and Frequently Asked Questions.* Ypsilanti, MI: HighScope Educational Research Foundation.

Schweinhart, L. J., et al. 2005. *Lifetime Effects: The HighScope Perry Preschool Study Through Age 40.* HighScope Educational Research Foundation. Ypsilanti, MI: HighScope Press.

Sebring, P. B. 2006. *The Essential Supports for School Improvement.* Chicago: Consortium on Chicago School Research at the University of Chicago.

Siraj-Blatchford, I., et al. 2006. Educational Research and Evidence-Based Policy: The Mixed-Method Approach of the EPPE Project. *Evaluation & Research in Education* 19 (2), 63–82.

Siraj-Blatchford, I., et al. 2008. Towards the Transformation of Practice in Early Childhood Education: The Effective Provision of Preschool Education (EPPE) Project. *Cambridge Journal of Education* 38 (1), 23–36.

Smith, A. 1991. *The Wealth of Nations.* New York: Everyman's Library.

Staiger, D. O. 2010. Searching for Effective Teachers with Imperfect Information. *Journal of Economic Perspectives* 24 (3), 97–118.

Tucker-Drob, E. 2012. Preschools Reduce Early Academic-Achievement Gaps: A Longitudinal Twin Approach. *Psychological Science* 23 (3), 310–19.

Tuttle, C. C. 2010. *Student Characteristics and Achievement in 22 KIPP Middle Schools.* Washington, DC: Mathematica Policy Research.

Wainer, H., and H. Zwerling. 2006. Logical and Empirical Evidence That Smaller Schools Do Not Improve Student Achievement. *Phi Delta Kappan* 87, 300–303.

Wainer, H., 2007, May–June. The Most Dangerous Equation. *The American Scientist*, 249–256.

Wasley, P. F., et al. 2000. *Small Schools: Great Strides. A Study of New Small Schools in Chicago.* New York: Bank Street College of Education.

Weisberg, D. S. 2009. *The Widget Effect: Our National Failure to Acknowledge and Act on Differences in Teacher Effectiveness.* New York: The New Teacher Project.

Wenner Moyer, M. 2013, Jan. 16. The Early Education Racket. *Slate.*

Werblow, J., & L. Duesbery. 2009. The Impact of High School Size on Math Achievement and Dropout Rate. *High School Journal* 9 (3), 14–23.

West, M. http://educationnext.org/misunderstanding-the-gates-foun dation%E2%80%99s-measures-of-effective-teaching-project/.

Whitehurst, G. 2009, October. Don't Forget Curriculum. *Brown Center Letters on Education*, 1–11.

Winkler, A. M. 2012. *How Strong Are U.S. Teacher Unions? A State-by-State Comparison.* New York: Thomas B. Fordham Institute.

Wolf, P. J. 2008, Mar. School Voucher Programs: What the Research Says About Parental School Choice. *BYU Law Review*, 415–46.

Woessman, L., & M. West. 2002. *Class-Size Effects in School Systems Around the World: Evidence from Between-Grade Variation in TIMSS.* European Econom.

Zimmer, R., et al. 2008. *Evaluating the Performance of Philadelphia's Charter Schools.* Santa Monica: RAND Corporation.

Zimmer, R., et al. 2009. *Charter Schools in Eight States: Effects on Achievement, Attainment, Integration and Competition.* Santa Monica: RAND Corporation.

INDEX